YORK

A City Under Siege

1644

YORK

A City Under Siege

1644

JOHN GEARS

A CIP catalogue record for this book is available from the British Library.

ISBN 978-0-9955850-0-3

Book layout and cover design by Clare Brayshaw

Cover image © Alvaro German Vilela | Dreamstime.com

Prepared and printed by:

York Publishing Services Ltd
64 Hallfield Road
Layerthorpe
York YO31 7ZQ

Tel: 01904 431213

Website: www.yps-publishing.co.uk

Appreciation

The publishing and writing of this book would not have happened without the love, support and sheer determination of Shirley, my wife for over 50 years. I owe her so much.

Note from the Author

As a lifelong lover of all things historical and a citizen of the City of York, it was inevitable I chose to explore how the siege of York in 1644 impacted upon its citizens.

Having lived in the city as a schoolboy throughout the Second World War, I was interested to explore if the citizen under siege had been affected any differently in 1664. I have to say the hardships encountered by the citizens in both conflicts were very similar.

I set out to write a novel which would show the reader the hardship and heartbreak experienced by the beleaguered citizens and the brutalities which occurred in the ensuing battle. There were surprisingly many acts of kindness and compassion witnessed both in the City and in the battlefield.

The story is completed.

> *"York a City Under Siege 1644" is a reality and I as a newly qualified octogenarian wish you hours of happy reading!"*

John Gears

CHAPTER I

History Project for Tom

Upon hearing the call *"Come in"*, Tom entered the classroom and walked slowly toward the table at which his History teacher was busy marking books. Mr Holt was a person of middle years and he had taught History at Seldon Road School for over twenty years. Tom had always enjoyed been taught by him, he had a gift of making History come alive. Mr. Holt put down his marking pen, turned to Tom and smiled.

Opening the drawer of the table at which he was sitting, he took out a file of papers, he flicked through the file and withdrew one typewritten sheet of paper, he turned and said, *"Now, when you have read this paper Tom, I am sure you will feel that the History project to which it refers will be of great interest to you"*. Tom took the proffered sheet of paper and started to read it, the title line was "The English Civil War", the sub title was "The Siege of York and The Battle of Marston Moor", The printed instructions went on to inform students that they should carry out research, to trace and describe how these events affected the lives of the peasants and soldiers on both sides and how significant had the The Battle of Marston Moor been in affecting English History.

When he had finished reading the sheet of paper, Tom sat down on an adjacent chair, he was deep in thought when Mr. Holt said to him, *"There are some excellent books in the School Library which have the English Civil War as their main theme"*, he went on to suggest to Tom that he could also obtain valuable information from the City of York Archives and also at the County Records Office where most of the information was stored on micro-film. Mr. Holt then gave Tom a re-assuring smile and said, *"Tom I have every confidence in you and if you need any further advice, please come and see me"*, Tom said, *"Thank you"*, he then turned and walked out of the classroom.

– o0o –

Tom's mother dropped him off outside the County Records Office and as he was getting out of the car she said to him, *"Don't worry, you will be fine and I will pick you up around 4 o'clock"*. At the Enquiry Desk inside the Records Office, Tom explained to the Archivist what type of information he was seeking, after discussing his needs fully with him, she then took Tom to a row of computers set down one side of room. She gave him an introduction on how the system worked and told him if he had any problem, he should ask her and she would give him further help. After a short while, Tom found that he was able to locate the various recorded lists, Births, Deaths, Marriages, without much difficulty and so he commenced his search. Whilst scrolling the deaths for the year 1620, one name seemed to jump out at him, Isaac Stackpole, born 2nd June, 1614, at Little Leake, near Thirsk. Tom set to work to check every aspect he could concerning Isaac Stackpole, it was as if he was transporting himself back in time.

Isaac Stackpole closed the wicket gate into position as the last of his ten sheep scurried into the pen at the back of his cottage, in the morning he would herd his small flock into Thirsk, to sell them at market. He would have to rise at daybreak, he wanted to be at the market early and it would take him around two hours to herd his small flock the five miles or so into Thirsk. He kennelled his dog in the lean-to shelter outside the door of the cottage, he went into the cottage where Rose his wife was busy preparing their supper. There was a large cauldron on the fire in the hearth, in it was a stew made from vegetables, potatoes and the chopped up flesh of two wood pigeons which Isaac had netted earlier that day. This stew together with the rough baked bread Rose had made would ensure they would have a substantial meal, Isaac went back outside and called out to Ann and Willie his two children who were playing in a small copse of trees a short way from the cottage.

It was mid April, 1644 and throughout the year there had been many skirmishes between Royalists and Parliamentarians throughout Yorkshire of which Isaac had heard about from passing travellers. When he and his friends met at Thirsk Market, they discussed the rumours they had heard. Isaac was loyal to the Royalist cause and he had learned earlier that day, when his friend Jack Grainger arrived back from York with Squire Fewster, they were back several days earlier than had been intended. Jack had told him that Squire Fewster had decided to return immediately, because he thought the Parliamentarians would attack and seize York. Sir John Bellayse, Governor of York, had been wounded and taken prisoner along with many of his Royalist solgers, following a battle at Selby, after he and his men had clashed with Parliamentarians led by Lord Fairfax. The Garrison at York was now sorely short of garrison solgers, the "trained bands" (of the Craft Gilds) would help in any fight to save their City, but, they were not skilled fighters. Isaac was not a soldier, he was a ploughman, but if Squire Fewster (his master) went to join the Royalist cause Isaac knew that he and his fellow estate workers would have to go as well.

Isaac and Rose (his spouse) had been together for over ten years and they had built their little cottage together, they had used stone which they had dug from the adjacent hillside, Isaac spent most of his working hours labouring for Squire Fewster who lived in the Manor House close by Leake Church. For his labours Squire Fewster supplied Isaac with victuals sufficient to sustain his family with and he had allowed Isaac to build the small rough stone cottage on a small holding of land. On the adjacent hillside, the Squire allowed Isaac to graze his few head of livestock. All in all Isaac felt there were many families in England in these troubled times who were far worse off than he and Rose.

The family had supper and then Rose put the children to bed, Isaac helped Rose whilst she had spun some wool, they were both worried about the fears in the local countryside that a large battle was now imminent, if the Parliamentarian's decided to attack York. Isaac comforted Rose and suggested that it was possible that York may surrender without a fight, but he knew that would not happen. He did not tell her that Squire Fewster had only that day instructed all his estate workers in the Manorship's of Borrowby and Knayton, to be ready and prepared to march with him toward York and to any impending battle when he needed them. Isaac went outside to check on the sheep and the poultry, a dog fox had attempted to enter the sheep pen only two nights previously, but it had made off empty handed when his dog had picked up the scent and his barking alerted Isaac. When he returned indoors Isaac doused down the fire with ashes from the hearth and then lightly sprinkled water onto the ashes, he then followed Rose to bed.

Isaac awoke at daybreak the next morning and went into the scullery, he poured some water from a pitcher into the rough hewn stone sink, he took off his smock and washed his body from the waist upwards. He went to the corner of the kitchen into which he had fixed slate shelves which Rose used to store food, after cutting himself two thick slices of rough grain bread which Rose had baked the previous day and cut a hunk from the goat cheese which Rose had also made, he looked up to the rafters and saw that there were still two more cheeses hanging upon which they had yet to start. He cut the hunk of cheese into slices and placed them upon the bread, he pressed the two slices of bread together and then he poured himself some water into a hewn a wooden mug, he sat down at the table to enjoy his meal.

After breaking his fast Isaac went across to the hearth by the fire grate, he riddled the ash into hearth and spread some dry kindling into the grate. He then reached forward and took his flint and steel from a hook on the chimney breast and after two or three attempts he succeeded in producing a spark which in turn ignited the small handful of hay which Isaac was holding against the kindling. This soon had the kindling burning brightly, he then placed some larger sticks on top of the kindling and when they started to burn fiercely, he placed two large logs onto the fire, he watched the fire until the logs began to smoulder, at which point he turned away from it, satisfied that it would be bright and hot and would enable Rose to boil water in the cauldron to wash clothes and cook with when she awoke.

He put on his smock and over that a leather waistcoat, he put a gaiter on each shin over his moleskin knee breeches and fastened them off by tying the attached leather strips around the back of his calves, he then put on a pair of worn heavy boots made of wood and leather.

Reaching up to the shelf high on the wall Isaac took down his travelling pack, this was made from sheepskin which was stretched around a sturdy framework of cut willow branches. He had decided to have his pack ready and waiting for when he needed it and that he would leave it in the lean to sheep shed and hope that Rose would not question it's purpose. From a rack below the shelf Isaac took his three hunting knives, from a cupboard he took an extra pair of coarse cloth knee breeches, then he gathered together a large wool blanket, a wooden plate, a hard leather tankard and a large bundle of thin leather strips, all of these he put into the pack. After tightly fastening the top cover, he then swung the pack over his shoulder and he was able to put his arms through the two leather carrying straps. He removed the pack from his shoulders and carried it into the sheep shed and hung it from a roof beam and finally covered it with a large piece of hessian sacking.

He took his crook from behind the door and went out of the cottage, he opened the gate to the sheep pen and coaxed the sheep out and drove them onto the track towards Thirsk. After half a mile he came to the cottage of Tobias Platt, they had been friends since boyhood, Tobe, as Isaac called him worked with Isaac for Squire Fewster. They greeted each other, then set off to walk to the Market at Thirsk. Tobe was pulling a rickety cart on which he was transporting two wicker coops containing chickens which he hoped to sell at the Market. Isaac felt that his own sheep would bring him a good price, they were heavier and in a better condition than sheep he had seen sold the previous week. He looked skywards, there was not a cloud to be seen, he was pleased, a fine day would encourage the crowds to attend Market.

When they got to the Market it was quite busy and a crowd of Butchers were around the sheep pens, Isaac herded his small flock over to an empty pen and secured the wicker gate . Mr. Trollop the auction Mart owner wrote Isaac's name and the details of his stock into the large ledger which he carried with him to each pen and made a record as stock was placed in the pen After making his mark in the book, Isaac wandered over to see Jack Grainger who had brought Squire Fewster to the Market in the heavy waggon. Thinking Jack did not look quite his cheerful self, Isaac asked him if he was ill, Jack said no, "*Im' just worried, Squire teld mi summat on't way 'ere*". "*What worrit 'e told ya*", asked Isaac, Jack sighed, "*Well, Squire ses a messenger came from York, he brou't a letter from t' Squires brother sayin York's under siege an 't Parliamentarians have demanded them ta surrender*". Jack paused and then went on to say, "*Squire thinks tha'll be a lot a blood spilt afore very long*". Jack told Isaac he would see him later and then moved away to find the Squire.

The selling of the livestock was taking place, not wanting to miss seeing his sheep sold, Isaac moved toward the sheep pens, bidding was brisk and Isaac was pleased when he got a good price for his sheep. He walked across to where the fowl were being sold and stood beside Tobe. When Tobe's chickens were offered for sale he got a little less for them, than what he had hoped. Mr. Trollop was sitting at his large desk which was standing on a strong wooden platform four hands above the floor. It was situated at the side of the door and from this high point he could see all that was taking place around the pens.

There was a line of six men waiting to receive their dues from Mr. Trollop, Isaac and Tobe took their place at the end of the line to await their turn. Whilst they were waiting, Isaac told Tobe of the news of the Siege of York, which he had heard from Jack Grainger. As they waited Tobe told Isaac of his fear, that if they had to go fight the Parliamentarians, who would care for his ageing parents if he himself got killed or maimed in a battle. Tobe was not married, but his mother and father were totally dependant upon their son to provide food and care for them. If he did not return in a day or so, they would not be able to look after themselves and would become ill. Isaac told him that when they got to the Manor House he would speak to his sister Nan who was a scullery maid in Squire Fewster's house, he was sure that Nan would agree to visit and give attention to Tobe's mother and father.

Mr. Trollop shouted out, "*You are next for you dues Stackpole*", he paid Isaac the amount of money for which the sheep had been sold, from which Mr. Trollop had deducted his own fee for selling the sheep. Tobe was similarly handed his dues and the pair moved away into the cluster of people. They had collected Tobe's handcart ready to commence their journey back, when Jack Grainger found them, he said, "*Squire ses, ya can 'ave a lift back wi us, if ya want*", they both thanked Jack and walked with him to the heavy waggon. The journey was un-eventful and little was said by anyone, they were all lost in their own thoughts.

When they turned into the kitchen yard at the side of the Manor House, Isaac saw Nan going into the wash house he called out to her and she turned smiled and waved as she waited for Isaac and Tobe to go up to her. Nan gave Isaac a hug and said to him, "*Is Rose and the kid's alright*", Isaac re-assured her of their welfare and then he explained to Nan the problem and worry Tobe had, concerning the welfare of his parents. Nan had a longstanding fancy for Tobe, because of her shyness she had never tried to get in conversation with him, she had admired him from afar. Isaac asked her if it would be possible, that whilst he and Tobe were away she might have time to give some attention to them. She said, *"I'll talk to Mrs. Hopkin, I'm sure she'll agree, Mrs. Platt had been Lady Fewster's dressmaker years ago"*. Isaac thought for a moment and then asked, *"Will you have time enough"*. Nan smiled at them both and said, *"Don't worry 'bout 'em Tobe, come what may I'll see the'er looked after"*. Tobe looked uncomfortable and was lost for words as he mumbled his appreciation to Nan.

As Nan turned to enter the wash house, the loud clanging of the fire bell rang out across the courtyard, looking round Isaac saw Jack Grainger was ringing it and the Squire was at the same time emerging from the kitchen door. With a wave of his arm he gestured his men to assemble at the loading ramp, which was at the front of the flour and granary store. When they had all gathered in front of him, Squire Fewster waited until the general chatter had subsided and then he spoke, *"I have to tell you that York is now besieged"*, there was at first a silence round the Courtyard, but this was quickly followed by loud chatter as the assembled men commented their thoughts to their neighbours. After a few moments and raising his voice slightly, the Squire said, *"Men, hear me, we must stay calm and await events"*. Silence prevailed around the yard, the Squire then went on to say, *"There will be difficult times ahead for all of us, I ask you all to be careful of what you say to any travellers who may stop and question you"*. He told them, *"Any stranger, may be an enemy to the King's cause, keep what you know to yourselves"*. The advice he had given to his audience had been quite a surprise to them and their concern showed on their faces.

Before he concluded the Squire reminded those who did not live at or near to the Manor house to take particular care to protect their families and their livestock. There could be danger and thefts by the stragglers from the Scottish Army who had a history of attacking lonely farmsteads to steal food and livestock and harm anyone who stood in their way. Finally he said, *"When plans are made for us to move toward York, you will all be told as late as possible, so make plans for your absence now"*. He then turned abruptly and went back into the Manor House. The courtyard cleared quickly as the men left in small groups discussing what they had been told.

Isaac left the yard with Tobe, who seemed shocked and very quiet as they made the journey homewards. When they reached Tobe's Cottage, Isaac tried to cheer Tobe up and make things seem brighter for him, he was not very successful, so he said his goodbye and set off to make his own way home. As Isaac was approaching along the track to his cottage, he saw Ann and Willi running excitedly towards him, as they got to him, he swept both of them off their feet and held them up, one in each arm. When they got into the small stockyard at the cottage, the children begged Isaac to let them help him to feed and water the goats, Isaac waited and watched as the children ran around with great excitement searching for eggs to collect.

The children searched everywhere and kept returning to Isaac to place their eggs into the leather bucket which their father was holding. When their task was completed the bucket was half full. They all then went into the cottage to show Rose the result of their work. After praising her children for their efforts, she sent them to play outside before supper. Turning to Isaac she said, *"W'ats matter y'r early"*, Isaac hesitated and then said, *"Ya know when we talked on't siege"*, he hesitated, Rose who was stirring the stew in the cauldron over the fire gave him a piercing look. He went on, *"Well Squire ses siege at York 'as started"*, Rose went and sat at the table, she started crying, she looked pleadingly at

Isaac and said, *"You shouldn't 'ave ta 'ave owt ta do wi' it, y'er a plowman not a soldier"*.

It saddened Isaac to see her so upset, he went over and sat down beside her, he took her hand and clasped her into his arms to comfort her and he whispered, *"I'll be reet, ah know ah will"*, she calmed a little and was attempting to dry her eyes as the children came dashing in though the doorway. She got up and said, *"Supper's nearly ready so ya can all swill y'selves at trough"*. Rose set the table and they all sat down to eat, even the children sensed the atmosphere, everyone was subdued and Isaac and Rose did not speak throughout the meal.

After Rose had put the children to bed, she joined Isaac who was sitting at the table, she said to him, *"Is all of em goin"*, Isaac replied, *"Aye, nobody sed owt agin it"*, she thought and said, *"Wat's Tobe doin' bout his Mam an Dad"* she looked at Isaac and he said, *"Wi talked ta Nan, she sed she'd give an eye to em"*. Rose stood and walked behind Isaac, she put her hands on his shoulders and said, *"When did Squire say ya'd be back then"*, Isaac shook his head and said, *"He didn't tell us, ah don't think 'e knows"*, Isaac turned on his chair and took Rose's hand and pulled her round so that she was sitting on his knee, he kissed her and hugged her and said, *"Look I'll be alreet, I'll tek care, don't worry"*.

Rose had her arms around Isaac's neck and she started to sob. Isaac comforted her gently and after a short while she stopped and said, *"Ah do 'ope nowt 'appens ta ya, ah don't think ah could bear it"*. Isaac lifted her chin with his hand and kissed her fully on the lips, she shuddered slightly with emotion and Isaac whispered, *"It'll be alreet, you'll see"*. He rose from the table and as he looked towards Rose, he said to her re-assuringly, *"Why don't ya go get into bed lass, I'll just go an see ta stock, then I'll come as well, ya know I'll need to be up a'fore daybreak"*. Rose once more gave a deep sigh and said to him, *"Ay well, don't be so long yerself"*.

When he got outside, Isaac checked the sheep pen and found the animals cowering in one corner, he realised that something, probably a fox was lurking nearby and the ewes were aware of it's presence, he knew he must do something to flush the predator out. Isaac went to the lean-to outside the back door of the cottage and let his dog out, he took him towards the small patch of scrub, nettles and brambles across the yard from the cottage, half way across the yard the dog shot forward, barking furiously and then skirted round the far side of thicket where he went into a down position. He was still barking and wagging his tail, Isaac now knew where the fox was, he called the dog to him, he instructed him to stay and Isaac went back across the yard and picked up a round wooden pole which was sharpened to a point at one end and was about an arms length taller than Isaac was himself.

Isaac grasped the pole in both hands, he sent the dog back round the thicket of brambles and then Isaac started violently plunging the pole into the brambles and scrub, suddenly there was a piercing squeal, he could feel the other end shaking and he held tightly onto the pole, then there was no movement at the end of the pole, he had killed the fox, that was one less to threaten his small flock. He pulled out the pole and returned it to it's position against the sheep pen, he was pleased with himself and he put the dog back into the lean-to and went back into the cottage.

When Isaac got into the kitchen he walked over to the fire and began to rake it, all the ash fell down into the space below the fire grate, he then took three or four pieces of peat from a large basket at the far end of the hearth and he placed them upon the red embers remaining in the grate, he then shovelled sheep dung on top of the peat. He paused and watched the fire for a moment or so and he swept up all the ashes lying in the hearth and put those on the fire, he watched until he saw smoke slowly escaping through from the top of the ash, whereupon he rose and walked across the kitchen and through the doorway of the wooden partition into the bedroom.

As he undressed Isaac placed his clothes tidily on the top of the heavy wooden coffer standing in the corner of the small bedroom area. The bed which Isaac had constructed was in the opposite corner, it was made of wood, it was fixed to the walls of the cottage at the head and on one side, stout wooden planks stretching from floor to rafters covered in the other end of the bed and by using a heavy woollen curtain along the front side of the bed the inside was completely enclosed. The mattress which was thickly filled with Duck feathers and down, rested upon timbers which were about knee high from the floor, after undressing, Isaac put on his long hessian nightshirt, then he drew back the curtain and got into bed.

As he laid down, Rose snuggled up to him and she whispered, "*Let's mek love*", Isaac put his arms around her, she was naked, she had removed her shift and nightdress which she usually wore in bed, Isaac was fondling her body and Rose was slowly pulling Isaac's nightshirt up his body, she whispered to him, "*Tek it off*", Isaac sat up and took off his nightshirt, she pulled him toward her on the bed. They made love passionately and they were both consumed within each other, after which, whilst they were relaxing in each others embrace they fell asleep.

A loud banging and shouting awoke Isaac, it was still dark and remembering the Squire's warning about the straggling Scots solgers, he rose quickly from his bed and darted to the cottage door. As he got to the door, there was more shouting and Isaac recognised the voice as that of Jack Grainger and he was speaking loudly and excitedly, Isaac removed the batten securing the door and opened the door slightly. He saw his friend was alone and so he stepped outside, after spending a few moments calming his friend down, Jack told him that the Squire had received an urgent message from his brother Sir George Fewster and it had to be forwarded on to York.

The message was for Sir Thomas Glenham, the Governor of York. Squire Fewster had instructed Jack to take the message and a speedy horse to Isaac, who was to ride as hard as he could to Sowerby, where he was to hand the message over to another messenger who would be waiting by the village duckpond to carry the message onward.

Jack went on to say to Isaac that a Beacon Light had been lit on the top of Sutton Bank, that is how the new messenger had been warned to await Isaac's arrival and there had been other beacons lit all the way to York, other riders would be waiting to take the message on.

Isaac noticed that Jack had tethered both horses to the rail in the yard, it was just breaking daylight, he gestured Jack to follow him inside, saying "*Ah'll have to get dressed and tell Rose*", he dashed into the bedchamber and quickly told Rose about his journey whilst he was putting his clothes on. When he went back into the kitchen Jack handed him the message, which was inside a strong paper wallet, which was clearly addressed to Sir Thomas Glenham, Governor of York.

Taking the parcel from his friend, they both went outside into the yard and Jack said to Isaac, "*Squire said the message would be safer if you put it into the secret pocket in the saddle cloth*", whereupon he lifted the saddle cloth and showed

Isaac a cleverly concealed compartment on the inside of the cloth, it was well disguised to the naked eye, unless a thorough close examination was made.

Isaac placed the package inside the compartment, he turned to Rose, embraced her and told he would be back in a few hours. Jack was holding the bridle of the bay gelding which Isaac was to ride, turning to Isaac he said, "*Ah wanted ta tek message but, Squire said ah wor too old, 'e wanted you 'cause ya fitter 'e said*". Isaac smiled, patted Jack on the shoulder and mounted the horse, Jack moved to the yard gate and opened it, Isaac rode the horse forward and with a cheerful wave to Rose, he galloped off down the track. Jack bade Rose good bye, he mounted his horse and headed off back to the Manor House.

At a steady gallop, Isaac skirted Borrowby and after passing the Water Mill at the fringe of the village he joined the road to Thirsk, he saw no one until he had ridden a mile or so beyond Borrowby. Then coming towards him from Thirsk he saw a large cart, the body of which was covered by a large brown coloured awning. Isaac recognised the waggon as one owned by Abe Brown a Thirsk tanner, Jeb Webb a friend of Isaac was sitting on the high seat holding the reins. They wished each other good day and Isaac said to Jeb, "*Is it quiet in Thirsk, 'ave you seen any round heads on't road*", Jeb said, "*Ah an't sin any t'day, but some on 'em rode thro't market square las' neet*". Thanking his friend, Isaac bade him good bye, turned and spurred his horse onward to Thirsk.

As he entered Thirsk, Isaac slowed his horse to a trot, it was still early and there were not many townspeople astir. As he crossed the bridge spanning Cod Beck, Isaac brought his horse to a stop, listening, he could hear the sound of many hooves, it sounded like a troop of horses coming trotting through the Market Place toward him. He urged his horse to walk forward and turned left and walked down a snicket, before entering a yard which would conceal him from the view of the troopers, whom he could hear approaching along the street towards the bridge over Cod Beck, he waited and listened as the clatter of hooves receded away from him.

Silence returned, Isaac urged his mount forward and they moved off at a walk into the Market Square. As he approached the Market Cross, Isaac saw Matty Morton the Town Constable who was bending over a figure lying on the ground. Reining his horse in, Isaac moved close up to Matty and said to him, *"Whats up Matty"*, the Constable looked up at Isaac and said, *"It's awd Raef Hobbs, sum o't round'eads ah jus' ridden thro' and one on em rode his 'oss strait at Raef"*. Raef was a man of heavy build and he was also fond of his ale, Isaac dismounted and helped Matty to lift Raef into a sitting position against the Market Cross. Although it was only breakfast time, Isaac could smell ale on Raef's breath, seeing that apart from being bruised about his body from the incident, Isaac felt the man would not need much further help.

Bading Matty farewell, Isaac remounted his horse and continued through the Market Place and thence took the road to Sowerby. He galloped the horse the two miles or so to Sowerby, but he slowed his animal down to a trot as he entered the village, everywhere was very quiet, Isaac was concerned, but not afraid, he approached the duckpond which was set back some yards from the maintrack. He saw there was a saddled horse grazing at the side of the pond, then, half in the water at the side of the duckpond he saw a body. He rode his horse forward to the rail fence around the pond, he dismounted his horse and the tied the reins to the palings of the fence.

Striding to the edge of the pond, Isaac bent down and saw that the man had been badly beaten, his clothing was torn and heavily bloodstained, he was barely conscious, Isaac grasped the man under the armpits and pulled him out of the water and upto the fence. After propping the man into a sitting position against the stout wooden support of the fence, Isaac took a kerchief from around the man's neck, he wetted the kerchief in the water at the pond and returned, to commence wiping the blood from around the man's face. The man was groaning and attempting to speak at the same time.

Isaac calmly re-assured the man, that he was no longer in danger, after a short time, the victim calmed and started to talk with difficulty. He said to Isaac, "*Ave ya brou't a message fa mi ta tek ta York*", Isaac replied, "*Yes, but w'at 'appened t'ya*", the man caught his breath for a moment and then went on to say, "*Ah wa' waiting fa' ya ta' get here, when t' round'eads got 'ere*", he stopped and took some deep breaths and said, "*Tha wanted message, 'an ah telled em ad gi'n it over ta next rider, an he'd gone into Thirsk ta get ta York that way*".

Realising he was facing serious problems, Isaac said, "*W'at did tha do then*", the injured man replied, "*Tha ripped all mi clothes lookin' fa t' message, when tha cudn't fin it, tha beat me up an' rode off ta Thirsk*". Isaac knew the man was not able to carry the message further on towards York, he said, "*Wat's ya' name*", he looked at Isaac and shaking his head, he slowly replied, "Rob Steel". Hoping Rob realised how weak he was to make such an important journey, Isaac said, "*Rob, ya can't tek tha message fu'ther ya too shuk up*", still shaking his head Rob said, "*I'll mek it, I'll git by*".

Isaac stood up, he realised Rob was trying to be loyal to his own Master, after thinking for a moment or two, he turned to Rob and looking down to him he said, "*Can ya ger up on ya own*". After struggling for some minutes Rob was unable to get to his feet, he looked at Isaac, then he sighed loudly and slumping back against fence post, said, "*I can't*". Bending down on his knees to Rob's side, Isaac said, "*Look ah can tek it, ya mun tell where ya wer teking it ta*". Catching his breath before he was able to speak, Rob said, "*Ah 'ad ta go ta Sessay, an meet at a big willo' tree*". Rising up once more, Isaac said, "*Am gonna tek it then, folk 'all be abawt soon an' tha'll look after ya*". Rob nodded in agreement, looking down at him, Isaac said, "*Tell ya Master, av tekken it on, reet I'm off then*". Isaac smiled down at Rob, then he turned and walked to his horse, wheeled the animal round and with a wave of his hand to Rob and rode off toward Sessay.

CHAPTER II

Urgent Message to Deliver

As Isaac left the village, he decided to make his way to Sessay by way of the field tracks, with which he was well acquainted and that way he might not meet any Parliamentarian solgers.

The sun was shining, and across in distant fields, Isaac could see workers hoeing amongst the crops. In a field to his left, a shepherd was using his dog to herd the sheep in readiness to taking them to Market. Ahead of him Isaac saw there was a closed gate, he decided to save time by jumping the obstacle, he gathered the reins in his hands set the horse to the gate and it made a perfect jump and landing. He saw a cart coming towards him, he checked his mount to a walk as he came up to the cart. The driver gave a friendly wave, he stopped his cart and said to Isaac, *"Tek care about a mile ahead, ah saw a tramp goin' tuther way"*, looking puzzled Isaac said, *"Wat wa 'rong wi him"*, the carter replied, *"He wern't a tramp, 'is clothes wern't mucki enough and 'e had a pistol 'idden inside 'is gansy, 'e wer up ta no good, keep cleer ov ''im"*. Isaac thanked the man and turning his horse once more trotted ahead.

Looking ahead Isaac saw the glint of the sun on the waters of Cod Beck as it meandered through the fields and pastures before it flowed onwards and was swallowed up into the River Swale. As he got to the edge of the beck he gently urged the horse to enter the water, which was but 3 or 4 hands deep at that point, the horse stood his ground and looked at the water splashing and eddying amongst stones and small rocks. Satisfied and confident, the horse stepped into the water and picked his way carefully across and away from the larger stone hazards. Reaching the other side the animal stepped from the water onto the low grassy bank and thence the lush green pasture of the field, steadied himself and waited until Isaac set him off into a trot.

They had travelled but a few paces when there was a loud bang, the animal was startled and reared upon his hindlegs and Isaac had great difficulty controlling and calming his mount. After a few moments of struggling, Isaac was able to get his mount under control and got the horse into a gallop away from the scene. He could feel his face burning and he realised that blood was running down his face, he was riding low in the saddle, his head was level with the neck of the horse. Isaac knew he had to keep riding as hard as he could away from the danger of any more shots. Some distance ahead, he spotted a copse of trees and decided that in order to check his wounds and to give the horse a little time to recover he needed cover and headed towards it. Upon reaching the copse, he slowed the horse and then stopped, before walking the animal into the cover afforded by the bushes and small trees.

Isaac tethered the horse to a small sapling, he quickly checked the flanks and legs of his mount and he was relieved there were no injuries. Isaac gently touched the injury to his own face, the blood was reduced to a trickle as it congealed. Looking about his hiding place and beyond, he saw the copse was on a slight gradient and he was able to see in the far distance the Cod Beck and a short distance away from it a figure was walking in Isaac's direction.

Turning to his horse, Isaac led the animal round the edge of the copse away from the sight of the distant figure, steadying the horse he again checked the animal over before he mounted and set off to gallop onwards to Sessay. As he rode he could still feel the searing pain in his cheek where he had been hit by the pistol ball, he brushed his cheek with the back of his hand and he was thankful when he realised the bleeding had stopped. Isaac cautiously approached the road from Thirsk to Dalton, the road was clear of travellers, he could see far to his right a herd of cattle being driven towards Dalton, he crossed the road and galloped quickly away from it.

Feeling discomfort from the wound to his face, Isaac slowed to a trot as he came to a fast flowing stream, Isaac knew that just beyond it was the road into Sessay. Crossing the stream Isaac continued his way, using the field tracks all the way into the village, he was fearful of meeting either round heads or Scots who were known to move about the country to steal food and livestock.

When he could see the houses of Sessay, he dismounted from his horse and walked with the animal, as he got close by the farms and houses he turned and approached a pathway which was bordered by overgrown hedges. The pathway took him right into Sessay and as he stood at the side of a cottage garden, he could see the large willow tree and standing under the tree was a figure. He was a Friar and he was wearing a brown habit which was secured by a white rope around his waist, the hanging surplus of the rope was knotted three times in the Franciscan style, which signified *Faith, Hope and Charity*. On his feet he was wearing rough leather sandals. He was a tall man, but he was thin and bony and he had gaunt staring eyes. Standing close by the Friar was a white coloured heavy horse which was tethered to the willow tree.

Isaac carefully looked along the road through the village in both directions, the few people who were gossiping or walking about the village street did not look suspicious to Isaac. Glancing again in both directions, Isaac walked his mount a short way along the street toward the Friar and when he got under the tree he reined in his horse and dismounted. Solemnly clasping his hands together the Friar bowed his head and looked without expression directly at Isaac, saying, *"My son, I have been awaiting your safe arrival, I see from your wound you have been in danger"* ? Isaac nodded his head and turning he stepped forward towards his horse under the willow tree , the Friar followed close on his heel.

Standing close up to the horse's girth, Isaac swiftly removed the paper wallet containing the message from it's hiding place in the saddlecloth and passed it quickly to the Friar, who, with equal speed cosseted the article deep within the confines of his habit. Isaac was convinced that any observers would be unaware of the transaction which had taken place, both men however then proceeded to carry out an examination on the withers of Isaac's horse. This activity had been quickly whispered to Isaac by the Friar and used to mislead any unseen observers into believing they were looking for an injury. The animal, having been found "free of injury" both men stepped forward to the Friar's horse which was patiently waiting to move on.

As they stood by the Friar's mount, Isaac said, *"Mi masta 'll wanna no, who ah gev 't message ta, w'at shall ah tell 'im"*? The Friar did not answer the question immediately, but concentrated his attention to untethering his horse and then passing the loose end of the white rope through the rope halter and knotting them together forming a crude but efficient rein. Checking the knot again, he turned, looked intently at Isaac and said, *"Tell your master that Friar Thomas is thankful."* He walked his horse away from the tree and then stopped, he gathered his rope rein in his left hand, and said to Isaac, "*I fear, I need your assistance, I need a leg up*". Isaac stepped forward and facing the Friar, he stooped, twined his fingers together forming a stirrup and then gestured the Friar to put his foot in it. The Friar safely mounted his horse, then walked the animal forward away from Isaac, without any further speech or gesture.

Isaac did not return to his own mount until he had seen Friar Thomas disappear from view at the far end of the village, whereupon he returned to the willow tree, unhitched his horse, then led the animal back to the same pathway by which they had approached the village. When they were clear of the pathway and the overgrown hedges, Isaac mounted and set off on his return journey to the Manor House. Feeling thirsty and hungry, he had not broken his fast before starting his journey, he decided to call at the small farmstead of Sykes Marton, a yeoman farmer he had met at Market and had become friendly with.

As Isaac approached the farmstead he saw Sykes coming out of the barn, he was carrying a plough blade to his cart, he placed the implement on the bed of the cart and turned and bade Isaac welcome. Isaac dismounted and tethered the horse within the barn, Sykes brought a leather bucket which he had filled with water from the trough at the side of the barn. The horse consumed the water greedily and emptied the bucket, Sykes removed the bucket and entering a stall a took a canvas nosebag from a peg on the wall and filled it with oats from a barrel within the doorway. Turning, he offered the nosebag to Isaac who hung the bag from the horses head, both men turned and walked away leaving the animal munching contentedly.

Upon leaving the barn, they walked across the farmyard to enter the stone built farmhouse, after passing through the outer door, Sykes led the way down a short passage and turned left into a large kitchen which was dominated by a very large table, which was situated in the centre of the room. From strong metal hooks in the ceiling beams, Isaac saw hanging an assortment of cheeses and sides of salted bacon and ham. Sykes wife Florrie, saw Isaac looking at the hanging food and said to Isaac, *"Ast tha eat'n lad, thu luks 'ungry ta me"*. Isaac smiled and explained that he had not yet broken his fast that day. She said, *"Well ya'd best git ta table wi Sykes an' a'll fettle ya summat ta eul"*.

Both men did as bidded and sat facing each other across the big table, Florrie took a large carving knife from a drawer in the far end of the table and a large platter from a wall shelf, she then left the kitchen, she immediately appeared back in doorway and said *"Is salted bacon reet fo' ya Isaac"*, he nodded his head and said, *"Aye, thank ya"*. Sykes listened intently whilst Isaac related his morning adventures and the circumstances of the injury to his cheek. Leaving his chair Sykes walked round the table and examined Isaacs injury. He saw that the musket ball had removed the lobe of Isaac's ear and grazed a furrow of skin away along Isaac's lower jaw bone. Upon completing his check of the injury, Sykes stood upright and said, *"Tha's bin reet lu'ky an't ya, tha wa' a fingers width away fra getting yersin killed"*.

At this point Florrie swept back into the kitchen the platter was laden with rashers of thick cut bacon and she had a basket of large brown eggs. Whilst Florrie was busy preparing the food, Sykes told Isaac that on returning home that morning from Thirsk market a troop of Parliamentarian soldiers had been checking everyone who they thought suspicious entering or leaving Thirsk over the Cod beck bridge and had roughly beaten a number of them. He then said to Isaac, *"Tha knows, ah think tha knew summat about thee or t'other messengers"*, Isaac thought about what Sykes had told him and he realised the troopers he had seen early that morning could have been looking for him. Isaacs thoughts were interrupted by Florrie as she loudly said, *"Cum on now, help y'selves grub's ready"*.

Throughout the meal, chat was centred around families and routine daily affairs which affected their local surroundings. Sykes told Isaac avoiding Thirsk completely would be his best plan when he continued his journey, he confidently predicted there would be no Parliamentarian troopers north of Thirsk and those in the area earlier in the day had probably now headed south towards York. They finished their meal and Isaac thanked Sykes and Florrie for their kindness to him and wished them well before bading farewell. At the door into the yard, Sykes held Isaac back by the arm, and said, *"Jus' stay in 'til 'ave had a gud luk about"*, Isaac waited within the doorway for a few minutes until he heard Sykes call to him. He crossed the yard and went across to the barn where Sykes was waiting, they went inside and they chatted whilst Isaac prepared his horse for the journey.

Isaac took the animal by the reins and accompanied by Sykes they went outside into the yard, they stood by the mounting steps, where Isaac again offered his thanks for the hospitality he had received, he then stepped up the mounting stone and seated himself comfortably in the saddle. He moved the horse forward at a walk, gave a cheery wave to Sykes and setting the horse into a trot he rode away from the farm. Because of what Sykes suggested regarding avoiding Thirsk, Isaac decided to ride towards Bagby and as he had done early that morning he kept away from the roads.

Keeping to a brisk trot and without incident he was soon approaching Bagby, he kept to the field tracks and did not enter the village. As he got to the north side of the village he chose a track that had thick hawthorn bushes on both sides and would conceal his presence from the hills to the east near Whitestone Hill. He maintained a good gallop along the track, until he came upon open countryside which he knew was well north of Thirsk, he changed direction and headed across the fields toward the road to Northallerton.

Still avoiding the road, Isaac made steady progress by keeping to the field tracks, he skirted round the north side of Borrowby and he soon saw the Manor House ahead of him. Entering the stableyard, Isaac walked the horse over to the mounting steps and dismounted, he handed the reins to the waiting groom and went around the back of the house to the kitchen court yard, after knocking on the door the cook Mrs. Hopkin invited him into the kitchen and sent a scullery maid to inform the Squire of Isaac's arrival. The maid returned and asked Isaac to follow her, she led him from the kitchen into the main entrance hall and then into a room to the left of the front door, she knocked upon the door and when called to from within, she entered. She opened the door and walked in, she waited at the door and bade Isaac to walk into the room, she then left the room and closed the door after her.

As he entered the room, Isaac saw before him Squire Fewster and his brother Sir George Fewster, they were standing around a large table which was covered in green material and there were three balls on the table, both men had in their hand a round wooden stick, the Squire was using his stick to hit one of the balls along the table. After the ball had stopped rolling, the Squire said, "*I think George, we should hear what Isaac has to tell us*", whereupon both men placed their sticks upon the table and went and seated themselves at a table near to the window. When the men were sitting comfortably Squire Fewster bade Isaac to tell them his story.

Isaac told the Squire and his brother of the exploits of his day, both men were very concerned when they were told of shooting and his injury, upon hearing that Isaac had passed the message to Father Thomas both the Squire and his brother expressed their relief, Squire Fewster said, "*The message is in safe hands, Father Thomas would give his life in the King's cause*". The Squire thanked Isaac for his efforts and told him he was very pleased with his conduct. After Isaac had left the room Sir George, said to his brother, "*Charles you have a good man there, I hope you look after him*", Squire Fewster nodded his agreement and replied, "*I have every trust in him, he is like his father, a man whom I would have trusted with my life*".

When he had withdrawn from the Squire's presence, Isaac made his way back to the kitchen and after crossing the kitchen courtyard he set out along the track to his home and family. When the cottage came into Isaac's view, the sun was starting to set, as he continued walking he gently touched his face and he could feel a raised weal, he knew Rose would be angry and concerned because he had been injured. The sudden and loud excited cries of children's voices, shattered the peacefulness of the countryside as Willie and Ann dashed towards him from their hiding place in a nearby elder bush. As they got to him, Isaac scooped both of them into his arms and carried them to the cottage gate.

Rose came to the cottage door in response to the children's shrieking and laughter, she smiled happily when she saw Isaac had returned and she too dashed forward and threw her arms around Isaac whilst he was still holding the children. She stepped back suddenly saying, "*What's up wi yer face*", whilst at the same time she was gently touching the recent injury. Isaac put the children down and put his arm around Rose's shoulders as they walked slowly into the cottage. Upon entering their home, Rose went straight across the kitchen to the fireplace and checked the food she was cooking for supper, Isaac crossed to the bench near the window and taking a leather drinking vessel from a line which were hung from hooks, which were fastened to the bottom of a small cup-board which was fastened to the wall above the bench. He filled his vessel with fresh water from a jug standing on the bench and had a long cooling drink.

After checking on the progress of the cooking food, Rose crossed over to where Isaac was standing near the window, she said, "*Reet, now 'ow did ya face get like that*", Isaac told her all the details he had encountered that day, Rose looked both frightened and angry, she said, "*Ya c'ud ah bin killed, 'ow c'ud I ah coped wi two kid's ta bring up on mi own*". Isaac tried, not very successfully to re-assure Rose, but fully understood her concern and the same concerns had passed through his own mind during the events of the day. Rose once again busied herself with the preparation and serving of the supper, Isaac took the children outside to the water trough where he supervised that both thoroughly washed their faces and hands and after he had sent the children back into the cottage he similarly dealt with his own wash.

Neither parent spoke of their worries during the course of the meal, they both listened attentively as their children chatted to them of their own adventures of that day. The dangers of Isaac's adventure would be discussed at great length after the children had been put to bed. Rose knew that Isaac had no choice but to do as the Squire ordered him to do, Isaac knew the worries and fears that Rose had for his safety and he spent a long time trying to re-assure her that he would take care of himself and return safely. Their concerns prevented Isaac or Rose getting much sleep that night.

Upon waking the next morning to a bright, sunny day, Isaac still had the worries of the previous night upon his mind and after carrying out his normal routine of preparations for the day he set out for the Manor House. His mind was still deep in thought and his step was very weary.

CHAPTER III

York Under Siege

On the 11th April, 1644, the Governor of York, Sir John Bellayse, whilst storming Selby, along with many of his men was taken prisoner by Lord Fairfax, this left the garrison at York at risk from attack and short of soldiers to defend the Citie. The Marquis of Newcastle, Sir William Cavendish upon hearing the news, decided to withdraw from Durham and to fall back on York, he entered the Citie with his men on the 16th April, 1644. The Parliamentarian Armies of the Lord's Leven and Fairfax arrived at York on 21st April, it took them three days to get their men into be*sieging* positions. Before the siege was started Merchants visiting the City had left hurriedly, most County landowners quickly returned home to protect their estates. Many others, Merchants and Gentlemen and their Ladies were unable to leave and remained in the City throughout the siege.

The besiegers did not however, have enough men to completely surround the Citie and a large section of the north east side of the Walls had to be covered by troops of Cavalry patrolling the area whenever they were able. Newcastle was thus enabled, on 22nd April, to send the bulk of his Cavalry out of the Citie to travel south to link up with other Royalist forces. Due to shortage of fodder for the horses, he retained only 300 or so of the Cavalry to supplement the 4,500 foot soldiers who formed the garrison. The soldiers were billeted about the Citie, the citizens who had to lodge and board them were paid but *4d* a day for their *diete*. This money was raised by the Common Council levying the Citizens, hoping to later recover the money from the Royal purse.

It was early evening, in mid May, 1644 and the citizens present in the Citie streets, appeared worried and tense as they went about their business, the normal laughter and gaiety of groups of neighbours gossiping and children playing in the passages and streets were no longer to be heard. It could be seen that normal routine of the lives of the citizens had changed dramatically since the middle of April, when the Citie had come under Siege from the Armies of Parliament (known as Roundheads) and they had started to come under regular fire from heavy cannon.

Besiegers had established a few Batteries of culverins and cannon on high ground at some points around the Citie. There had been many houses and workshops damaged by heavy fire from this type of ordinance, only two days previously the spire of St. Deny's Church in Walmgate had been smashed after being hit by heavy shot. Citizens had been killed and injured. Many of the workshops and dwellings without the Citie Walls. had been fired by defenders to clear the areas around the Bars and those properties close to the walls. This was intended to deny from Parliamentarian besiegers use of them as a shield to conceal any activity to lay mines under the defensive strong points around the Citie, or make a surprise attack.

A large magazine was established at the Clifford's Tower and along with the Castle Mills Postern, extra defensive earthworks had been put in place. A lot of this work had been carried out by the various Gild craftsmen voluntarily and as requested by the Governor of the Citie, Sir John Glenham. Five Sconces *(which were defensive Forts)* had been constructed by means of raised earthworks, measuring about four score yards long and two score yards wide and defended by over one hundred soldiers with a battery of cannons.

All of these fortifications were outside the Citie walls and each of them were at least some four hundred paces or a little more from the Citie. Because of the presence of these Sconces, many Citizens in the early weeks of the siege were enabled to graze their livestock on some of the strays outside the Citie Walls.

Luke Watts, a Cordwainer was in his workshop in Trinity Passage, off Gudramgate, he laid to one side the riding boot he was making, he tidied his workbench, he could hear his wife in the kitchen preparing their evening meal, he knew the food would be sparse, but nourishing. No one was starving, but food was likely to become scarce. Luke went into the kitchen and sat down at the table which was already laid and his wife Ann brought the food comprising of *(soup, boiled carrot and dandelion leaves and slices of wholemeal bread and a wedge of cheese each)*, to the table.

They each ate their meal in silence, Ann was still grieving the death of their five year old son Tim who had died of a fever two months previously and her baby which had been stillborn three weeks previously (caused, Luke thought, by the shock of Tim dying so suddenly). When he had finished his meal, Luke took his 'gansy' from the hook behind the kitchen door, he told Ann he had to go to Havers Lane to visit the Cordwainers Hall and promised her he would be back as soon as he could.

He walked into Gudramgate where he met with Ralph Twist a fellow Cordwainer, together they walked toward

Monke Bar and as they reached the Bar they encountered John Cundill, who was elderly, very lame, much overweight and he was also the Parish Constable, he was checking the security of the Sally-port which was set in wall of the Barbican of Monk Bar, John told them that he had just locked up after allowing a mounted messenger from the Earl of Newcastle to leave the Citie by that route. The absence of leaguers outside that section of the Wall resulted in small troops of Roundheads making very occasional patrols.

Messengers leaving the Citie on horseback were seldom intercepted by the patrols. The nearest Parliamentary solgers were encamped some distance away, close by Heslington and Fulford. Luke and Ralph left John Cundill to his task and then climbed upon the the Citie Wall. The Gild of Cordwainers had been given the task of watching for any activity the besieging Parliamentarians might use to attack or commence tunnelling in order to lay a mine under the wall along that section of the Citie Walls. York like London and some other Cities, had "trained bands" of citizens and craftsmen who were ready to resist attacks on their Citie. The Masters of most of the Craft Gilds in the Citie were now arranging training for their members for this very purpose.

Luke and Ralph walked along the wall from the Monke Bar to Layerthorpe Postern, they looked over the Wall and from the Heslington area they saw smoke rising over the treetops. The Roundheads had lit fires to prepare the food for their evening meal. There was no movement along any of the tracks approaching the Citie Wall. They encountered Karl Milstead who was on patrol of the Walls (Karl was a journeyman Cordwainer who worked for Moses Akombe the Master of the York Guild of Cordwainers).

From his belt Karl unfastened his leather flask, he uncorked it and took a long slow drink of ale from it, he offered Luke and Ralph to share in his refreshment, they declined and he re-fastened it to his belt. He told them that Horace Richardson was patrolling the far end of their section toward Layerthorpe Postern. Luke asked him if his duty would finish before the Company drill in Cordwainers Hall was over, Karl told them that he and Horace were on patrol until dusk and then they were both going home.

When they got to Layerthorpe Postern, both Luke and Ralph exchanged greetings with Horace, they then left the Walls and went into Hundegate and then to Cordwainers Hall in Havers Lane. As they entered the Hall, Luke estimated it was about half full of their fellow Cordwainers, most of whom were in possession of self made roughly assembled Pikes. Members of the garrison from the Clifforde Tower were present and shortly everyone quietened when the Sergeant of the Garrison shouted for their attention and began explaining the drill positions they would need to use to defend the Walls using their makeshift Pikes. He told the men they would be alongside the members of the garrison who would have muskets.

The drill went on until half past the hour of eight and the men were then dismissed by their Master Moses Akombe and in their straggling groups set off to make their numerous ways home. As the groups were leaving the Hall, Moses Akombe was standing aside from the door and he was conversing with the Company Clerk and the Sergeant of the Garrison of Cliffords Tower. Upon seeing Luke approaching the door, Moses called out to him and beckoned for him to join them.

When Luke joined them, Master Akombe said, "*Luke, Sgt. Hogg will need a lodging and I have decided that he will be billeted with you and Ann*", Moses introduced Luke to Sgt. Hogg, who then went off in company with the Clerk to collect his pack and equipment which was in the Clerk's side-chamber. Whilst they were away Moses said to Luke, *"The Chamberlain will pay the 4d a day which is your due, for the cost of his diete whilst he is with you"*.

Carrying his pack, Sgt. Hogg rejoined them and he and Luke set off to walk to Trinity Passage. Luke knew that Ann would not be happy with the arrival of Sgt. Hogg. As they walked through the streets Luke was quiet and thinking how he could best deal with Ann's re-action. Sgt. Hogg, however, was happily explaining to Luke the extent of the defences of the Citie, he was not aware that Luke was not listening to a word he was saying.

They walked through Bedern and into Gudramgate, where, very noisy chatter and laughter was heard coming from within the inns and alehouses they passed, most of whose occupants were solgers from the Garrison, who when they were not on duty, frequented the premises with their comrades. Some local wenches of ill repute were often in company with the solgers, drunkenness was common. The keepers of the taverns still open, brewed their own ale and intoxicants (most of them of dubious content). A lot of the ingredients for brewing were starting to become scarce. As they turned into Trinity Passage they could hear shouting and laughter from within the nearby Bedern Hall, which had been the refectory of the Vicars Choral, but, now housed clergy who had either been disgraced or were regularly in a drunken state.

Luke explained to Sgt. Hogg that Ann (because of her recent heartbreaks) might be upset at his presence in her home. Upon opening the front door Luke invited Sgt. Hogg to step inside the shop, he then closed the door, shot the bolts across and set into their retaining brackets the heavy iron security bar across the door. Picking up the oil lantern,

Luke led the way across the workshop towards the kitchen at the rear. As Luke opened the kitchen door, he called out to Ann and upon stepping into the kitchen he saw she was across at the fireplace, she was stirring the contents of a cooking pan, which would be their Supper.

Ann straightened up from her task and turned to face him, she gave a gasp of surprise and ran quickly toward him and with a cry of delight, she threw her arms around Sgt. Hogg's neck. He similarly embraced Ann and lifted her off her feet and swung her round. When he stopped and she was able to regain her feet, she half turned to Luke and said, *"This is my Uncle Josh, I have not seen him since I was a child"*. After several moment's of embrace Ann stepped back and looking closely at Sgt. Hogg, she remarked, *"Uncle, when I was a little girl you always looked like a giant, I was sometimes frightened"*. Joshua Hogg smiled and taking his cloak from his shoulder he hung it behind the kitchen door, he turned and went to the fireplace, he pulled forward a chair and sat opposite Luke.

Supper was taken at a slow pace, due to the numerous questions asked and so many memories exchanged of instances of sadness and laughter as they looked back on earlier times. Joshua Hogg had been the youngest brother of Ann's mother and he had run off when he was thirteen. He arrived eventually at the edge of the Moors near to Whitby. Where after being found by a shepherd, who had used him to watch over sheep grazing on the moors above Whitby and had habitually and cruelly starved and beat him. As he grew into manhood, he again ran away and he eventually arrived in London. He joined the King's Army and became a Pikeman and after gaining the trust and respect of his fellow soldiers he was given the rank of Sergeant.

Joshua told them that this War would never be won by either side, there would be losers and they would be the ordinary common people, they had and were, being forced to fight and die in battles that they neither wanted or understood. He said if the King lost, the people would suffer for many years at the hands of Parliament. Ann asked him how long he thought the Siege would last and would the Parliamentarians "fire" the Citie if they ever breeched the Walls. Joshua told them the siege was weak along the North side of the Citie because the Earl of Manchester had not yet arrived with his Army. The approach to the Citie in that area was only guarded by irregular patrols by troops of mounted Parliamentary soldiers.

The Scot's if they got into the Citie, would rampage and were likely to plunder, rape and get drunk he told them, but, he thought Lord Fairfax, whom he knew to be a fair man would try to keep any occupying Army in check. They talked on until the midnight hour, which they heard being shouted in the street outside by the Constable John Cundilll, they then retired to rest for the night. At such short notice Ann told Joshua that a garret room was the only suitable space in the house where they could accommodate him, she led him up the stairs and when he saw the room he told her it would suit his needs.

When Ann returned to the marital bedchamber both she and Luke talked a little longer, as they settled down to sleep, Luke realised the arrival of her uncle, had made Anne more cheerful than she had been for many weeks. Luke awoke at daybreak, Ann was not in the bed, he dressed and made his way down to the kitchen. As he entered the kitchen he heard Josh's heavy booted footsteps coming down the stairs after him.

As Luke was putting another log onto the fire, Josh walked into the kitchen and bade both Luke and Ann a good morn. They all took their places at table and Ann ladled generous helpings of gruel onto their platters. Josh told them, that from that morning, because of the siege, Sir John Glenham after discussions with the Lord Mayor, was arranging for many foodstuffs to be collected from the homes of the Citizens and held in Clifforde,s Tower, to be redistributed fairly among everyone in the Citie, when it was needed.

After breaking their fast, Luke went into his workshop and after taking down the shutters, he stood on the doorstep, he saw Trinity Passage was very busy, his neighbours were busy preparing their wares for sale. He shouted greetings to his opposite neighbour Will Wright, a butcher who was standing on the cobbles outside his open fronted shop laying out his joints of meat. After an exchange of banter and laughter, Luke turned back inside and started his days labour. In a short while Josh came from the kitchen, he had on his cape, his shoulder belt containing his shot and at his waist hung a strong leather vessel containing his black powder, he was carrying his musket in his right hand. He bade Luke farewell and Josh set off to make his way to the Clifford's Tower.

Luke worked steadily throughout the morning and as noon approached he had finished the pair of riding boots he had been working upon. He polished the boots and carefully placed them in a soft skinned carrying bag. He took off his apron and put on his leather jerkin, he went into the kitchen and said to Anne, *"I have to go to the Common Hall"*. As he spoke, the sound of cannon fire could be heard and Ann said, *"Please be careful"*. Smiling, Luke said, *"Ay, ah will"*.

Walking down Gudramgate towards Kings Church, Luke passed by the right side of the Church and continued into Shambles. Horses were restless within the shafts of their carts due to the noise of the distant cannon fire, the Butchers who traded in that street, were not standing outside their shops exchanging their usual banter with their fellow traders. As he turned right from Shambles, he walked along the Pavement towards All Saints Church, Luke saw coming towards him a crowd of people they were jostling on the roadway in Coppergate near to the Church.

As he got to the Church he saw that some in the crowd had injuries and open wounds and most of them were in a panic. He then saw one of his friends Keit Starkey, he was trying to push his handcart which he used in his craft as a Plaisterer, he was going in the opposite direction to the crowd. Solgers from the Garrison were trying to calm people in the crowd and other bystanders, they were urging them to move on and return to their workshops or homes. Keit told Luke that the Butter Market in Micklegate had been hit by cannon fire, some people had been killed and many had been injured, he had been told to go to the Butter Market to help with rescue and to remove rubble on his handcart

At the solgers bidding Luke left his friend and continued his walk along Ousegate onto the bridge, ahead of him on his right at the south end of the bridge stood St. Williams's Chapel, from the clock tower of the Chapel Luke saw that the time was nearly a half after twelve. He walked passed the Chapel door and entered the next door into the Council Chamber, he spoke to the Constable who told him that the Lord Mayor Edmond Cowper was at the Clifford Tower. Luke left the riding boots with the Constable and as he left the building, he decided that before he went back to his workshop he would walk on into Micklegate to the Butter Market to see if he could help. From the Common Hall he turned right to walk toward Micklegate, on the other side of the Bridge, stood the Debtor's Prison, very few of the small window's had any glass left within them,

When he got to the Butter Market, Luke saw that all the injured people had been taken from the area, he saw Keit again, he was struggling to push his handcart, which had been fully loaded with broken stone and rocks back through broken stone debris into Micklegate. Luke went over to Keit and helped him to push the heavy load. Keit said he had been told by the Garrison souldiers to take his load to the Layerthorp Postern, the Wall was fallen at parts in that area and was in sore need of been made stronger. As they pushed the cart along they were often passed by horse drawn carts carrying out the same task.

As they struggled along with the heavy cart Keit said that those badly injured had been taken into St. Martincum-Gregory Church. those who could walk had been sent to Holy Trinity Church in Micklegate. Solgers had told Luke that the cannón had been on Houlgate Hill and had been firing over the Bishop's Fields. It had been silenced after being hit by cannon fire from Citie defenders at the Sconce outside the Citie on the London Road. Upon their arrival at the Postern at Layerthorpe they found that many of the craftsmen who were in the Trained Bands of the Citie were hard at work to make the Wall stronger, everyone around seemed cheerful and determined. They all appeared to be comrades together, they were not going to be starved or frightened into surrender.

When the cart was unloaded they could still hear the noise from cannon explosions away in the distance. They decided this firing would be from the Sconce on London Road. After leaving Keit, who was returning to the Butter Market, Luke made his way back to Trinity Passage. As he walked through the Citie streets, he saw many citizens moving warily, most kept close to buildings ready to take shelter quickly. Fear and anxiety showed clearly on the faces of most women, but, strangely the children appeared excited at what was happening, as if it was a new game. Luke wondered what sorrows lay ahead for the good Citizens of York.

As he entered his workshop Ann came through from the kitchen, she told him that Garrison solgers led by Uncle Josh had visited, they had been ordered by Sir John Glenham (Governor of the Citie) to check all properties in the Citie in order to seize food and flour which they were to take to the Cliffords Tower for storage.

When they left they took with them two bags of bran flour and a barrel of salted Pork, she had managed to hide two more sacks of bran flour in the log store, along with a large matured cheese. Dried vegetables they did not take, Uncle Josh had told his men there was not enough quantity. Chickens in the backyard were not taken, they only took food which could be stored. Luke told Ann that it was right that food should be taken and stored, so that when food stocks were really low, everyone would get a fair share of what was in the store at Clifford's Tower.

Because of his late return from having helped his friend Keit, they had their mid-day meal late. Luke told Ann of all the damage and injuries which had been caused that morn. After his meal Luke returned to his workshop and set to work making boots which were part of an order received to supply strong footwear to be used by the Trained Bands of the Citie. Moses Akombe the Master Cordwainer had shared the order equally amongst all the Craftsmen in the Gild.

As he was concentrating on his task of of cutting out welts, the workshop doorbell clanged a merry jingle as his friend Ralph Twist entered into the workshop from Trinity Passage, he was carrying a canvas sack over his shoulder. They exchanged greetings and Ralph placed the sack upon the workbench and took out a brace of coney's *(rabbits)*, he said to Luke, "*Ah went out from t' Sally Port last neet an' set snares, ah got three brace, so ah thout thou cud ave a brace*". Luke thanked him warmly, they would he thought, make a tasty supper, the skin's he would cure and use them as lining for winter boots, many of his gentlewomen customers felt they needed the extra warmth and comfort afforded by the fur on the skin's.

After they had a quick chat concerning ye most recent events of the siege, they arranged to meet that evening at Cordwainers Hall, where they were to receive further training in the role of "trained bands". Finishing the boot he had been working upon, Luke picked up both coney's (they were two large bucks) he went through into the kitchen, Ann was preparing vegetables for supper, he showed her the coney's and commenced skinning both animals, ready for Ann to cook them.

It was late afternoon and Luke took his leave, telling Ann he would return before "Great Peter" tolled six o' the clock from the Minster bell tower. He left Gudramgate and went into Bedern, as he passed Bedern Hall (the refectory of the Vicar's Choral) he heard shouting and raucous laughter coming from within. The occupants were probably, as happened quite often in a drunken state. He walked down the snickleway, passing St. Saviours Church and continued into Fossgate, he then turned into Foss Yard and went to the workshop of his Gild Master Moses Akombe.

Upon his arrival, Luke was welcomed by Moses, who then turned and then stretched his leg once or twice (as if he had cramp) before he seated himself on a stool and bade Luke to seat himself on the other stool at the workbench. When they settled themselves comfortably, Luke said to Moses, "*Master, ah bin giv'n ah brace o' coney's , fro' Ralph Twist, he'd snar'd em on't grass banks o't moat next ta Wall at*

Monk Bar". Moses smiled and said, *"Yes, I know, Raef gave me a brace as well"*. Luke shifted his posture on the seat and said, *"Well Master, ah bin thinkin', food a'll be 'arder ta get, as t' round'eads try ta force us ta surrender"*.

Moses gazed at Luke with great intent and said, *"Pray go on"*, Luke continued and said, *"Well Master, ah think, if t' Court of Assistants sez yea, wi cud av t' members working t'gether catching more coney's, 'n salt 'em 'n put 'em in barrels to keep 'til needed"*. Moses in a thoughtful mood gazed at Luke and said, *"Luke, you have told me of a good way of increasing our food stocks, I am sure, when I advise the members of the Court of Assistants, they will agree with the idea, the Lord Mayor will also I think, support your idea, thank you Luke"*.

Rising slowly from his seat and again stretching his leg, Moses said, *"I will discuss this with the members of the Court tonight"*. Luke thanked the Master and feeling pleased with his efforts, Luke departed from the Workshop.

When he got back to his own workshop, Luke after tidying his bench went through into the kitchen, Ann was preparing supper, cannon fire could be heard, Luke went through the kitchen door and into the yard. He listened and judged that the noise of the cannon was from the area of Lamel Hill, they were probably once again being aimed at Walmgate Bar. The firing stopped and he went back into the kitchen, Ann told him that supper was ready, she said, "Ah think wi'd best 'ave owers, an ah can leave Uncle Josh's in't stewpan". Luke told Ann of his visit to Moses Akombe, Ann said, *"Ya can't get a meal that tastes better than a gud roast or stewed coney"*. They were just finishing their meal when there was a loud knocking on the front door, Luke got up saying to Ann, *"That 'ill be Josh, ah think"*.

Upon opening the door, Luke was quite surprised to see standing before him, John Cundill, the Parish Constable.

Luke bade his visitor to enter the workshop. John was both elderly and lame, his stature was bowed and his official staff of office was very useful in aiding him to walk.

He shuffled into the workshop and whilst leaning heavily against Luke's workbench, he said, "*Luke, I ast ta ask ya summa*t," he turned and pushing backwards he was able to rest his rump partly on the workbench, after a deep breath he said, "*Ay ave ta be 'lected back ast' constable round here, an I ave ta get two Freemen ta send letters ta Lord Mayor telling him, am fit fa job*". Luke readily agreed, in spite of his lameness he knew John Cundill could do his job and he knew he was an honest man.

Luke said to John Cundill, "*Ah"ll mek sure 't Lord Mayor gets a letter.*" Ye Constable smiled his appreciation and said, "*Thank ya Luke, yunno ah bin t' Constable in this Ward fa two score years or more*". Luke said, "*Ah ya sure ya strong enough ta manage it still*". John adjusted his posture upon the bench and after taking a deep breath he said, "*Ah can talk sense into most folk but if they tu'n nasty, folk around come an' 'elp me*". Taking another deep breath he stood up from the bench and after clasping Luke by his arm in thanks he turned and made his way through the door and into the street.

After locking the workshop door, Luke returned into the kitchen, Josh was sitting at the table eating his supper, he turned to look at Luke and said, "*This rabbit tastes good, it is nice to eat some meat that does not taste salty*". Luke sat down on a spare chair opposite and told Josh of his visit to see Moses Akombe and explained the idea he had discussed with his Gild Master. Josh nodded his agreement and said, "*That is a good idea, stocks in the Food Store for the Citie are good at the moment, but rabbits could be very useful in a few weeks as stocks are used.*"

Whilst Josh got on with his meal, Luke looked through his Money Book to check the amounts of unpaid Bills that had arisen since the siege had started. Luke knew his customers well enough to know they would settle their debts after the Siege was over. Most of the Citizens were keeping hold of their money if they could. Many craftsmen and traders were, where possible, settling theirs debts by exchanging goods or services with their fellow traders.

CHAPTER IV

Crisis for Tobias

As Isaac approached Tobe's cottage, he became concerned, there was no smoke curling from the chimney, this was very unusual, every day as Isaac approached the cottage there was always smoke swirling from the chimney.

The last thing Tobe did each day before heading to his work, was to bank up the fire with a log or two, then cover them with sheep dung and wet ashes, this method usually ensured that the fire kept going all day, Tobe knew that even warm and pleasant days his mother and father, because of their frailty, often felt cold. The absence of smoke alerted Isaac, he knew something was wrong, he ran forward to the cottage and as he got to the gate, he saw the front door was standing wide open.

When he entered the cottage he shouted out for Tobe, but, his friend was not in the cottage, he saw Tobe's father, (Ned Platt) was lying on the kitchen floor near to the fireplace, he was lying on his back, his face was ashen grey and he was not breathing, when Isaac placed his hand upon old man's face and forehead the skin was cold to his touch. It was clear to Isaac that Tobe's father was dead, Isaac rose and walked across the kitchen and looked into the other room, there was very little light in the room, the only window being very small. From the doorway Isaac looked back into the kitchen, on the mantle shelf he saw a small candle dish containing a stub of tallow candle. He went across and picked up the dish and taking a spill from the mantle shelf he placed it carefully into the fire and dying embers and eventually obtained a flame from which he lit the candle. Going back into the bedroom, Isaac saw a bed in the far corner, moving toward it he saw there was a small huddled figure sitting on the bed.

It had been some time since Isaac had actually seen Mrs. Platt, she looked so frail, but he realised she must be at least 50years old and he had seen so many elderly people like her who had become ill and weak. Isaac knew she could no longer hear and Tobe had told him that her sight was now very poor. Whilst he was thinking what he could do next Isaac heard the sound of voices coming from outside the cottage. He went back to the kitchen and as he got to the cottage door, he saw Tobe standing beside Jack Grainger's waggon, he was helping Mrs. Hopkin to step down from the high seat of the waggon. Jack Grainger was busy at the side of the waggon, he lifted a large size square shaped basket onto his shoulder and started to walk toward Isaac, who was still standing at the cottage door, Isaac nodded to Jack and stepped out of the doorway and walked slowly over to the waggon, where Mrs. Hopkin was busy smoothing out the folds of her dress, whilst Tobe looked despairingly at Isaac as he approached them.

When he got to where Tobe was standing, Isaac clasped his arms around his friend's shoulders and expressed his sympathy, Jack came out of the cottage and returned to the waggon, turning to Isaac he said, *"Isaac, w'ile Tobe tek's Mrs. Hopkin int' cottage can ya giv' mi an 'and wi t' trestles an t' big planks*". Nodding, Isaac moved away from Tobe and when Mrs. Hopkin took hold of his arm, Tobe walked with her into the cottage. As Jack and Isaac were taking the trestles and large plank from the waggon, Jack said to Isaac, "*Tobe got ta Manor House afor' it got light, all wor in darkness, so, he sat an' waited int' barn until Will Thornton ternd up e'rly fa work*".

Isaac looked at Jack and said, "*Ow's 'e teken it, da ya think*", Jack raised his eyebrows and said, "*Ah don't think 'e know' w'ats 'appened, 'es in shock*".

After they had unloaded the waggon Jack told Isaac that Squire Fewster had sent Mrs. Hopkin to lay-out Mr. Platt and to dress him in a shroud and tie him up in sack-cloth ready for burial. When Jack and Isaac had carried everything into the cottage and set up the plank and trestles in the kitchen, they gently lifted the body of Mr. Platt onto the plank, both men withdrew quietly outside and waited at the waggon. Whilst they were waiting Isaac asked Jack what was to happen when Mrs. Hopkin had completed the laying-out, Jack informed Isaac that the Squire had told him to take the body straight to Leak Church and set up the trestle table near to the Baptism Font and lay the body upon it and leave it there. The Squire was sending for the Parson to arrange a Funeral.

Both men turned when they heard Mrs. Hopkin call, she waved them forward toward the cottage. They moved forward and joined her at the doorway, she whispered to them, that she had finished laying-out Mr. Platt and that she would take Tobe into the bedroom and help him to see to his mother, whilst Jack and Isaac removed the body, the trestles and the remnants of sackcloth from the cottage. Mrs. Hopkin turned and they followed her into the cottage, she took Tobe by his arm and led him through into the bedroom and at the doorway she turned her head and gestured to Jack and Isaac to take the body to the waggon.

Both men nodded to her solemnly and turned to commence their task, they each went to a different end of the trestle table and took hold of the shoulders and feet with their hands, with an affirming nod to each other they lifted up the body, then shuffled gently and quietly outside, where they placed the body onto the waggon and covered it with a canvas sheet, they re-entered the cottage and then brought out the trestles, planks and sackcloth remnants and then after putting them on the wagon they awaited the return of Mrs. Hopkin.

After a short while they saw Mrs. Hopkin come out of the door of the cottage and she turned and started to talk to Tobe who was standing on the doorstep of the cottage, he looked such a sad and forlorn figure as he listened to what Mrs. Hopkin was telling him, after a few moments she gave him a hug, turned and walked slowly toward the waggon. Jack got onto the waggon at his driving side, Isaac took down a wooden box from the wagon and helped Mrs. Hopkin to step onto it, from whence she stepped onto the waggon after taking the firm hand offered to her by Jack, who was standing on the waggon in behind the high seat. Isaac climbed over the side of the waggon using the wheelspokes as steps. Making sure Mrs. Hopkin was comfortable on the high seat at his side, Jack took up the reins, upon hearing the click of Jack's tongue the horses walked on, both Jack and Isaac gave friendly waves to Tobe as the waggon was turning.

Leak Church was close by the Manor House and as they approached, Mrs. Hopkin asked Jack to take the waggon into the kitchen courtyard of the Manor House before going to the Church. Entering the gates of the Manor House, Jack flicked the reins and instructed his team of horses toward the kitchen courtyard by calling out *"for'ard lads"*. The horses moved forward at a walk and needed no further bidding they took the waggon straight into the courtyard and halted at the side of the loading ramp. Mrs. Hopkin was able to step straight from the waggon onto the ramp without assistance, after which she turned to Jack and said, *"Please wait here for me, I'll not be long"*.

Turning as he stood up Jack said to his friend, *"Isaac ah think I'll tek yon sackcloth back in t' stable, can ya tek tuther stuff in la kitchen"*, both men jumped down and commenced their tasks. As Jack got back to the waggon, Isaac was just coming from the kitchen onto the loading ramp, as he sat down on the high seat Jack saw Mrs. Hopkin coming towards the waggon from the direction of the kitchen garden, she was carrying in each hand a large bunch of various bright coloured flowers. Jack got down from the waggon and when she got to him she asked him to place the blooms carefully onto the waggon. When Jack got back onto the waggon, Mrs. Hopkin had seated herself comfortably on the high seat, Isaac was sitting behind her with his back against the waggon side.

They made the short journey to Leak Church in sombre silence which was not broken until the waggon stopped outside the Church and Jack said, "Mrs. Hopkin, shall wi tek flowers in fust an' then ya can sort 'em, til Isaac an' me 'ave got tresells set up", the lady nodded her agreement and she set off to enter the Church, after they had each carefully picked up a bunch of flowers Isaac and Jack followed her. Whilst Mrs. Hopkin was looking for suitable vases in which to display the flowers, Isaac and Jack returned outside to the waggon, they each picked up a pair of trestles and returned with them into the Church. They set the trestles in place next to the Baptismal Font and Jack paced out, that there would be sufficient space to safely approach the trestles, before they returned with the body of Mr. Platt on the large planks, which they had bound together with strong rope. After slightly altering the position of the trestles, both men agreed they had got it right.

With Isaac leading the way both men left the Church and went back to the waggon, before moving the plank, Jack suggested that it would be safer if he secured the body to the plank with a piece of sackcloth tied around it, Isaac nodded his agreement. Jack climbed onto the waggon and when he had found a suitable piece of sackcloth from within the box under his high seat, he said to Isaac, *"Reet if ya can just lift plank up a bit, I'll push sackcloth throu' an' tie it round"*. After completing this task Jack got down from the waggon and the two men, carefully and slowly lifted the plank and carried it and the body into the Church. As they got to the trestles, Mrs. Hopkin was waiting and with the help of her occasional words of guidance, the planks and body were laid across the trestles. Mrs. Hopkin then placed vases of flowers on the plank at the head and foot, she stepped back and all three of them stood for a moment with bowed heads, before turning and leaving the Church.

Outside the Church, Mrs Hopkin told Jack she would walk back to the Manor House, Isaac sat on the high seat next to Jack and they drove in silence during the short ride to the stableyard. A stream bubbled over pebbles and large stones as flowed down from the hills, passing, but a short distance from the rear of the Manor House, in periods of heavy rainfall the flow of the stream became a raging torrent. The Squire had decided to divert part of the stream in order to form a lake, so that when there was a period of drought there would always be water for use in the Manor House itself and the farmyard. Isaac and Tobe together with other estate workers had been working since early Spring digging out meadow land about three chains from the Manor House (this would form the bowl of the new Lake).

Jack headed his cart over to the crater to join the rest of the men, their arrival caused a few comments about their lateness, but, when Isaac told them of the tasks that Jack and he had performed that morning, their good natured ribaldry turned swiftly to sympathy, most of them had known Tobe's father.

CHAPTER V

Building a lake

Isaa saw that the middle of the hole was as deep as a man was tall and it levelled out as it got to the edges. The men were lining the floor of the new lake with clay which could be dug on the surrounding hills. Turning his head, Isaac saw his friend Will Thornton leading his horses and waggon back to the hillside, when he caught up with the waggon, Will asked him how Tobe was dealing with the death, Isaac related to him the arrangements that had been made and how the shock of the death was affecting their friend.

When they reached the pick-up point for the clay at the bottom of the hill, there was, about two chains above, a scarred ridge which ran across the hillside and then dipped slowly down to form a rugged gully about three chains or more long. At the top of the gully a team of men were busy digging clay from the dry watercourse along the ridge and loading it onto stout wooden sledges. When full, the sledges were lowered by the men below controlling the descent by using rope pulley's wrapped around stout posts hammered into the hillside. An earth ramp had been made at the end of the descent, this enabled the sledges to be manhandled onto the waiting waggon's and then carted back to the lake site.

After assisting Will to load his waggon, Isaac took a shovel and scrambled up the hillside and joined the men who were digging the clay, seeing that there were enough diggers, Isaac joined the group who were loading the clay onto the sledges. It was toiling work and all were ready for the stew and rough bread (which had been sent up from the Manor House) for their break which was taken taken some time after mid-day. When they had finished their refreshment, work was resumed and continued until late in the afternoon, when dark clouds were looming in the sky above them. Whilst they paused in their work Isaac and his group saw approaching them, Mr. Thomas Strong, who was the Estate Bailiff for Squire Fewster, he stood below them and shouted, " *We look set for a heavy storm, the Squire wan'ts you all off the hillside, finish work for the day*", all the workers were keen to comply with the instruction given to them and were quick to prepare to make their various ways home.

Before most of the men had got off the hillside, the storm struck, amidst a very heavy downpour of rain, bright flashes of lightning lit up the sky and loud claps of thunder quickly followed. On the cart track at the bottom of the hill, Will had hastily covered the waggon with a large canvas sheet, which was placed over and secured to the wooden stanchions and crossbeams which he had also put in place to support the sheet. Will shouted to the men to climb aboard the waggon, the whole group scrambled onto the waggon and sat or squat under the canvas awning. The rain was still falling heavily and torrents of water were cascading down the hillside, meanwhile Will patiently coaxed his team forward for the short journey to the Manor House.

Upon entering the stable yard, Will drove the waggon straight into the large barn, his wet and dishevelled passengers got down and many of them grabbed handfuls of straw and briskly rubbed their sodden clothing in an effort to dry off. After a few minutes there was a shout from near the large entrance doors to the barn informing everyone that the rain had stopped and that prompted people to leave in small bedraggled groups.

From a pile of dry hessian sacks standing in a corner, Isaac picked one up and took it with him, it would help to cover his head and shoulders if there was a further storm as he made his way home. As he approached Tobe's house, Isaac saw a small cart coming toward him, Jack Grainger was the driver and Squire Fewster was his passenger. Isaac stepped slightly off the track and gave a wave as the cart trundled passed him and continued on to the Manor House.

Just as Isaac was about to knock on the door of Tobe's cottage, the door opened Tobe was standing on the threshold, he stepped backwards and bade Isaac to enter. Upon stepping inside Isaac saw a young girl across the kitchen at the fireplace she was busy stirring the contents of the large cauldron which was standing on the hob at the firegrate. Tobe told Isaac that Mrs. Hopkin had spoken to Lady Fewster about Mrs. Platt's health and the circumstances Tobe had now found himself in. Lady Fewster had told Mrs. Hopkin, to make such arrangements as she thought necessary to deal with the problem. The young girl was a scullery maid and she had been detailed by Mrs. Hopkin to attend to the needs of Mrs. Platt by attending at the cottage for an hour each morning and evening to feed and nurse her.

Thinking of the burial Isaac said, *"Ave ya sin Parson Grimley"*, Tobe replied, *"Ah f'un him int' chu'chyard at midday, an 'e sez ah can't bury mi dad int' chu'chyard, co's ah can't pay, e' sez he'll ave' to go in't corner o't field wi 't rest o' poor"*. Isaac said,

"When ah ya diggin' grave then", said Isaac turning to his friend and Tobe said, *"Jack Gainger told 'mi he'd get Will*

-55-

ta 'elp im an' they'd do 't job tonight after work". He paused and gathering his thoughts, he said, *"Squires just bin ta say, he's letting me off work t'morrow, an ah can 'ave t' burial w'en t'uthers ah finished work"*. Isaac asked Tobe if he wanted any other help, but Tobe assured Isaac that he felt they could manage. They clasped hands and Isaac gave his friend a pat of comfort on the shoulder, before turning and making his weary way home.

When Isaac got home he told Rose of the events of the day and of his thoughts and sympathy for his friend. He was quite subdued and he had to make a real effort to respond to the excited cries of his children who were at play when they called for his attention.

He decided that before supper, he would take the children on a walk up the hill to check the fencing of a field, where he intended to summer graze his sheep. They left the cottage and in the yard Isaac called his dog which quickly appeared from the barn and ran after the children as they skipped along the path. As they approached a long sandy bank at the side of the track, Isaac saw large groups of rabbits scurrying back into the adjacent burrows. The breeding season had, Isaac thought, added greatly to the numbers of this rabbit colony and would be a big help to providing food in coming months.

When they got to a copse of small trees and bushes, Isaac took out his knife and cut a bundle of strong saplings and sharpened each of them at one end. Willi and Ann had scrambled through to the other side of the copse and Isaac heard them shouting excitedly, putting his bundle of saplings at the side of the track, he then made his way to where his children were. The grass and vegetation had been burnt away a short distance from the copse and Isaac saw there were a great number of bones from small animals and birds scattered about the area.

Turning, Isaac saw his children were standing within the copse, their attention was drawn to an area where the floor was covered with a thick layer of straw. Lying upon this patch of straw was a bedraggled figure, Isaac shouted to the children to go wait upon the track. As he bent down beside the figure, Isaac knew immediately that he was looking at a dead man. There were maggots wriggling on his face, they were exiting from his mouth and nostrils and a strong smell of rotting flesh could be smelt in the air around the scene. The straw area where the body was lying was fenced on three sides by hurdles, made by intertwining thin willow together to form a trellis onto strong saplings the structure was completed by a fourth similar hurdle placed across on to of the top them forming a roof. The structure was large enough to offer shelter for two medium size men.

This structure had clearly been made and used by the wayfarer lying dead in front of him, who in life had not wished to be discovered. Isaac could see and feel that the straw was wet and smelly, the ash from the fire was cold and damp to the touch. Returning to the the track and calling for the children to follow him, Isaac picked up the saplings and went the short distance to the field where he had intended to check the fencing, he placed the bundle in the field near the gate. Calling to the children, they all made their way back to the cottage.

Isaac was not happy about the presence of the camp and body he had found, the circumstances of the death he found even more worrying. He was probably a "leaguer", who had deserted from the Scottish Army and had been heading northwards to get home, when illness overtook him. When they got back to the cottage Rose was about to serve supper. Later after the children had gone to bed, Isaac told Rose of the makeshift camp and the body he had found. He told her not to venture up in that direction or let the children out of her sight for the next few days, he could have died from the black death, pox or fever.

Isaac awoke early next morning and after breaking his fast and foddering and watering his stock, he set off for the Manor House. Upon arriving, he made straight for the large stable where he knew he would find Jack Grainger tending to his charges. He told Jack of the discovery he had made the previous day and asked his friend what he thought he should do about the body. Jack who was standing beside a wooden bench, continued in his task of filling the nosebags which were placed upon the bench, when he had filled the last one, he turned to Isaac and said, *"I'll tell tha' w'at ah'do, but gi' mi 'and to feed these 'osses ferst"*.

When the horses had been fed, they returned to the bench and Jack said, *"Wi' 'ave t' tel't Squire, bout it"*. He paused whilst he fastened his gaiters to his legs, he then said, *"Ah think yon body, shu'd be cuv'erd in lime and burned in a pit at t'edge o' field"*. Jack stepped forward and took his smock coat from where it had been hanging on wooden peg on a nearby upright wooden roof beam. He put the garment on and turned to Isaac and said, *"Reet, ah ya ready, wi'll go t' see t' Squire"*.

They left the stable and walked across the stable yard, walking round the barn they entered the large kitchen yard and approached the kitchen door. As they got to the door Mrs. Hopkin appeared on the threshold, she said, *"Good morning Jack, good morning Isaac, is it the Squire you are seeking"*. Will nodded and said, *"Ay is 'e about"*, Mrs. Hopkin said, *"Yes, he has broken his fast and he is in the Library writing letters, I will take you through"*. At the door to the Library she motioned to Jack and Isaac to wait, she knocked upon the door and upon hearing the responsive call from within she entered.

After a few moments she withdrew from the room and beckoned Jack and Isaac to enter, the Squire was sitting at a long oak table, he had in his hand his quill and he was writing in a large calf-skin bound ledger. He placed his quill onto the inkstand, moved the ledger to one side and looked up at his two workers. He then said to Jack, *"Mrs. Hopkin has told me you need my advice, what is the problem"*, Jack and Isaac looked uneasily at each other, before Isaac said, *"I f'und ah body yesterday, an ah thou't, tha sh'ud no 'bout it, Master"*.

Squire Fewster questioned Isaac closely about all the circumstances surrounding the discovery and when he was satisfied he had all the necessary information, he rose from his chair and walked over to the fireplace. After spending quite some time pacing back and forth in front of the fireplace, he returned to his seat at the table. He sat down and spent a few more moments in thought, he then looked up at both men. Setting his gaze upon Isaac he said, *"I am pleased with your actions yesterday, as you rightly say the corpse could be a danger to the health of all in our community and you were right to bring it to my attention"*.

The Squire got to his feet and walked over to the window where he looked out over the countryside, in the distance the Woundhills were to be seen, the tops of them were emerging slowly as the morning sunshine dispersed the mist which had shrouded the tops since daybreak. Turning, he walked back to the table, where he again seated himself. After some shuffling movements and finally satisfying himself that he was in the most comfortable position he sat up straight, placed his clasped hands upon the table and looked once more at Will and Isaac. He took a kerchief from the pocket of his breeches and slowly he mopped his brow, before returning the item back to his to his breeches pocket. He then said, *"I have decided what I want done, I want you both to listen carefully to what I say"*.

He took a drink of water from a glass which was upon the table close to his right hand, he cleared his throat and then said, "*I am concerned that the death of this of this person may have been caused by some fever, or even the plague, I want to be certain that all risk is removed, I don't want it spreading about the entire area*". Taking another drink from his glass he went on to say, "*Both of you go to the copse and before you leave, see Mrs. Hopkin and she will find some leather gauntlets to cover your hands when moving the body*". Pausing, he again cleared his throat, he then continued by saying, "*You must dig a pit and build over it a large fire, make it, big enough and hot enough to burn all the body and after it has fully burned and all the ash and fragments have fallen into the pit, I want you to fill in the and cover it with heavy rocks*".

Squire Fewster rose to his feet and said, "*Go now and do as I have bidden, when you see Mrs. Hopkin ask her also, to give you some suitable linen to mask your mouths and noses whilst you are handling the corpse*". The pair turned and left the room closing the door quietly behind them. They made their way through the house to the kitchen and told Mrs. Hopkin of the Squire's instructions to provide them with gauntlets and suitable masking linen. She bade them to wait outside in the porchway whilst she gathered the articles they required. Some minutes later she appeared at the kitchen door, she handed a hessian bag to Jack and said, "*Just you two take care of yourselves, whilst you are doing whatever it is you are supposed to be doing*". Both men nodded in agreement, but, despite Mrs. Hopkin enquiring glances, they omitted to mention the nature of the task they had been given. As the men turned toward the porch way to walk back to the stable, she said, "*Think on and be back in time for poor Ned Platt's burial*".

With Isaac's help, Jack soon harnessed the horses into the waggon and they set off on their journey to deal with the task ahead of them. During the journey both men refrained from discussing the task they had been given, but they were both deep in thought about possible infection to which they may be subjected. When they arrived at the copse. Jack removed the team of horses from the shafts and hobbled them some distance from the waggon, both men then took their spades from the flatbed of the waggon and after marking the size of the pit they required they began digging. The soil was very light in composition and was easy to work, they stuck doggedly to their task and with the sun high above them indicating the arrival of mid-day. They stopped and took stock of the length and depth of the pit they had created, they decided that it should be deeper than waist deep. Resuming their work they excavated more soil and very soon, after again checking the depth, they decided it was deep enough.

Jack suggested to Isaac that they should go with the cart to the large wood a mile or so further up the track to get fallen trees and branches with which to build the fire. Isaac agreed with his friend and after re-harnessing the horses in the shafts, they set off up the track. When they reached the wood, Jack drove down a rough track where he knew there were piles of substantial sized logs, he told Isaac these would be ideal to build the big fire they would need. They came to the first pile, there were about a score of sturdy logs as long as a man was high, with obvious delight Jack said, *"Ah teld thee, jus' w'at wi need"*.

Both men set to work loading logs and branches onto the waggon, they took regular breaks to slake their thirst and get their breath back, for it was it heavy and tiring work they were doing. Jack gave careful thought as the space on the waggon was filled with timber, finally he turned to Isaac and said, *"Ah think wi'v en'uff on fa' this load"*. After replacing their axes and gansies back onto the waggon both the men climbed up onto the high seat and they set off to return back to the copse.

As they arrived back at the copse they saw another waggon approaching them. As he got down from the waggon Jack said to Isaac, "*Ah dun't 'no w'at Will ah's cum fa*". Will drew his team to a halt in front of Jack's team and got down from his high seat. Turning to Jack he said, "*Squire sez ah's got ta gi' ya a bit a 'elp*". Jack grinned and said, "*We'd best ger on then*", whilst Jack and Isaac started unloading their timber, Will started taking bundles of straw from his waggon, the Squire had told him to take the load with him to help get the fire burning.

Jack and Isaac sorted the less sturdy of the branches and placed them criss cross over the pit and Will followed them placing bundles of straw on top. Larger logs were then chosen and again Will placed a thick layer of straw over them, when the pyre was about shoulder height, Jack and Isaac decided that it was time to place the body onto the pyre. They each wrapped around their mouths and noses the linen Mrs. Hopkin had given them and then their gauntlets upon their hands. They moved the body onto the pyre and then gathered together all the debris scattered about the makeshift camp. This was also placed onto the pyre. After placing further branches onto the top they similarly stood branches and logs against all the sides. All three men stepped back to view the results of their efforts.

After taking their few minutes break during which all three men took a drink of ale from the cask under Jack's high seat, they turned their attention to lighting the pyre. Jack had taken the tinderbox from his waggon and he set about using kindling to make a small fire away from the pyre. Whilst he was busy sparking a flame, he asked Isaac and Will to make some torches from straw and kindling. With deft use of the flint and steel he successfully sparked a flame to some straw which quickly spread to the kindling. He built the fire up with thicker kindling and the fire started glowing contentedly.

He saw his companions had made a score or more of torches and called to them, "*Ah think wi can bu'n it now*". All of the men took a torch in each of their hands, they all lit their torches together and went to the sides of the pyre and lit the straw along the bottom edges of the pyre and repeated their actions until the pyre aided by the strong breeze started to burn fiercely. The heat and smoke forced them all to step back several paces and each used a long handled pitchfork to push back burning logs into the flames to prevent them rolling off the sides of the pyre. After a time the embers of the lower burning branches started to fall into the pit.

To keep the fire burning fiercely they placed further logs on top and around the sides as necessary, the men only approached the pyre when it was necessary, they all stood back for comfort from smoke and heat. Looking skywards, Isaac judged from the position of the sun that it was well passed mid-afternoon and remarked to his friends, "*Ah think wi out't put rest o' straw on ta keep it flaming*", Will said, "*Aye, an' ah got a barrel o' goose fat on't waggon, that'll mek it flare up*".

Seeing his companions nodding agreement, Will went to his waggon, followed by Isaac and Jack who unloaded and carried the remaining straw near to the pyre, Will lifted down the barrel and rolled it forward. All three men took up their pitchforks and spread the straw evenly on the ground along both sides of the pyre and far enough away not to catch fire. Then Will liberally poured the fat onto the straw as he walked around the pyre, the men standing apart from each other commenced pitching the saturated straw onto the flames. The flames shot high into the air causing all three men to jump back hastily to safety.

With the fire burning fiercely, the men stood back watching the result of their exertions, very soon the fire ash and debris started to drop into the pit below the pyre quite quickly and they frequently had to move forward to push back blazing branches back onto the fire. As they stood watching, the intensity of the heat started to get cooler and there was but two or three hands in height of fire above ground level which consisted almost entirely of glowing embers.

When the top of the pyre became just a smouldering blanket of ash, Jack said, *"Ah think, wi can start ta rake it flat int' pit now"*, as a result of the raking, the embers fell into the pit, the hot ash was some way below ground level. Will said *"Ah brou't some clay an' muck from t' new pond, that'll fill it in"*. As Will went to move his waggon and team into position, Isaac went with Jack and his waggon about four furlong up the track where there was a pile of large stones which had been removed from the field as a result of recent ploughing.

Will very soon had his waggon into position alongside the pit and was shovelling the clay and soil debris into it. When he had formed a mound above the pit he moved his waggon and removed one of his heavy horses, he led the animal over to the newly formed mound and commenced to walk the animal over the top of it. The weight of the animal very soon levelled the area and he was satisfied with the result. Will was just replacing the horse back into the shafts when Isaac and Jack returned with their load of stones. They dismounted from the waggon and inspected the levelling Will had just completed, Jack turned to his friend and said, *"Tha's med a good job on that Will, now if tha giv' me an' Isaac a hand wi' thes' 'ere stones wi can all on us get back 'ome"*.

The men quickly covered the new grave with the stones and after tidying the area and loading their tools back onto the waggons, they set off to return to Leake for Ned Platts Funeral. Will and Jack's men got their team's moving at a brisk speed and they got to the field at the side of the Church just as Tobe and a group of estate workers approached from the Manor House. Isaac, Will and Jack all quickly jumped down from the waggons and joined the other mourners assembled with Tobe at the side of the grave and after Parson Grimley had said prayers then they all joined in a burial chant. After the Burial service most of the mourners turned and followed Parson Grimley from the field. Isaac, Jack and Will stayed and filled the grave in, whilst Tobe stood in silence watching them. When they had finished Jack told Tobe he would drop him off at his cottage on his way to taking Isaac home. There was little said on the journey, Tobe's two friends thought it was best to leave him to his own thoughts. After dropping Tobe outside his cottage, Jack and Isaac continued in sombre silence until Jack stopped his waggon outside the gate to Isaac's home and allowed his friend to dismount and after saying their farewell's he set off back to the Manor House

As Isaac entered the gate Rose appeared at the cottage door, he shouted to her, *"Keep t' kid's in, ah'm off t' beck, ta bath mi sen"*. He went first into the store shed and took from a hook, an old smock and a pair of breeches, which he kept there to use, whenever he needed to wash himself down at the beck, whenever he got home and he was (up t' nav't in muk and blather).

He went down the hillside to the beck, he took off his boots and stripped off all his clothes, whereupon he walked into the fast flowing water. The water was about six hands deep and and he knelt and laid in the water, vigorously rubbing his body with his hands, ensuring he washed the whole of his body. He then took the clothes he had been wearing, item by item and thoroughly washed and them and squeezed them out as tight as he could before folding them and putting them onto the bank. He put on his dry smock and britches and his wet boots and made his way back to the cottage.

After supper he talked with Rose about his day, he told her of what the Squire had instructed them to do with the corpse up the track and then he talked of Ned Platt's burial and the ungodly way Parson Grimley had dealt with Tobe. Rose asked him a few questions about who was at the burial, but, showed no interest regarding the mysterious corpse up the track. Isaac knew she was always uneasy whenever fever struck around them, she was fearful that it would strike at her family members, he did not pursue the subject. As the sky darkened before bedtime, Isaac went outside and checked the poultry and sheep were settled for the night and he filled their water troughs. Returning inside the cottage and damping down the fire in the grate, he made his way wearily to bed.

CHAPTER VI

Siege Tightened Around York

After the arrival of the army of the Earl of Manchester, the Citie was completely surrounded by leager Armies on 3rd of June, 1644. For citizens and everyone besieged within the Citie, this meant that stocks of food and supplies would eventually be completely used up and York would have to be yielded to the besiegers. The Earl of Newcastle knew that food supplies they already had would last (with careful sharing) for many more weeks, but he hoped that Prince Rupert and his Army would arrive long before that time. Salvation of the Citie and the King's subjects within it, depended upon the speedy arrival of Prince Rupert and his Army.

In order to stall Parliamentarians Armies from making an immediate attack upon York, Earl of Newcastle sent out from the Citie messengers, ordering them to ensure they were captured by the leaguers. Messages they carried were intended to mislead Parliamentarians into believing the citizens were starving at that time and that Newcastle intended to seek a parley to discuss terms of surrendering the Citie to Parliamentarian forces.

Ye whole purpose was to delay attacks on the Citie and misleading leaguers, thus gaining more time to allow for Prince Rupert's arrival. When Newcastle knew his messengers had been taken, he sent letters to Halifax, Leslie and Manchester, seeking a meeting to discuss terms for him to be able surrender the Citie to them. Their Lordships Halifax, Leven and Manchester upon their receipt of letters from Newcastle seeking to Parley with them, gathered at a hastily arranged meeting at Halifax's Headquarters at Heslington Hall.

After much discussion they drew up their terms for the surrender of the Garrison and for the Citie to be yielded to them within twenty four hours, failure would result in a full bombardment of the Citie using all the Batteries of Artillery they had surrounding the Citie at this time. This document was duly delivered by messenger to Newcastle, never having intended to surrender the Citie to the Leager Armies, Newcastle sent a further letter, in which he advised that it was not possible for him to agree to their ridiculous terms. He asked for a parley with them and that a cease fire should be upheld until sensible agreement could be reached.

Following a further Meeting between the Parliamentarian Generals, they agreed that a "peace" Meeting should take place. They sent news of their decision along with the names of who their representatives at the meeting would be to Newcastle. He in turn forwarded to the Parliamentarians the names representing his Army and also, those of the Governor and the Citizens of York.

Tentage was erected on Scarcroft Stray and was some four hundred yards without of Micklegate Bar. The site of the Tents was an equal distance from the London Road Sconce (held by the Royalists) and the Sconce at Nun Mill (held by leagers) defenders from both Sconces had clear sight of the Parley area.

A cessation of fighting had been agreed, it was to be three hours before the commencement of the Parley. Parties of Commissioners from both factions who were each to be accompanied by 100 Musketeers arrived to commence the Parley at three of the clock in the afternoon. From the outset, discussions from both sides were forceful and heated and continued right into the evening. At nine of the clock in the evening, Parliamentarian Commissioners presented their conditions to the Royalists, to take to the Earl of Newcastle. Anger and bloody oaths were expressed by the Royalists who refused to take the proposed terms away with them. General Lesley sent the Message to Newcastle in the very late hours that evening. Upon receiving the letter and reading the terms laid out, Newcastle sent his reply, in which he said, "*As a person of Honour I cannot possibly condescend to any of these propositions*".

The breakdown of the "parley" was the cause of much ill-will between the trained bands of craftsmen guarding the Walls and the leagers. Each evening at dusk and taking advantage of the half-light many leagers using what cover was available moved closer to the Walls. Their intention was to shout insults and threats to the Citizen defenders, who in response had on more than one occasion managed to drench unwary leagers who had closed right up to the Wall in excrement and urine by tipping buckets of it over the Wall. It was common practice to place buckets at suitable points on the Wall to enable the men and sometimes women on duty, to relieve themselves without leaving their posts.

Before the leagers completely surrounded the Citie on the 3rd June, mail delivery had been affected, Postmaster's throughout the country had been forced to suspend collection and delivery of mail in many areas which became beleaguered or where spasmodic fighting frequently occurred between the opposing Armies. However, throughout the siege in York, letters were secretly sent and received by the Royalist Generals and even by prominent Gentlemen and their entourages who had been caught in the Citie.

The Ambassador from Venice was one such "captive", who along with his servants and advisors, had been resident in the Citie at the time of the siege was laid. Throughout his stay in the Citie, he used his own Servants to carry his messages to and from London. On one occasion a returning Messenger, who had travelled from London by ship and landed at Scarborough, was pursued near Buttercram by a leager patrol from the Earl of Manchester's Army.

After capture the Messenger was taken to the Fort at Buttercram where after being questioned and his Message Satchel examined, he was held overnight. The next day he was taken to York, his capture was felt to be important, he was taken before the Earl of Manchester. The Earl and a various number of his officers, questioned the man over a period of several days. Believing the Messenger and the messages in his possession were genuine correspondence for the Honourable Ambassador from Venice, Manchester sent a message with one of his officers, who was not bearing arms to the Citie Wall, where he was to seek audience with the Earl of Newcastle and deliver the letter to him.

In his letter, Manchester sought confirmation that the Ambassador was in the Citie and if true, would the Noble Lord allow the captured Messenger to enter the Citie and meet with the Ambassador. Newcastle and the Ambassador were friends and Newcastle was aware that his friend had been sending and receiving Messages to and from London and Venice since the Siege had started. Newcastle, replied giving his approval to the request.

Ye Governor of the Citie, Sir Thomas Glenham, had very soon after the Citie had become beleagerd sought advice and suggestions of those Citizens who had the special skills and knowledge of the approaches to the Citie and surrounding countryides, which would enable them to escort Messengers. Ye Lord Mayor, Sir Edmund Cowper, after seeking help from the Master's of the Trade Gilds in the Citie, was given the names of a number of Tradesmen who had the skills and wanted to help the Citie in it's time of crisis.

Those Citizen Tradesmen, commenced their task of safely escorting messengers away from the leager encampments. Official and important Messages, both in and out of the Citie were set in code, a small number of Messengers were caught and put to considerable pain by the leagers in order to obtain information.

One such Citizen volunteer was the ferryman at Lendal ferry who had a wide knowledge of the River Ouse and the River Fosse and of the becks and waterways feeding into them and his work had given him both boating skills and knowledge of the times and heights of the tide. His escorting of Messengers usually ensured their safety when they departed or approached the Citie in darkness, after the midnight hour.

Ye ferryman had been born and bred in York and from boyhood he had gathered a full knowledge of traversing quickly through the system of fields and streams which had developed around the entire Citie walls. After choosing his safest and quickest route he always sought assistance with the Constables John Cundill and Christopher Foster to leave the Citie on foot with any messenger he was guiding, by using the Sally port at Monk Bar.

Upon entering the field system and heading north westerly he was able to take them after walking about one and a half miles, to the River Foss. At this point he had hidden amongst a dense clump of bushes his small rowing boat. Using the rowing boat he was able to make safe progress with his passenger a further two miles up the river to a small isolated farmstead occupied by his sister and her husband, Ray Jonson from the farmstead the messenger was able to continue his journey upon the horse upon which he had arrived. Ye ferryman was paid a generous fee for his services, from which in turn he then paid Ray Jonson for the livery and forage. Messengers journeying south to London, mostly rode eastwards to Scarborough, from whence they could board ship, which was a safer and quicker way for them to complete the journey to the Capital.

At this time, the Citie had been beleaguered for nearly two months, as far as they were able, Citizens adapted their lives to changes in their lifestyles, adults and children alike had grown used to the noise of cannon and musket fire, which they endured on most days. Garrison solgers and Citizens trained bands all took their part in Watches, patrolling the Walls both night and day. If and whence the enemy was seen advancing towards the Citie in large numbers, alarm was to be raised by loud ringing of hand bells, which were kept in the watchtowers and sentry points.

Despite shouted anger and oaths exchanged each day between Leagers and Garrison solgers on the Walls, incidents of kindness and charity sometimes took place. Two boys from within the Citie, not above 12years old, decided one sunny afternoon, that they would wander along the banks of the River Ouse towards leager lines at Acomb Landing, hoping they would be able to see the bridge of boats. There were many stories abounding the Citie, that leagers had built such a bridge. They left the Citie at North Street postern, telling the watchman they were going to gather eggs from nests of ducks and water hen along the river bank. He told them not to wander very far upstream, because high tide on the river was in two hours time and they might get cut off.

A short time after setting off, they realised the that the incoming tide was causing the water to rise and they were no longer able to walk along the water's edge paddling their feet. They scrambled up the bank and continued walking toward the landing at Akomb. They soon encountered water filled pits of the Brick Kilns, it was a hot day and the boy's sought to cool themselves by swimming in one of the bigger pits. After much excitement they decided to get out of the pit, whilst trying to get out they realised the water level was much further from the top than they had realised and the sides were to slippery to get a grip.

Despite their struggles to get out of the pit they could not, they began to panic, they started to shout for help, they became tired, were becoming weak and their shouts for help went unanswered, they supported each other in the water. Were they were going to die!

Approaching on horseback some distance upstream from them were two leager solgers of Lord Leven's Scottish Army. As the men got closer they heard shouted calls from the boy's. Spurring their horses forward they trotted up to a pit in which two boy's were trapped. In an instant they realised what danger the boy's were in, they leapt from their horses, both men throwing themselves onto gravel at the edge of the pit and grasping outstretched hands of each of the boys, pulled them up to safety. Fetching blankets from his horse, the older solger gave one to each boy and indicated they should dry themselves. Still shivering, mostly with fright, the boys dried themselves and very shyly put their clothes back on.

Remounting their horses, both men bent forward and with outstretched hands they each pulled one of the boys up behind them onto their horses. Both horsemen walked their horses forward toward the Citie Walls.

As they approached North Street postern each man reined in his mount and stopped well out of musket range. One of the men indicated to the boys to jump down and he himself dismounted. Taking his musket from his shoulder he placed it slowly upon the ground, his actions could be plainly seen by the sentinels on the Citie walls. With one boy on either side of him, they set of walking very slowly toward the postern. Ye watchman who had seen the boys leave the Citie, came out from the postern and walked toward them.

In spite of the Watchman having difficulty understanding the Scottish accent of the solger, he did by a mix of speech, hand gestures, nods and shakes of the head, explain the nature of the escapade of the boys to the Watchman. Using similar means to those used by the solger, the Watchman expressed his thanks for the efforts they had made in safely rescuing the boys. To show the true warmth of his thanks, the Watchman took hold of the solger's hand and shook it warmly. After gesturing to both boys they set off to walk to the Postern Gate at Lendal, the Watchman turned to follow them and gave a friendly wave to the solger as he did so.

At Supper that evening, Josh told Luke and Ann about the incident concerning the two boys. He told them that the Watchman after he had issued stern warnings to the boys, had visited the Garrison and reported the incident to the Captain of the Guard. An entry was made by him into the Watch Record Book. Sir John Glenham the Governor of the Citie, was very interested in that report and had commented, *"In these times of hardship and killings, it is pleasing for me to hear that human compassion still abounds"*.

Mary Ward a devout Catholic had returned home to York in 1642, where she had taken up residence in Heworth

Village. She had spent many years travelling across Europe where she had set up small convents of teaching nuns. Illness had forced her return and some followers and her servants resided at her home with her. When the Siege had been laid in April, Mary resisted the pleas of her friends and followers to retreat into the safety of the Citie. Following the arrival of advanced regiments of the Earl of Manchester's Army in Heworth village and canon and musket fire was being exchanged between the leagers and the Citie defenders, death and damage was occurring in the village.

Stories abounded of the solgers of Manchesters Army robbing and beating villagers and travellers trying to retreat into the Citie. Mary decided that for the safety of her followers they would have to move into the Citie. Because of her illness, Mary was confined to her bed, upon which she was carried from the village of Heworth and through groups of leager solgers who were cooking or eating their evening meal around a number of camp fires. She was accompanied by her servants and followers, who were carrying bedding, clothing, pots and pans and as much else as they could. On their journey into the Citie, not one of their group was approached or stopped by leager solgers. Mary Ward stayed in the Citie throughout the siege and received treatment from her Doctor to relieve the pain from the body "stones" from which she suffered.

At this time, the Corporation of the Citie was kept busy with problems arising from the Siege. Ye Lord Mayor Edmund Cooper, often had great difficulty in controlling the Meetings of the Corporation which took place in the Common Hall on the Ouse Bridge. Many of the Aldermen were also Master of a Craft Gild in the Citie. Arguments and disagreements, all too often arose in meetings of the Council in the Common Hall, when the Aldermen from a

Craft Gilds felt certain decisions, which had been proposed to strengthen the Citie's defence would damage the trading opportunities of their particular Gild.

There were some groups of Citizens, including some of the Aldermen, who favoured the Puritan style of Worship, but they were a minority. Ye Clergy of the Minster and the Parsons and Vicars of the Churches in the Citie largely led and controlled the worshipping choices of the majority of the Citizens of York at this time.

Complaints from the Citizens were frequently made to the Garrison Governor, concerning brawls, thefts and rapes allegedly carried out by drunken solgers. Ye Earl of Newcastle had tried to ensure the garrison solgers within the Citie were kept in control. He had instructed that groups of his Whitecoats would patrol the Citie, by night and day.

Drunk and unruly solgers were routinely taken to the prisons at Monk Bar or on Ousebridge by the Parish Constables or Watchmen. From whence the Whitecoat patrols would take them to the Clifford's Tower and there await the Governor deciding their fate.

CHAPTER VII

Walls Breached

Throughout the siege, Sunday morning Service in the Minster had always been well attended by citizens and visitors, (Lord's Knights, Gentlemen and their Ladies from adjoining counties, including the Venetian Ambassador and his entourage, along with Scholars and Merchants from London and lands across oceans and seas, all were beleaguered within the Citie throughout the siege). On Trinity Sunday, 16th June, 1644, York minster was again crowded, there was near to a thousand worshippers, many Garrison soldiers were present in this large congregation. As noon approached many worshippers were becoming restless and longing for the Sermon to come to an end to allow them to stretch aching limbs and joints.

A thunderous bang from outside the Minster caused shouts and screams of bewilderment in the congregation, followed by a clattering of heavy boots upon flagged floor, as the members of the Citie Garrison and Trained Bands dashed from the great West door of Ye Minster in order to repel a feared attack from the leagers.

Sgt. Josh Hogg was one of the first of the Garrison solgers to get onto the steps outside the West door of the Minster, he saw a pall of dark grey smoke climbing above house rooftops to the North, in an area beyond Bootham Bar. He and his group had left their weapons upon a cart at the corner of Petergate, guarded by two of his solgers. He saw they were jostling around the cart as they sought and armed themselves. Josh dashed across to them, he quickly armed himself with his musket pistols and shot. He heard loud musket fire coming from the area from whence he had seen the smoke rising. Josh called his men to follow him and he set off running toward Bootham Bar, as they got to the Bar they could hear shouting and screaming and many, many, loud bangs as muskets were fired at them, many of the shot missiles striking and bouncing off the stonework of the Bar. All the noise indicated there was a battle taking place in the area of the orchard behind the King's Manor and the Bowling Green near to St. Mary's Tower.

Looking around Josh saw hundreds of Garrison Solgers and Trained Band citizens dashing along with them toward the Bowling Green and St. Mary's Tower. As they arrived at the wall at the corner of the King's Manor garden, Josh was shocked, he saw a breach had been made in the Citie wall in the yard of the King's Manor, near to St. Mary's Tower and the leaguers had entered through it. There were bodies lying on the rubble of the breach, across from the Bowling Green and smoke was still rising from St. Mary's Tower which now did not have a roof.

Shouting orders to his men, Josh led them into the walled garden of King's Manor and joined the Whitecoats (the Earl of Newcastle's men), they were firing their muskets and pistols at leagers who were trying to climb over the wall from makeshift ladders and others still scrambling over the breach in the Citie Wall made by cannon fire and it was about a furlong from St. Mary's Tower. There were scores of bodies lying on the ground around the bowling green and many more near to and amongst rubble of the breached wall. Josh and his men could hear moans and wails from wounded solgers, they could see severed limbs lying some distance from the nearest bodies. It was a pitiful, depressing and sickening sight of carnage and death.

Suddenly, above clattering noise from musket fire and distant cannon fire, Josh heard a commotion of loud shouting and musket shots from without the Walls, sounding as if coming from an area outside of St. Mary's Tower. As shouts and noise grew louder, he saw approaching from his right through the breach in the walls, a large force of Whitecoats. Another large body of Whitecoats and trained band members had also approached through the gates onto and across the bowling green area. Leaguers still fighting, found they were cut off from further re-inforcements and were surrounded and eventually they were taken captive, they numbered about two hundred.

All the prisoners, looking weary and dishevelled were assembled into columns and guarded by Whitecoat solgers they trudged away to be confined in the Clifford's Tower. With his group of men Josh joined groups of trained band citizens in helping to rescue wounded solgers from both sides, many had serious wounds, they took them by handcart to the Hall of St. Anthony and the Hall of the Company of Merchant Adventurers where they received treatment and as they continued with their task, Josh noticed that apart from the occasional sound of a musket shot and the moans and cries of the injured, there was a stillness and quietness spreading across the streets, people had gathered in small groups and were speaking quietly together as the wounded were wheeled passed them.

Even as Josh and his men were making their way to the Hall of St. Antony, they were, at intervals passed by a Barber or Surgeon dashing to help the injured at the Hall.

As they had left the scene of the breach, Josh had noticed a number of Vicars, Parsons and other members of the clergy ministering to the relatives who had found their family members amongst the dead.

Upon arrival at the Hall, Josh passed their two casualties (one of whom was a roundhead trooper) to the care of two townswomen. Before leaving the Hall, Josh looked about and saw that there were many more townswomen busy helping the Surgeons and Barbers as they went about their grim task of amputating limbs and removing musket shot from wounds. Deciding his men were not required at the Hall, Josh rejoined them. Outside he espied the Lord Mayor, Sir Edmund Cowper approaching he was walking alongside a cart being pushed by members of the Citie Trained Bands.

As they were heading back to the area of King's Manor, Josh heard his men discussing the wounded man on the cart which the Lord Mayor had accompanied, when he asked, the men told him the wounded man was Colonel Sam Brearley, a stalwart citizen of York. As they marched down Ogleforth, loud cannon fire could be heard, distant cannon fire could be heard responding as they continued. When they arrived back at the King's Manor, they heard loud explosions, which were coming from north of the Citie, leagers must have established a Battery in Clifton, most shots however were falling short of the Walls.

Josh saw that many men from the "Trained bands" of the Citie were busy working to repair damage in the Wall where it had been breeched. They were making it up with loose stonework earth and sods, he took his men further down the Wall. A cannon battery defending the Citie, was on the flat roof of the tower St. Olaf's Church, it was no longer firing, there was total silence from the roof. When they reached the Church, Josh cautiously climbed the makeshift ladder onto a flat roof. There was only one cannoneer crouching down on the platform, upon reaching his side Josh saw that he was trying to pull back onto the platform another soldier who was injured and unconscious.

Calling to his own men, Josh ordered two of them to join him upon the roof, after much effort they managed to pull the man onto the platform. He was dead, a musket wound could be seen in the centre of his forehead, blood was trickling from it down his temple. The body was then fastened with ropes and with much difficulty lowered to the ground. He detailed two of his men to carry the body away from the Manor gardens and pass it on to the Trained Band members who were dealing with casualties.

The Cannoneer was but sore and angry, because of the death of his mate at the hands of the leagers, he was swearing oaths and he begged Josh to give a man to assist him to resume his battering of the enemy. Josh readily agreed and detailed more of his men to go back and seek out cannon balls and return with them. The Cannoneer pointed out the puffs and cloud of white smoke swirling above the treetops about four hundred yards away, the enemy were still firing. Making adjustments to the set of the barrel of his cannon the man shouted for the gun to be loaded and then with a great roar and a huge swathe of white smoke the weapon was fired. The Cannoneer, was pursuing his task with a determination and ruthlessness that was enshrined in anger.

His bombardment was still in full flow when the men Josh had detailed returned with a cart loaded with cannon shot. The sight of the new supply of ammunition seemed to spur the Cannoneer to continue his bombardment with a greater anger. Suddenly he stopped shouting and pointed ahead toward the distant tree line, Josh looked to where he had last seen the smoke, he realised there was no smoke and there was no noise of explosions from that area. The opposing Battery had been silenced, the Cannoneer began roaring with joy and this was accompanied by the rousing cheers of Josh and his men.

When a relieving crew of Cannoneers arrived at the Battery, Josh gathered his own men together and they made their way slowly back through the gardens of King's Manor intending to return to Clifford's Tower. Suddenly, just as they approached an apple tree which was laden with unripened fruit, a Musket pistol fell from the tree and landed on the grass right in front of them. Josh and his men scattered and sought cover behind nearby trees and then furtively changed their positions until the apple tree was surrounded from a safe distance.

When Josh saw his men were in safe cover, he shouted instructions for the fugitives hiding in the tree, to throw down all their weapons. There was silence and no movement upon the tree. Josh then shouted again, advising that if after a count of ten their weapons were not surrendered his men would be ordered to fire into the tree. Again there was silence and then after a shout from up the tree saying *"Don't shoot"*, there were a series of clatters and thuds as an assortment of weapons fell from the tree. Then again silence, Josh shouted toward the tree, *"Who are you and how many of you"*. *"We are but two solgers of the 'leager Army"*, came the quick reply. *"Climb down in peace, we have you completely surrounded"*, Josh shouted to them.

After a noisy and oath provoking descent through the tree branches two figures finally dropped tiredly from the tree onto the ground. They were quickly taken prisoner, their weapons taken from the ground and confiscated by Josh's men. They then moved away from the tree and took the prisoners back to Josh. Looking the prisoners over Josh was quite happy they were leager solgers. He said to them, *"So we have caught you stealing the King's apples"*. This caused great laughter among Josh's men. Before leaving the scene Josh ordered all of his men to fire two shots up into the apple tree. This order did not cause the prisoners to register any noticeable concern. Josh gave the order and the shots were fired, Josh thought that either there were no more leagers hiding in the apple tree or his men were unlucky marksmen.

Reforming his men back into a column with the prisoners in the centre, Josh marched them back to Clifford's Tower. There was still occasional exchanges of cannon fire from the west and south of the Citie. Battery fire from Clifford's Tower was being directed toward Halifax's batteries upon Lamel Hill.

Since the mine explosion at Marygate Tower, Ann had been helping with the wounded solgers from both sides at St Anthony's Hall, she had never before seen such horrible injuries and suffering, but, she overcame her feelings and horror to give the best care she could to those suffering solgers. She became strong to support those who had undergone surgery for limb loss and wounds from bullets. To those who were near to death she gave strength and hope and comfort. There had been no time for her to think or worry about Luke and Josh, but, her patients were now comfortable and she was now weary and worried for the safety of her loved ones.

A Barber/Surgeon who was accompanied by Mabel Carter a neighbour of Anne, approached her. He gave Anne his thanks for her help and care and told her she was tired and must go home and rest, he said Mabel would take over from her. Ann withdrew wearily and made her way to the Chamberlain's room where all the ladies who had attended to offer their help had left their Bonnets and Cloaks. Upon entering the Chamberlain's room Ann took her bonnet and cloak and moved across to a standing mirror, she was shocked at her image, she looked bedraggled, her dress and petticoat were spattered with blood and various other stains. Whilst she was walking home after leaving St. Anthony's, Ann realised she had learned a lot that day, about life and about death, but most of all, about herself. Hoping all would be well when she got there, she trod her weary path home to Trinity Passage. Arriving home, Ann entered by the kitchen door, the workshop door from the street, they never used on the Sabbath day.

She raked the ashes from the fire into the grate below and then placed logs and kindling onto the fire, after the logs were burning well, she placed the cauldron of cold water onto the hob above the fire. As Ann passed the door into the workshop, she paused and was appreciative of the smell of new leather emanating from within the workshop, she moved on across the kitchen and stepped into the larder. Upon leaving she was carrying a slab of Brawn (which she had cooked and left to set the previous day) also a large round of white crumbly cheese and a loaf of rough grain bread, which were placed on the table. After again checking the fire, she placed a pan containing potatoes, cabbage and carrot onto the second hob over the fire.

Whilst setting the table for tea, Ann heard the sneck of the yard gate being lifted and the clunk of boots crossing the yard. Looking up as the door opened, she saw Luke on the threshold and about to walk into the kitchen, he had a broad smile across his face. He walked across to her and hugged her tightly, the emotions of her day caught up with her as she felt the warmth of love from her husband was giving her in their embrace. Stepping back from her Luke placed his palm under his wife's chin, she had a serenity he had never noticed before. He kissed her upon the lips and then moved away to the sink to wash before tea.

Luke told Ann he had spent the day helping Kiet Starky and many other craftsmen and citizens to build up again the Citie Wall where it had been breached, they would be safe that night because extra solgers and lookouts had been posted, but much more work would be needed.

Just as Ann was about to serve the food onto the table, she heard Josh cross the yard and when the kitchen door swung open, both she and Luke were pleased to see him safe and uninjured. Josh gave each of them in turn a huge clasping hug of greeting. After they had all re-assured each other that none of them had sustained any injury carrying out their various tasks, they settled at the table and the meal was eaten with little conversation.

When the meal had been consumed and Ann had cleared the table, they each in turn related their experiences of the day. Josh was able to tell them that the leagers, had also been tunnelling under Walmgate Bar to place a second mine there. Ye leager tunnellers were heard digging by Garrison solgers on duty in the Barbican above them. When this had been reported to Sir John Glenham the Governor of the Citie, he had ordered a shaft to be dug and the tunnel to be flooded.

The leagers, Josh told them had lost over 50 men killed, a similar number wounded and over 200 taken prisoner, to save the Citie food, Josh said the prisoners would be handed back. Amongst Garrison soldiers and citizens there had been more than thirty killed (most of them Whitecoats of the Earl of Newcastle's Regiments) and included six officers, there had been above forty wounded in and around the Bowling green and Ye Manor gardens. It was not thought that any of the citizens or Garrison solgers had been taken prisoner.

Ye following morning, by 7 of the clock, Ann left the workshop in Trinity Passage to return to St. Anthony's Hall in Aldwark , she wanted once again to help in whatever way she could, to help the wounded and dying. Josh had left at daybreak to return to the Clifford's Tower and Luke had jobs to finish in his workshop, before returning to help with repairing the breech in the Wall. As Ann approached the entrance to the Hall she espied a coach waiting outside. She stopped and waited just short of the Hall door, she saw two gentlemen were stepping from the doorway into the street.

They stepped forward to the coach and entered it, Ann knew one of the gentlemen was the Lord Mayor Edmond Cooper and she thought the other one was the Governor of the Citie Sir John Glenham. Ye coach moved slowly but noisily away, the metal rimmed wheels making a clatter upon the cobbles of the roadway. As Ann was stepping forward to enter the Hall, she noticed two whitecoated slogers who were pushing a cart, they turned through the large Archway leading to the rear Courtyard of the Hall.

Ann entered the Hall and walked toward the Chamberlain's Room. She knocked upon the door and a female voice bade her to enter, upon entering Ann was surprised to see sitting at the table was Mistress Akombe who she knew very well, her husband Moses like Luke was a Cordwainer. Mistress Akombe welcomed Ann and bade her to take a seat next to her at the table.

As Mistress Akombe was explaining to Ann the lists of wounded which she had written on the sheets of paper in front of her. They were interrupted by an urgent knocking upon the door and when invited, entry was made by the two white coated men who Ann had seen outside the Hall. Ye taller of the two men said to Mistress Akombe, *"Wi'v bin sent fra, garrison ta tek bodies back, ah think thes' three"*. She rose beckoning Ann to do likewise, she said, *Come this way, I am afraid they have not yet been (made ready) for Burial"*. She led the group down a corridor and then entered a side chamber. There were a number of bodies, a dozen or more lying upon the floor each was covered by a sheet of hessian sacking.

Mistress Akombe turned to Ann and said, *"Are you prepared to help me enshroud the three dead soldiers"*, Ann nodded her agreement. Checking her list Mistress Akombe identified the bodies by the numbers written on paper labels which were pinned to the cover over each body. Turning to the two white coated soldiers Mistress Akombe asked them to lift and carry the first body she had identified to a large oak table at the side of the Chamber.

Checking again the number on the sheet with the number on her list, Mistress Akombe saw that the name of the dead person was Robert Bowman. Pointing to a pile of large newly made sackcloth bags. She said to Ann, " *Each of those bags has a name and number painted onto a leather tag, which is stitched onto the top corner"*. Ann followed her over to the sacks and they soon sorted through and found the bag bearing the name Robert Bowman.

Returning to the table with the bag Mistress Akombe stood at one side of the table and motioned Ann to stand at the other, she then laid the bag lengthwise on the table at the side of the corpse. The bag was only sewn up the front one foot from the bottom. She then said to Ann, *"If you pull him onto his side toward yourself, I will push his feet into the bottom of the bag and then I will pass the side nearest to me upwards and push it over, so that it faces you"*. When they had completed that part of their task, Mistress Akombe said, *"Good , now you pull that edge toward you, whilst I lower his body back down toward me"*.

When the corpse was lying back down on the table, Mistress Akombe said, *"Good , now I will pull him onto his side toward myself and you push your side of the bag upwards and lay it the length of his body"*.

When this was done, Ann lowered the body back down upon the table whilst Mistress Akombe held her side of the bag tightly pulling the edge toward herself. Straightening the edges of the bag together so that they overlapped down the middle of the bag. Mistress Akombe went across to a shelf on the wall and came back with two large needles already threaded with good strong twine, Ann recognised immediately the needles were the same type as Luke used to sew leather uppers onto the welts of boots and shoes. Passing Ann one of the needles, the good lady then said, *"Well my dear, if you start up from the feet I will come down from the head, I think we will use saddle stitch"*.

They completed the task quickly and then Mistress Akombe supervised the two white coat solgers whilst they were taking the body to the cart and then to bring the second corpse back. The two ladies worked well together and the second body was soon enshrouded and placed onto the cart. After they had similarly enshrouded the third body and the Whitecoats had gone away the two ladies returned to the Chamberlains room. Bidding Ann to follow her, Mistress Akombe led the way though the ground floor corridors to the kitchen, which was set at the back of the building, overlooking a paved quadrangle.

At the far end of the kitchen underneath a large chimney breast, was standing a large metal brazier containing half burnt logs with glowing red embers. There were three strong metal arms secured to the wall behind and on either side of the brazier. From one of the arms which had been swung round over the fire was hanging a cauldron, in which was simmering beef tea. Approaching the brazier and taking hold of the leather handle of the metal linked chain which was used to withdraw the arm and the cauldron from the cooking position Mistress Akombe carefully swung the cauldron away from the heat. Leaning over the cauldron, her nostrils captured tasteful aroma of herbs and beef drifting upward toward her.

Taking the ladle from a peg on the wall, she turned and smiling her approval said to Ann, "*Could you please bring over two of those bowls standing on the shelf over there*". Ann took the bowls to her and she immediately became aware of the meaty and herbal aroma of the simmering beef tea. Ann watched as Mistress Akombe ladled from the cauldron and filled both bowls. Passing one bowl to Ann she said, "*I think we will have some rough grain bread and a slice of goats cheese with this.*" With their bowls, bread and cheese, the two ladies seated themselves at the large table away from the fire. They consumed their meal with very little conversation between them, other than Ann complimenting Mistress Akombe on the taste and quality of the Beef Tea.

After clearing away and washing their bowls and spoons Mistress Akombe said, "*Well, Ann my dear, when I spoke to the Surgeon earlier he told me he expected four or five more of the wounded to die from their wounds, I think we had better go and see him*". Upon entering into the main Hall, Ann saw makeshift beds set against each side wall and two more rows set head to head to each other down the centre of the Hall.

Espying two men speaking together at the far end of the room Mistress Akombe motioned Ann to wait and she herself walked slowly down the aisle of the Hall between the two lines of beds of wounded men towards the medical gentlemen at the end of Hall. She approached the elder of the gentlemen and became involved in conversation with him. After a few minutes she returned to Ann. She said to Ann, "*The good Lord has taken two of the solgers and the Surgeon feels sure our Lord will also be taking the third one within the hour"*.

After helping Mistress Akombe to complete the enshrouding of the other three solgers, Ann was leaving the main door of St. Anthony's Hall. As she descended the steps she heard coming from the Minster, the bell of Great Peter booming out the noon hour over the Citie. As she made her way home, the streets she walked along, were strangely quiet. Few people were about, the attack upon the Citie Wall's the previous day, had brought to them the realisation of the peril and danger that all within the Citie were in.

Entering Trinity Passage, she espied Luke, he was standing outside the workshop door and he was locking it. She called to him, he turned toward her and smiled, turning he unlocked the door again.

They entered the workshop and Luke told her that the Cordwainers were to spend the afternoon helping to strengthen the City Wall from St. Mary Tower down to the river and the work might require working on into the evening.

When Luke reached the Bowling Green area, he espied Moses Akombe and his fellow Cordwainers in the far right hand corner near to the damaged Marygate Tower. A wooden scaffold platform had been erected alongside the Wall and as large stones were sorted from the debris they were hauled by carts to the scaffold and were then set in place by the two Stonemasons working on the scaffold. Luke joined his fellow Craftsmen in removing debris and hauling all the suitable stones to the Wall.

By mid-afternoon Moses called upon his men to take a break and they all partook of a tankard of ale drawn from a barrel which had been provided for their use by William Foster, Innkeeper of the Star Inn, Stonegate. Whilst enjoying his refreshing ale, Luke saw down the whole length of Marygate to the river, where other Craft Guilds were also busy strengthening sections of the Wall.

At supper that evening Ann and Luke listened as Josh explained how serious the threat to the Citie had now become, but news of the approach of Prince Rupert with his relieving was expected expected very soon. Luke asked Josh how he knew this news was true, Josh told him that in spite of the leagers presence it was still possible for messengers to get into and out of the Citie, right under the very noses of the leagers.

CHAPTER VIII

The Journey to York

Isaac was working with Tobe and six other of their fellow workers in the lush meadows on the gently sloping hillsides leading from Borrowby, travelling slowly up the hill toward them, Isaac saw Jack Grainger leading his pair of heavy horses and the large empty haywain. Both Jack and Will Thornton, had since early morning been leading their teams pulling full loads of hay back to the Manor House, where it was stacked and covered, to be used, when needed as fodder for the stock.

Upon reaching Isaac, Jack halted the team, then he patted each horse in turn and whispered into their ears, before he reached under the high cross seat and give each animal a nosebag. Turning to Jack he then said, *"Squire ses, wen ah cum back from this next load, I 'ast ta tek all on ya back wi me, 'e wants all on us in't yard ta tell us tell us summat"*.

Complying with the Squire's instructions, Isaac and his fellow workers, sitting atop of Jack and Will's haywains, returned to the Manor House and after placing the loads from both haywains onto the stacks, they all made their way into the rear courtyard. There already assembled, were twenty or so of their fellow workers, greetings were exchanged as they all mingled amongst their friends. Seeing Jack and Will were sitting very comfortably upon an empty waggon at the side of the courtyard Isaac and Tobe moved across and joined them. There were rumours and wild stories spreading all around the courtyard and excitement showed on the faces of all those, there assembled.

A hush descended upon the courtyard, after the fire bell outside the back door of the Manor House was rung by Squire Fewster, all eyes turned in his direction as the Squire walked up the ramp onto the stone loading bay.

The Squire was looking solemn, as he cast his gaze around the courtyard at all his workers, he pondered how many would not come back, would any of them survive, himself included. He looked toward his wife who was standing on the small terrace behind him, he looked skywards and then he began to address them, *"Loyal servants"*, he said, *We are in dangerous times, you all know that the Parliamentarians have been laying Siege to York since April"*, the assembly expressed a murmurs of agreement, *"If York falls, the King's cause in the North of England will be seriously harmed, will we allow that to happen"*? A loud chorus *"No"* echoed around the courtyard, he went on, *"Are all of you with me to go to York to fight for the King's cause"*? There were resounding shouts of agreement from the workers, followed by some cries of *"Long live King Charles"*.

He paused for the chatter right around the yard to stop and then he regained their attention by saying, *"We have been hoping that Prince Rupert could take his Army to relieve York and I have heard news of his approach to the border with Lancashire and in but a day or so he will be outside York and we will go to York to join him"*. His audience started cheering loudly, the Squire raised his hand and the assembly quietened down and he said, *"Are you all with me"*? The Squire glanced around the assembly, there did not appear to be any dissent from his audience, finally he said to them, "*All of you must make preparations for the care of your families and any stock you have*".

The Squire turned, he rejoined his wife and they both went back into the Manor House, the estate workers split up into their smaller groups and commenced their various discussions on what the Squire had told them. Isaac and Tobe got down from the cart and were about to go to the kitchen yard when Will and Jack called to them from the cart. Will asked Isaac if he and Tobe would give them a hand in the stables before they set off for home. They needed to prepare and part load two waggons in readiness for their imminent departure, they would be able to complete the loading themselves later, after the Squire had given them his full instructions concerning what would be needed to be taken in the waggons on the journey to York". The other estate workers had now started to make their way in two and threes towards their homes, their talk however was still centred upon what the Squire had told them.

Returning with Jack and Will to the stables workshop, Isaac was surprised to see the front end of the largest of the waggons was raised from the floor and fastened by means of two heavy chains hanging on pulley's which were secured to the strong oak beams of the stable roof. As Jack and Will set about changing the wheels, Tobe asked Will what the problem was, Will replied, "*Squire ses we'll ah ruff ground ta go ovver, so 'e wants stronger front weels on both o't waggons*". Isaac asked, "*So Jack w'at ya want an' mi an' Tobe to do*", Jack replied, "*That pile o' round stakes an'the barrels and ropes need stacking ont' other flat bed ovver theer*". The two friends bent to their task and very soon had the stakes, barrels and ropes loaded onto the waggon.

Tobe shouted across to Jack, "*Is tha out else afore wi go*", Jack paused in his work then shook his head and said "*Ah can't think of owt, ya'd best get off 'ome*". When they got to the doors of the barn Isaac and Tobe shouted to their friends and waved their goodbyes.

When Isaac arrived back home, he sent the children out to gather the eggs and then calmly broke the news to Rose of his departure for York on the following day. She listened quietly to Isaac, she did not say anything but moved toward him and after throwing her arms around him she embraced him.

When Isaac awoke next morning, daylight was just breaking, he got out of bed without waking Rose, he dressed and went outside. He went across to the sheep pen, the animals looked in good fettle and he knew Rose was perfectly capable of seeing to them until he returned. Upon going back into the cottage, he went to the fireplace, the fire was still smoking, he raked it and placed some kindling on and it started to burn, on top of that he placed some small logs, they quickly started to smoulder and then burning as bright flames appeared. He filled the metal cauldron with water from the water butt outside the cottage door and put it onto the grid over the fire, he went to the stone sink and had a wash before he prepared his food to break his fast. As he was partaking of his food, Rose came in from the bedroom. She busied herself at the hearth, she was ill prepared for the parting she would soon have to face, Isaac meanwhile picked up his travelling pack and started to re-fill it with the items he would need whilst he was away.

When he had completed his task with his pack, Isaac went across to the stone sink where Rose was busy washing platters and pans, he took her into his arms and embraced her, he said to her, "*Ya know I 'ave ta go don't ya*", she looked at him with pleading eyes and said, *"Yes, but i'm worrid ya won't cum back ta me"*. He sighed, *"Look ah'll be back in a week, but ah need ya ta luk after t' kids an t' sheep til' ah get back"*. She looked up at him, *"Ya know ah will"*, she said, he gave her a long lingering kiss, then he turned picked up his pack and made for the door and strode towards the gate at the side of the track towards Leake. At the gate he turned and saw she was standing at the cottage door, he gave her a re-assuring wave and then set off towards the Manor House.

As he approached the Manor House, Isaac had a heavy heart and he wondered to himself why he was involved in this war, why could he and his family and his friends, not be allowed to live their lives happily and peacefully like they used to. As he turned through the gates of the Manor House Isaac saw Tobe in the crowded courtyard talking to Will Thornton, he made his way to where they were standing. They exchanged greetings and Tobe said to Isaac, *"Squire 'as teld me I as t' go on't wagon wi Will, an' you ave t' go on t'other wagon wi' Jack Grainger"*.

Ye fire bell started ringing and a hush descended on the courtyard, all eyes were fixed upon the Squire as he started to speak, he firstly informed each person what their tasks were to be and then went on to explain that the task of his group would be to support the infantry and protect the baggage and supplies camp in the rear. Finally he said, *"We are setting off in ten minutes, we are going to Thirsk, where we will join forces with my brother Sir George Fewster and his men and then we head for York"*.

He strode down the ramp from the loading bay and walked across to where a young ostler was holding his horse beside the stone mounting block, he checked the girthband, mounted the horse and walked it across the courtyard to where his wife was standing with Mistress Hopkin (the cook) and the rest of the household servants. Lady Fewster stepped forward and approached him, as she did so, she handed to him a lace kerchief which she had removed from her head, she said, *"Please take this my favour dearest, God be with you and come back safe"*. The Squire took the proferred favour, he fastened it to his sash, he turned the horse and trotted toward the gate. As he got to the gate he stopped and signalled for his men to follow, they moved toward him as a column, six ranks in three's each man carrying a makeshift pike. The column was followed by the two wagon's each pulled by two heavy horses, at the gate they turned onto the road to Thirsk.

As he sat on the cross seat of the rear waggon , Isaac's mind was thinking deeply of the consequences to his family, should he fail to return. Jack Grainger, meanwhile, unaware his audience was not listening to him, was advancing his view that Fire was the best weapon of war. Jack, went rambling on explaining, to no one in particular that a barricade of stout sharp pointed hurdles set behind a burning trench would stop any Cavalry charge. Continuing Jack said, *"Ya see Isaac, 'osses like most animals tek fright o fire"*, Jack then asked the opinion of his two horses, who both snorted in response to his question, he turned again to Isaac and said, *"Aye fire 'ud stop em dead"*. Isaac's thought's were far away from what Jack was telling him, he was worried how Rose would cope in his absence and he was more than a little nervous of what his own fate may be in the forthcoming battle.

The Squire led the column into Borrowby, when they got to the Square he called a halt outside The Wheatsheaf. He dismounted from his horse and turned, he waved to Jack Grainger to move forward with his waggon. Jack clicked his tongue and his pair of heavy horses pulled the waggon forward and Jack halted them on the cobbles outside the

Wheatsheaf. The Squire said, *"Jack have you left that space in the middle of the waggon which I asked for"*, Jack replied, *"Aye Squire, ay 'ave"*. A large figure over two rods tall and of ample proportions appeared in the doorway of the Wheatsheaf, it was the innkeeper Harry Bosomworth, he smiled at the Squire and said, *"Morning Squire, ah ya pickin' up them two 'ogsheads of Ale, ah ave em ont gantry in't backyard"*. The Squire replied, *"Thank you Harry, Jack will bring the waggon round into the Yard"*.

Jack flicked the reins and the two powerful horses responded and the heavy wagon was pulled slowly forward and into the yard at the side of the hostelry. Jack halted the horses at a point where the side of the waggon was adjacent to the stone gantry in the yard, he stood up and stepped onto the shaft of the waggon and then onto the gantry, he removed the pinions and lowered the centre of the three drop side pieces onto the gantry. Harry was already standing on the gantry and he called to Jack, *"Reet Jack leave it ta me"*, *and then will very little effort"*, he pushed the casks one after the other onto the other onto the waggon and securely wedged them into place. When he had finished he shouted, *"Reet Jack that's fettled em, i'll see ta sides after ya pull move on a bit"*. After he had seen Harry lift up the side pieces and replace the pinions, Jack gave a flick of the reins, and the horses moved forward and they again took up their position at the rear of the column.

As their group approached Thirsk, Isaac noticed there were many more people than usual were making their way towards the Market Place, looking ahead, Isaac could see Squire Fewster at the head of the column as it went across the stone hump back bridge over the Cod Beck. Townspeople, many of whom Isaac knew, were waving and shouting good luck as the column passed by and continued on into the Market Place, where the men and the waggons came to a halt behind where the Squire had reined in at the right hand side of the Market Cross. Isaac saw there were three other columns about the size of their own waiting in the Market Square, Squire Fewster, after dismounting from his horse made his way over to where his brother was standing with his own men and waggons.

Isaac was gazing across the Market Square toward the throngs of bystanders surrounding the assembled columns, Tobe turned round to look back at Jack and Isaac on the waggon behind him and shouted, "*As ta seen yon Cannon on't back ah Squires brothers waggon,* Isaac looked in the direction that Tobe was pointing and he saw a huge trunk of metal pointing upwards, it was mounted onto a sturdy oak base and it had solid wooden wheels. Isaac had never seen a cannon before and he was quite impressed by how big it was, it was much larger than he imagined it would be.

Turning to look at Jack he said, "*It's bigger than ah thout it wud be*", Jack replied, "*Som off em ah bigger than that, wen ah was in York a'fore start o't siege Squire teld me that York cannons was't as big as't Siege Cannon Lord fairfax wud 'aveta fire on York*". As Isaac looked across the Market Place, he saw that the Squire and his brother Sir George Fewster had joined the leaders of the other two columns and the group became quite agitated as they were speaking. Squire Fewster suddenly turned round and with a sweeping gesture toward the crowded Market Place he again faced his companions and spoke to them, they all nodded in assent and then turned simultaneously as a group and headed across the square and entered The Ox Hotel.

With the Squire leading the way, they entered a large comfortable withdrawing room on the left hand side of the large hallway. They busied themselves removing their gauntlets and their colourful headgear, each of which was bedecked with an abundance of large feathers, they each carefully placed their property on a long settle which was near to the fireplace, the mantle and surround of which was richly carved, they seated themselves around a large circular table adjacent to the window, a young scullion boy was busy on the other side of the room trimming the wicks of a large number of oil lamps arranged on a table in front of him. Sir George looked toward the boy and shouted to him, *"Be off with you lad and bade your Master to attend upon us"*, the boy with a look of fear on his face darted from the room to comply with Sir George's instruction.

The group were busy chatting, a figure bustled through the doorway missing his footing as he did so which caused him to stumble, he stopped for a moment and as he approached the table, he was already apologising for not being present upon their arrival. He was a person of some three score years, his hair was sparse, his face was round and slightly jovial looking and his body had a suggestion of portliness. He was under two yards tall and his demeanour toward his guests fussy, after again expressing his apologies to Sir George, he said,*"Welcome, I am Rufus Baldric, how can I serve you Gentlemen"*, Sir George said, *"Innkeeper, provide us with victuals, we need to break our fast"*. Rufus bowed (almost as if in Prayer) and in haste he shuffled backwards through the door.

Squire Fewster addressed his brother and said,*"In the orders you received, were they quite clear that we and our men should join up with and be responsible for the defence of the baggage and stores waggons"*. Sir George replied, *"Dear brother, the instructions I received were quite clear, namely that all four of us, together with our men were to defend the waggons and stores, a further instruction was attached that all our men were to be ordered, that a strip of red material was to be attached on their left shoulders, in order to identify them".*

Squire Fewster was about to speak again, but checked himself, he espied Rufus Baldric entering the room, he was carrying a very large wooden platter containing food and he was followed by a pretty serving wench carrying another platter containing large jugs of ale and drinking vessels. Rufus fussed around his guests, placing the platters, vessels and food carefully onto the table and then adjusting very slightly the position of one or two of them. Sir George became somewhat irritated by Rufus and said to him, *"Don't dither Innkeeper, kindly withdraw".* Rufus stepped backwards and again bowing excessively he withdrew from the room.

Sir George poured himself some ale into a large pewter goblet, he partook of several of the thick slices of bread from the platter, (it was still warm and was not long out of the oven) he reached for a dish containing wedges of a crumbly white cheese (made locally and very popular) he placed some cheese onto a slice of bread and then liberally spread some onion and fruit pickle on top. His companions similarly prepared their food and there was silence around the table as the group broke their fast. They each ate their fill and when all the food had been consumed the Squire refilled all of their drinking vessels with ale and they sat back and relaxed.

Squire Fewster opened his waist pouch and took from it a pipe made from briar, the stem was some two hands in length. Again from his waist pouch he took a soft leather bag with a drawstring, he opened it and from it he took an amount of tobacco and carefully rubbed it on the palm of his hand, he followed this by carefully packing the tobacco into the bowl of the pipe. The Squire looked toward the doorway and saw the serving wench waiting across the hallway, he shouted, *"Come hither wench, I need a lighted taper"*, the girl walked quickly into the room and went to the fireplace, from a vase she took a spill (a very thin strip of wood about three hands long) she put it into a flame in the fire and it began to smoulder in a red glow. She walked across to the Squire and he leaned forward as she placed the smouldering end of the spill across the bowl of his pipe, he began to inhale and quite quickly, the pipe produced smoke which the Squire exhaled.

Meanwhile other members of the group (with the exception of Sir George had followed the Squire's lead) and had similarly prepared their pipes ready to smoke, the girl went to each of them in turn and proffered a light from the spill. When she got to the last of the smokers in the circle Simon Gorstung, she tried to step away as he threw his arm around her waist and pulled her forcibly onto his knee, his pipe clattered to the floor as he pushed his hand down the top of her bodice and started to fondle her breasts. She cried out fearfully, begging him to release her, there was a loud crash as Squire Fewster's chair fell backwards. The Squire had re-acted immediately, when Gorstung had caught hold of the girl, he had jumped from his chair and bounded toward Gorstung, he had drawn his sword and he shouted, *"You scoundrel, unhand the wench at once"*, there was a look of utter surprise on Gorstung's face as he complied with the Squire's instruction. As Gorstung released her, the girl ran shrieking from the room, Squire Fewster replaced his sword into this scabbard his sword, turning once more to Gorstung, who appeared to be quite un-nerved at the response the Squire had made toward him, the Squire glowered at Gorstung and said, *"Never again, in my presene be so un-gentlemanly, or you will surely feel cold steel"*.

Sir George intervened to restore order, he said to Squire Fewster, *"Calm down Charles, she is only a serving wench,,* she probably enjoys the attention,, I am sure Gorstung meant no harm". He then turned toward Gorstung and said, "We have important work to do, you will apologise to my brother, won't you"? With a sullen look on his face Gorstung mumbled an apology to Squire Fewster, at which Sir George said, "Now, can we please recommence our discussion, we must examine the best and safest route".

Walter Minton (the fourth member of the group) adressed his companions,"Gentlemen, we must keep to the quieter roads and lanes to avoid any chance of meeting troops of Roundheads who may be in the area, they have stopped and plundered from many carts and waggons which they have stopped in recent weeks". Gorstung nodded his head in agreement and said, "We have to find a safe place to cross the River Ouse, before we reach York.". Sir George then said, " I have been advised that Oliver Calvert, who owns land on both sides of the river at Aldwark, uses a large raft to ferry his carts and livestock across the river and he is a King's man". Squire Fewster commented, "Aldwark would be then our best crossing point".

Their discussion of the various routes and problems was concluded when Sir George sadid, "Well Gentlemen, are we agreed that our route will be by way of Sowerby, Dalton, Sessay, Brafferton, Helperby, Flawith, Aldwark, Thorp Underwood and on to York"? Seeing his companions nodding their agreement, Sir George smiled and said,"Very well gentlemen, let us go to give our support to King Charles". They rose and collected hats and gauntlets from the settle and as they were doing so Rufus Baldric entered the room.

He bowed to Sir George and said, "Sire, I hope my humble fayre was fulfilling for your needs". Sir George replied, "Innkeeper, you have provided good plain wholesome food", he rummaged in his waist pouch and then turning to his brother said, "Charles have you two crowns to give the

Innkeeper?" Squire Fewster similarly placed his hand within his own waist pouch and withdrew coins which he handed to Baldric, who with some hesitancy accepted the proffered coinage and retreated from the room, bowing to the group until he reached the safety of the hallway. Sir George strode from the room closely followed by the other members of the group.

As they exited from the hotel into the Market Place, they had extreme difficulty making their way through the crowds, which had increased in number since their arrival. When they reached their respective waggons instructions were shouted to the waggoners and columns alike, Squire Fewster went across to his own waggons and said to Jack Grainger, *"We are making for Sowerby first, we will rest and water the horses for a short time when we get there".*

When all the column's of men had reformed in front of their respective waggons, Sir George raised his arm and signalled the baggage train to follow as he moved his horse forward into a walk. As they moved off the cobbled Market Square and turned right toward Sowerby, the crowd of onlookers started to cheer and there were many shouts of *"Long live King Charles"*, Isaac felt quite fearful as he sat high up on the waggon seats at Jack Grainger's side looking down at the crowd. He wondered how long, if ever, before he would be in the Market Place again.

Jack meanwhile was busy shouting greetings down to those members of the throng of bystanders whom he recognised. Isaac as he looked ahead guessed that the whole baggage train would be at least six chains long, after they had left the area of the Market Place the onlookers were less crowded and stood in small groups and the further they progressed they only saw occasional inhabitants either walking or pushing their carts toward the Market Place.

As they passed through Sowerby there were very few bystanders at the roadside. A calm seemed to have settled over the members of the column as they marched through and then left Sowerby behind them, and the noonday sun was high above them, the two heavy horses pulling the waggons were snorting loudly as they walked and constantly swished their tails to move off swarms of flies, which had followed the column since they had left Thirsk. Suddenly Isaac heard a commotion ahead and he saw Sir George was directing the leading column from off the road toward a large thicket of trees and beyond which Isaac could see the sunlight glinting a reflection from the surface of the "Cod Beck" (a rivulet running from near Dalton onto the moors above Ellerby). By this time Squire Fewster, together with Gorstung and Minton had ridden forward to join Sir George and after a few moments Minton rode forward across the fields following the leading column as it moved toward the thicket. Isaac saw the columns and waggon disappear behind the shield of the thicket

Just as the Squire's column was approaching the turn off point, Isaac saw Sir George and Gorstung turn their mounts and ride off toward the thicket where the other columns had gone. As their waggon drew up to the Squire he rode alongside and said to Jack, "*We are going to stay here for about an hour to water the horses and let you men have a rest and some victuals*". Jack nodded acknowledgement of the message, he then flicked the reins and clicked his tongue and his two charges responded and pulled the cart toward the thicket. When they approached the other seven wagons, Jack talked to his team and skilfully put pressure on his reins with one hand and none on the reins in his other hand and his horses gently pulled his waggon round and drew up alongside Will Thornton's waggon, Isaac and Jack jumped to the ground and Isaac went over to speak to Tobe.

Jack unhitched the horses from the shaft's, he then removed the harness and other tack from he team, he led a rope through each bridle and set off to the Cod Beck, on arrival at the bank the other drivers and grooms had allowed their charges into the water, which at that point was a little over knee deep. Jack drove a picket into the ground with a heavy hammer which he had taken from a leather saddlebag which he had placed across the horses back before he left the waggon, he secured a rope from one horse to the stake and after removing his boots Jack walked the other horse into the water, where with the use of a woollen cloth he commenced to wash down the mare, who was standing taking her fill of the cooling water. After completing his task with the first animal, Jack repeated the procedure with the second one, before leading them back to the shade of the thicket, where he hung a bag of oats around each of their necks.

As he sat down at the side of his waggon, slaking his thirst, after which, Jack started to eat his thick slices of bread coated with beef fat. As he finished eating, Isaac approached him from a throng of men who were gathered around one of the other waggons, he was carrying some pieces of red material, Jack saw they were cloth strips. Isaac passed one to Jack and said, *"Wi 'ave ta wear em ta show which side wi with"*, Jack watched Isaac put the strip onto his left shoulder and then make slight adjustments by tying it under his armpit and then pulling it down slightly until he was quite satisfied it was in the right position. Jack put his own strip on his shoulder and tied it in one quick movement and said to Isaac, *"Ah don't no as thal do us any good"*. Looking around the makeshift camp Jack could see that all the men were gathered in small groups whilst they similarly adorned themselves.

All heads suddenly turned as the sound of a hunting horn drew their attention to where Sir George and his companions were standing beside their picketed horses, there were many arm gestures and signals and Jack said, *"Ah think ther afta us ta put 'osses back in shafts"*, Isaac nodded and said, *"Ah think tha's reet"*, they saw as they looked along the line of waggon's that the grooms and waggoners were removing the horses from the pickets, Jack similarly went to his two heavy horses to release them, Isaac went to the waggon where Jack had hung the gear for the horses, between them they replaced all the gear onto the horses, they then slowly backed each horse into the shafts and hitched them up, they picked up their own packs and placed them back onto the waggon, they climbed up onto the waggon and as they sat on the high seat they saw that all the other waggons appeared to be re-horsed and ready to go.

Whilst they were waiting both Jack and Issac were looking in the direction of Squire Fewster, who was still in earnest conversation with his brother. They saw Sir George stride away in company with Minton toward their horses, they mounted and then signalled to their respective men and waggons to follow as they moved off. Squire Fewster and Gorstung continued in conversation and then they too walked toward their horses, they mounted and each went to the head of their column, after looking to observe the preparedness of everyone, Squire Fewster walked his horse forward and waved his arm for his column to follow. Gorstung's column followed on behind Jack and Isaac's waggon, looking back Isaac saw that Gorstung and his column were about a chain behind them, Squire Fewster turned left heading towards Dalton.

CHAPTER IX

Strangers Arrive

Rose had watched as Isaac walked away from her down the track, she had waited until he was lost from view and then she turned and went back into the cottage. She awoke Ann and Willie and overlooked them as they washed in the hot water she had poured into the sink from the cauldron which had boiled on the fire, after which she gave them some boiled oats and sheep's milk with which to break their fast. After finishing their meal she sent the children outside telling them to find and gather the eggs laid by the hens and ducks. Whilst the children were out Rose cleaned the cottage.

Rose was busy making cheese from sheep's milk, the children played happily enough in the yard outside, suddenly they ran into the cottage shouting excitedly, she calmed them down and Willie said, "*Ma, two men ar' ont' way upt' track*". When she got to the door of the cottage Rose saw that the men in question were about a furlong down the track and walking quite slowly toward the cottage, Rose moved forward and stood at the gate into the yard to await the visitors. As they got to her, Rose saw they were both dishevelled looking, one seemed to be about two score years old or more and the other looked much younger, Rose judged him to be about a score and five years old. They were not dressed in breeches but wore some type of woven material that looked like a woman's skirt, both were wearing leather jerkins and were carrying heavy staffs and each had a pack upon his back. They had red/sandy coloured hair and Rose noticed immediately that the elder of the two was extremely pale and he looked as if he was about to collapse. The younger man started to speak to Rose, she did not understand what he was saying, whilst she was shaking her head to indicate she did not understand, the elder man slumped to the floor.

As the younger man crouched at his companion's side, Rose dashed into the cottage and returned with a pitcher containing water, she passed it to the man, who tried to pour some into his companion's mouth and also rubbed some onto the man's forehead. He then tried to ease the elder one into a sitting position and as he was doing so, he was speaking to him in a strange halting language that Rose did not understand. She could see that the older man was sweating and gasping for his breath, she caught the younger man's attention and by her lifting the elder man's feet and gesturing that he grasp the man under the armpits they managed to lift the man into the small byre and made him comfortable on a bed of straw, Rose indicated that she was leaving the barn and signed by laying her head upon her flat palms that it would be better to let the man sleep.

She then left the barn and when outside she called for the children and they went into the cottage, she was frightened the men may be a danger to her and the children, she decided she would have the dog in the house through the night, she knew the dog would attack the men if they threatened the children.

After giving Ann and Willie their supper and put them to bed, she boiled some oats and milk, which she took on two wooden platters into the byre, the elder man was asleep, but he was no longer gasping for his breath, his companion was dozing at his side, as Rose moved toward them the young man stirred and looked at her. Rose smiled at him and handed him a dish and a spoon, he took the dish and started to eat the nourishing oats, he gobbled the food hungrily and the dish was soon empty, he set it down at his side and moved across to check on his companion, he placed his hand on the man's forehead and turned to Rose and smiled, Rose moved closer and she could see the man was no longer in a fever and his breathing was normal. Rose knelt at the side of the man and gently shook him, he stirred and opened his eyes, she smiled at him as she helped him to sit up, she passed him the dish of oats and a spoon and he nodded his thanks and slowly started to eat.

Whilst he was eating his companion was asking him question's and he just nodded in reply, until suddenly he stopped eating and shouted in anger at the younger man. Rose jumped back toward the door in fear and as he struggled to his feet he was shaking his head at Rose and clasping his hands as if in prayer, he then smiled at her and then turning towards his companion he spoke angrily to him.

Eventually his anger calmed and his attitude became became more friendly and they spoke less loudly, the older man turned to Rose and he was smiling as he pointed to himself and said, "*Duncan*" and then pointed to the younger man he said, "*Rory*", in a smiling responses and pointing to herself she said, "*Rose*". Still smiling she turned and left the byre, she went to the cottage, she got a large pitcher and filled it with water and along with some bread and two leather drinking vessels she returned to the byre.

The bread and the pitcher of water, she placed on a trestle in the corner of the byre and gestured by lifting her hand upward towards her mouth that they should drink, she turned to leave the byre and as she did so waved her hand slightly and said, *"Goodnight"*, they both murmured a response which she did not understand. Before she went into the cottage she called to the dog and when he got to her she took him to the cottage door and with a length of rope tethered him to the door frame. She busied herself damping down the fire and then prepared for bed, she felt calmer and happier than when the men had arrived that morning.

Rose awoke with a start, she heard the frantic barking of the dog outside, it was daylight and she heard loud voices. She quickly got out of bed and threw her cloak over her shoulders and hurried to the cottage door, when she opened the door, she saw two men, they were wearing what looked like metal jerkins and helmets and had pistols fastened in leather holders across their chests, she decided they must be Roundhead troopers. They were struggling to rope one of Rose's sheep, one of the troopers had a knife in his hand, Rose shouted them to stop, they turned and looked at her, they shouted to her to go back into the cottage. Rose dashed forward and caught hold of the arm of the trooper with the knife. The man turned and furiously stabbed Rose several times in her arm and shoulder, he then thrust her away and she fell to the ground, she did not move, but the trooper jumped and landed with both feet upon her left ankle, there was a sickening crack, he then viciously kicked her head.

The man then turned his attention back to the sheep, he saw a wild looking man who was lumbering towards him carrying a long pole which had a sharp point at the end. He instinctively tried to jump sideways out of the way, but the sharp point caught him in the throat and as he was propelled backwards, he fell to the ground, the point of the pole had penetrated straight through his neck and he was impaled to the ground, lifeless. Upon seeing the attack taking place, the second trooper had drawn his pistol, but before he had time to prepare it to fire, he was struck by a knife which became embedded in his upper arm.

The knife had been thrown by a second wild looking man, who upon seeing the trooper drop his pistol, ran forward and he was carrying another dagger type knife, he caught hold of the trooper around the neck he pulled his head back and cut the his throat several times and let the body fall to the ground. He then went across to join his companion who was kneeling on the ground where Rose had fallen, he was gently calling her name, but she did not respond, she was covered in blood, they gently lifted her and carried her into the cottage, they saw her bed and laid her upon it.

Duncan, the older man told his companion Rory to fetch some hot water from the cauldron over by the fire, meanwhile he started to check Rose's injuries (he had often aided wounded comrades by binding their battlefield injuries). Rose was still not conscious and she had cuts and bruising on her left temple where the trooper had kicked her, the wounds in her upper arm and shoulder were still bleeding, he took his knife and cut away the material of Rose's dress around her arm and chest, her breast was exposed, but he did not pause in his task, he folded the material he had cut away into his hand and soaked it in the leather jug of hot water and cleaned the wounds as best he could, he then bound the wounds tightly with material he had cut from Rose's shift.

The wounds on Rose's temple, Duncan found not to be deep and he bathed the area gently around the bruising, upon checking the ankle he found the foot was in a twisted position and the ankle was swelling rapidly, he was sure bones were broken within the joint. Duncan gently took hold of the foot and turned it toward it's natural position, Rose groaned painfully, he showed Rory how to hold the ankle in position and he went off searching into cupboards. When he returned he had with him two flat thin pieces of wood about as long as his foot, (Rose used them for mixing and shaping her cheeses) he placed each piece either side of her ankle along her leg and bound them tightly, the foot stayed in it's natural position. They covered her with wool blankets and left her to rest.

Whilst Duncan and Rory were in the kitchen deciding where best to lay the bodies of the troopers to rest and what they should do with the horses, Willie wandered in, he was leading Ann by the hand, she was weeping and looked confused. Rory told Duncan to keep both of the children in the kitchen, he then dashed outside and dragged the body of the trooper whose throat he had slit into the barn, he dumped it into a corner and covered it with straw. He went back outside and similarly dragged the body of the second trooper into the barn and dumped it at the side of his compatriot and again used a large amount of straw to conceal the bodies.

When he was satisfied they could not be seen, he left the barn and crossed over to the large wooden water butt near the cottage door, taking a leather bucket he filled it and returned to the spot where the bodies had lain and threw the water onto the ground hoping to disperse the pools of blood. After several buckets and much brushing, he decided that that he could not improve on the result he had achieved. When he got back into the kitchen he found Duncan had calmed the children and he was busily preparing oats and milk for them to break their fast.

CHAPTER X

Incident at Dalton

As they approached Dalton, Sir George led the column down a by-road in order to skirt round the village. Some distance beyond Dalton, Jack said to Isaac, *"Lisssen canst tha 'ear owt"*, Isaac cocked his ear and away to his right he heard shouting and then pistol shots. The column halted at Sir George's signal, Gorstung rode forward and he and Sir George conversed.

Isaac saw six men from the first column move forward and line up at the side of the road, Gorstung spoke to them and then one of the group came running back down the column, it was Jake Bowyer a friend of Jack Grainger. He ran past Jack's wagon and approached Gorstung's men, as Jake came back accompanied by six of Gorstung's men, he shouted to Jack, *"Sir George thinks a troop a Roundheads is up front ow us, wi 'ave ta go an check"*.

When they reached the head of the column, the group of eighteen or so selected men set off to follow Gorstung as he trotted his horse forward toward the noise. Isaac saw them enter a plantation of trees and then they were lost to sight. At this point in the main column, the waggoners and grooms were jumping down and giving their horse teams buckets of water, after Jack and Isaac had seen to their team they went over to chat to Will and Tobe on the waggon in front. Suddenly they heard screams, mingled with shouting from beyond the trees. Isaac said to Tobe, *"What's up ower theer, ah wonder"*.

As Gorstung's group had entered the plantation, he had ordered his men to spread out in a straight line, they then moved forward through the trees, when they reached the far side of the plantation, they saw that four or five roundhead troopers were in the yard of a small farm, the farmer and his family (his wife and two daughters) were kneeling in front of one of the troopers who appeared to be giving orders to his comrades. They responded by starting to light makeshift torches from the flames of a small brazier standing in a corner of the yard, the farmers wife and his daughters began screaming in terror.

Gorstung quickly realised that it was the Roundheads intention to burn the farmhouse and buildings, he shouted to his men, *"Let's take them"*, he drew his sword and galloped forward, his men were in close pursuit. Gorstung headed straight toward the trooper in charge and smote him a fierce blow across the chest which threw the man to the ground. Jumping from his horse he dashed forward and thrust his sword several times into the prone figure. The remaining troopers had dashed across the yard to where their horses were hitched, Gorstung's men however, with their rough made pikes were brutal and killed all the troopers before any of them were able to mount their horses. Gorstung turned and saw there was no further fighting and moved toward the farmer and his family.

The farmer suddenly shouted, "Beware Sire", Gorstung half turned and the trooper whom he had thought he'd killed was on his knees and he was pointing his pistol at

Gorstung, there was a bang and Gorstung fell to the ground, his men ran to his aid, alas, he had died instantly when the shot had entered his brain.

Jake Bowyer took charge, he talked to the farmer and his family, the farmer assured Jake he would arrange for Gorstung to have a decent Christian burial and thanked them for saving the lives of his family and preventing the burning of his farm. Jake took his leave and slowly led the men back to the waiting column leading the dead man's horse by the bridle.

When told of Gorstung's death Sir George Fewster was quite shocked and questioned Jake concerning the circumstances, Jake told how the farmer was arranging for a Christian burial for both Gorstung and the Roundhead troopers. Sir George re-acted quickly and called for the columns to reform and then gave the signal to move forward, he was worried that further Roundhead troopers could well descend upon the area in search of their missing brethren.

The column moved at a fast pace, it was the intention of Sir George to move as far as and as fast as he could from the area, before making camp for the night. By using field cart tracks they successfully passed by Sessay and Brafferton, as they were making a detour around Helperby dense smoke was arising above the treetops ahead of them. Sir George halted the column and Walter Minton and Squire Fewster rode forward to confer with him, Sir George said, *"Gentlemen, I am uneasy, we do not know the cause of that smoke, we could be exposed to attack if we remain in a long column"*.

Both Minton and the Squire agreed with Sir George's fears, Minton suggested that the waggon's flanked by twenty or so men should drop to the rear and proceed with caution. The main column splitting into two groups would meanwhile proceed forward at speed. This plan was agreed and orders were quickly given to re-group the waggon's and Jake Bowyer was placed in charge of the waggon's and instructed to proceed cautiously.

Sir George, Squire Fewster and Walter Minton, checked their men were in attack formation and then trotted their horses forward with the two groups of men following at the jog. At a point some fifty yards short of the plantation Sir George halted, and gave instructions that the men were to approach the plantation in line abreast. Sir George signalled the advance and cautiously led his men through the plantation. As they broke through the trees it was to see a large farmstead burning fiercely and parts of it already collapsing. They continued cautiously forward and as they approached the burning barn Sir George saw there were some bodies lying on the ground. He immediately halted the formation and shouted to six of his men to go forward with him, Sir George dismounted he did not need to check the figures on the ground, they were dead, it was a sickening sight.

There were four bodies, two males and two females, the older male, probably the farmer was lying in a grotesque position, his hands were bound behind his back, his left leg was severed from his body at the knee. The second male was younger (probably the farmers son) his hands were similarly bound behind his back and a noose was tight around his neck, the other end of the noose was fastened to a wooden lintel in the doorway of the barn, it had fallen away from the door frame which though partly in situe was badly burned. The two females, were, in Sir George's view mother and daughter, they were lying but a yard or two apart, their hands also had been bound behind their backs, their clothing was disarranged and blood soaked, they had probably been raped and then shot. Sir George was sickened by the barbarity of the injuries and the ruthless killing, he thought to himself how this innocent family, following their daily routine and not a threat to anyone, had been so tragically drawn into a conflict not of their making. He was appalled at the inhumanity of mankind.

He turned to the men around him, some of whom were openly expressing their anger, he told them to save their anger and retribution for the coming battle ! Acting upon Sir George's instructions, the group pulled forward a cart (which because of it's distance from the fire was intact). They cut the bonds from the victim's and solemnly placed the bodies upon the cart. Whilst two of their number were despatched to find digging implements, the remaining four pushed the cart away from the farm buildings and came to a halt at the side of a cultivated flower garden, set away at the rear of what had been the farmhouse, but which now was just smouldering rubble. Meanwhile Sir George, who had tethered his horse, was approaching them, he was in the company of the two men who had sorted out an assortment of shovels. At Sir George's behest they commenced digging a large grave near to an apple tree in a corner of the garden, the remainder of the column's under the direction of Squire Fewster and Walter Minton had formed a human chain and buckets of water were being passed along to douse those areas which were still burning.

When Sir George had decided that the grave was large enough, he got the men to place the bodies in the grave alongside each other, when that was completed to his satisfaction, they all stood solemnly around the grave and Sir George said prayers, he then turned and indicated the men to commence filling the earth back into the grave and for them to make a cross with which to mark the grave when they had finished. He then strode over to converse with Squire Fewster and Walter Minton.

Squire Fewster told his brother that he and Minton had set the men to douse the flames throughout the site and there were just a few places where partly burned timbers had fallen onto smouldering ash and re-ignited, but those apart, the fire was burned out, the men had not found any more bodies, but there were some animals and fowls in the adjoining fields. It was early evening, the sun was low on the Westerly skyline, Sir George said, *"I think we should consider making camp, what are your opinions Gentlemen"*, Minton said, *"I have an elderly uncle who has a large house by the river near Myton, this is but a mile or so away, we would surely be most welcome there"*. Sir George nodded his agreement and turning to his brother said, *"How do you favour that option Charles,"* he took a moment or so before he replied, *"How secluded is your uncle's property Walter, how likely is it that Roundhead troopers would pass that way"*. Walter Minton answered immediately, *"The property is extremely isolaterd, anyone unfamiliar with the locality would be unlikely to suspect that it existed"*. Squire Fewster after a little further thought said, *"In those circumstances George, I feel it would meet our overnight needs and allow us to set off shortly after daybreak tomorrow"*. Turning in his saddle, Sir George said, *"Minton lead us to your Uncle"*.

Before leaving the farmstead Sir George selected two of his own men to remain, he instructed them to care for all the livestock they found, *"Do as I bid men, until we return"*, he then ordered all the column's to reform and with Walter Minton leading they set off to Myton. He led the column off the main by-ways around lush meadows and eventually after detouring around a vast forest of oaks, a large Mansion stood before them. Minton signalled the columns to stop, he rode back to Sir George and his brother and said, *"I suggest Sire, that we leave the column's here with Bowyer in charge, whist we three explain our needs to my Uncle*". There was agreement with this suggestion and they rode forward and approached the house. Minton took them round to the rear of the house and into a quadrangle containing stabling on three sides. Stablemen and ostlers came forward and held their horses, they dismounted and Minton said to the elderly stableman, "*Hobman, see these animals are rubbed down, fed, watered and bedded down for the night*". Turning to his companions Minton said, "*This way Gentlemen*", they followed him to the side of the house and through a large canopied doorway which in turn led to a wide hallway, from which access could be gained on one side to the Kitchens, the other side afforded access to a Withdrawing Room and thence to the Dining Room.

Minton carried on straight down the Hallway until they came to the main Hall which was dominated by an imposing marble Staircase, turning off to the right Minton knocked on the door and a voice from within bade them to enter. They stepped into a comfortably furnished Sitting Room, at the far side of the room sitting in a carved oak chair with views out of the large bow shaped window sat an elderly gentleman, he rose upon their entry and moved slowly and with great difficulty toward them. His frame was stooped, he was sparse of hair (the little he had shone like silver) he looked painfully frail, but his eyes sparkled with alertness and determination, he greeted Minton and was then introduced to the Squire and Sir George. When they were all seated Minton commenced to acquaint his uncle (a former Naval Captain, Ralph Minton) with the object and needs of their visit to his house. He invited them to accept his hospitality for as long as was necessary in their quest to aid the King. Ralph Minton then moved over to the fireplace, in an alcove at one side of which stood a large gong suspended from a carved stand, he took a bound leather hammer which was hanging on the stand and with it struck the gong twice, the noise boomed around the room.

When Ralph Minton had resumed his seat, Sir George complimented him upon the elegance of his home, he thanked Sir George for his kind comments. He told them that he had inherited the property at the death of his wife's father and went on to say his wife had died a number of years ago. A knock at the door halted his story, he bade the caller to enter, Ralph Minton informed his visitors that before them stood his Steward of many years Oliver Hancock, he then proceeded to instruct Hancock to prepare accommodation for the visitors and ensure that their comfort was attended to in every possible way. As Hancock left the room to carry out his Master's instructions, Walter Minton took leave of his Uncle, explaining his need to return to the waiting columns to guide Bowyer to the best location where camp could be made for the night. He informed his companion's that he would also arrange for their travelling trunks and coffers to be brought from the waggon's.

When he arrived at the stable yard Walter Minton sought and found Hobman the stableman and explained to him his needs, Hobman called out to a young ostler, when the young lad stood before him, he said to him, *"Put those two ponies int' shafts o' small cart and then do Mr. Minton's bidding"*, Minton waited until the boy had completed his task and had climbed onto the seat board of the cart and then he himself joined him. He bade the boy to drive over to the waiting column's and when they reached the head of the column, Minton instructed Bowyer to signal the column to follow the cart. Minton turned to the boy and said *"Take the track that passes the pond and then go on down to the river bank."* There was a large hay meadow which had been harvested and the hay had recently been carted away. After ensuring that the trunks and coffers were all gathered together and placed on the cart, Minton instructed the ostler to return to the Mansion.

After Minton left, Isaac and Jack Grainger jumped down from their waggon and moved forward to check with Tobe and Will Thornton on where to make camp. Will Thornton said, "*Squire, gav' orders ta Jake Bowyer that waggon's 'ad ta be drawn up in a square, an 'e suid sentinels 'ad ta be placed owtside, an' wi all 'ave ta stop int' square*".

Isaac looked up the column, he saw the waggon's were being placed in position to form a square, he said to Jack, "*We'll mek a start Jack*". As Tobe and Will led their horse team and cart to join the square, Jack and Isaac similarly moved their team into position. After feeding and watering their charges, the teamsters throughout the column picketed their charges for the night and then along with all the men in the column, they partook of their own victuals. Men from each group, Sir George's, Minton's and Squire Fewster's had prepared and cooked the food on their own group fires, throughout each group men used their own hot drink herbs which they had gathered from adjacent hedgerows, they then immersed their nettle, dock or mint leaves in hot water from the fire and after imbuing, enjoyed their hot drinks.

It was a restless night for Isaac and he was awakened several times through the night, because of men arguing or coughing or horses being restless. The general camp noises awoke Isaac at dawn, there was banter and argument among some groups and laughter and horseplay amongst other groups, yet other groups were practising combat with staves and makeshift pikes which they had fashioned themselves, but nevertheless looked quite fearsome.

Isaac noticed that many men from the column were enjoying a swim in the river, he decided to join them. The water when he entered it was not too cold, after swimming back and forth across the river a couple of times, Isaac left the water and was standing on the sandy bank observing the groups practising combat, when he suddenly he heard angry shouts from the area of the waggon's, he saw Tobe and Jack Grainger struggling on the ground with another person next to Jack's waggon. Feeling the need to go the aid of his friends, Isaac dashed toward the waggon, as he arrived Tobe and Jack were manhandling a third person, a man whom Isaac did not know to his feet. Isaac said, *"Wat's up Jack"*, still breathless from the struggle Jack gasped, *"This swine 'as drunk Squire's ale"*.

As Tobe and Jack were trussing the hands of the thief behind his back, Isaac saw the man vomit as he lay on the ground. Once again Jack and Tobe hauled the man to his feet, but he just slumped forward back to the ground, he was drunk. They lost patience and dragged him under the waggon to await the Squire's punishment.

– o0o –

Squire Fewster awoke before dawn, he lit the candle on the small writing slope and from within his coffer withdrew his diary, he recorded all the events of the previous day and gave specific directions to identify, for his own future guidance the farmhouse where the family had been so callously 'put to death'.

He then went on to record his hopes and fears in the coming conflict and concluded by appending the date 30th June, 1644. After replacing his diary to his coffer, he knelt and commenced his private prayers. The light of day filtered into the room around the edges of the wooden shutters, the

Squire went across to the shutters, he pulled them inwards to let in the daylight and made them secure , he observed how the room appeared to change it's character in daylight, in contrast to the eerie shadowed room which candlelight had previously created

After completing his toilet and dressing, Squire Fewster proceeded downstairs and as he entered the Dining Room he saw his brother and Minton were already breaking their fast. He wished them a good morning and joined them at the table. Sir George turning to his brother said, *"Minton suggests we will make better progress keeping to ye field tracks to avoid those damned Roundheads, do you agree"*? Charles Fewster nodded his head in agreement. The steward Hancock entered the room and enquired of Charles Fewster for his dining requirements. After discussing his preferences with Hancock, he decided upon Gammon steak cooked over the griddle and a goose egg fried, this was to be accompanied by boiled oats in cows milk, baked bread, spread with cheese, all produced on the farm.

After the breaking of their fast, the trio completed their preparations and oversaw the carriage of their trunks and coffers by the ostlers to the stable area. Thence they returned to rejoin their columns. Squire Fewster rode over to Jack's waggon and as Jack held the horse, his master dismounted. Turning to Jack, Squire Fewster said, *"Are we ready to move Jack"*, in reply Jack said, *"Wi ar' Squire an wi 'ave a thief ova theer"*, pointing to the prostrate figure under the waggon. Looking in the direction Jack had indicated Charles Fewster saw the body on the ground at the side of Jack's wagon. Turning again to Jack he said, *"Do you know his identity"*, Jack shook his head, the Squire then said, *"Find Jake Bowyer, bade him to attend upon me"*. Jack ran off quickly and returned accompanied by Jake. Pointing to the figure on the ground, the Squire said, *"Bowyer, do you know this man"*?

Upon stooping Jake turned the man's head and said, "*Ay Squire, e's wi Mr. Minton, 'is name is Archer*". Squire Fewster instructed Jake to acquaint Mr. Minton of the man's deeds and tell him I will decide the punishment when the man awakens" Turning to Jack, he said, "*Get some help and throw him in the waggon*". Their task completed Jack and Tobe returned and found Isaac had commenced fixing the traces and the bridle onto one of Jack's horses and with Jack's help they soon had both animals prepared and waiting in the shafts.

The eight waggon's moved forward and lined up, the men had formed into their respective column's and in response to a forward gesture with his arm by Sir George Fewster at the head of the column, this motley assembly of the King's loyal subjects moved off for YORK and the impending battle. Along with a group of six chosen men, Walter Minton was riding some distance in front of the main body in order to warn of any threat from Parliamentarian patrols. Everyone was in sombre mood and like many others, Isaac was thinking of home and of Rose and the children, he hoped his fate in the coming days would allow him to return to them safely.

Minton and his small group approached Flawith cautiously, Minton sent his Steward ahead to check for the presence of Parliament troopers. As he approached the duck pond he beheld a young maiden with a yoke on her shoulders from which hung her milk pails. He reined in his horse and said to her, "*Fair maiden, have you espied any troops of Parliament through the village today*", she smiled and answered, "*Sire I have not, but a troop rode furiously through two morns ago*". Turning his horse, he thanked the girl and trotted back to inform Walter Minton. Upon receiving the news, Minton bade one of his men to wait and inform Sir George that the way was clear. He spurred his horse and with his men entered Flawith, they saw the milk maid selling milk at the door of a cottage and she waved gaily to them as they trotted on through the village.

Minton was uneasy as they rode along the byways, there were so few travellers and little sign of any farming activity in the fields they passed. A mile or so after Flawith, just as they rounded a copse of trees, Minton saw a figure hanging from a rope fastened to a branch of a large oak tree. Along with his men, Minton dismounted and instructed the most agile member of his group to climb the tree and cut the body down. The youth delegated to the task quickly climbed the oak and after sitting astride the branch, he commenced to shuffle forward and upon reaching the point where the rope was secured, he cut it. The body plummeted earthwards and struck the ground with a heavy thud. Minton saw immediately that the corpse was quite badly mutilated where predatory maggots and crows had already commenced their destructive work. In a hollow in the ground adjacent to the oak, the earth was quite soft, Minton bade his men to dig a grave with their makeshift pikes.

The victim had been bound hand and foot and he was not wearing any footwear, glancing around the scene, Minton saw at the edge of a bed of nettles a leather type object. He went over to the spot and picked the object up, he saw it was a flat worn leather case which had to two retaining straps, it bore the coat of arms of His Majesty King Charles. Upon looking into the case, Minton saw it was empty, who had killed the messenger, who had taken the messages, Minton sensed very strongly the hand of Parliament was involved. When he saw the grave had been dug deep enough, he ordered the men to place the body in the grave and fill in the soil. Their task completed, Minton said a short prayer before remounting and moving on.

The remainder of their journey to Aldwark was uneventful and Minton halted his group just outside Aldwark to await the arrival of Sir George and the columns. The sun had not yet reached its mid-day zenith and the sky was bright blue and cloudless. A stream reasonably deep and with very clear water ran through a meadow a little way from the main track into Aldwark, Minton instructed his men to picket their horses and then start fires to enable the main group upon their arrival to commence cooking a meal.

Upon the arrival of the main groups Sir George led them straight into the area that Minton's Party had prepared. Sentinels were posted and then riders and drivers gave their fullest attention to their equine charges, watering, rubbing down and feeding. Squire Fewster had detailed other men who had no responsibility for horses to get cooking cauldrons and food supplies from the waggons. By the use of leather buckets another group of men quickly filled the cauldrons with water from the stream, salted beef (cut in small pieces), chopped turnip, sliced onions, chopped carrots, sliced cabbage, were placed in one cauldron. Oats were boiled in another cauldron and water boiled in a third cauldron (men used the hot water to make their various own brews of herbal beverages), to complete their meal rough whole grain bread and cheese was available.

After eating their fill, Isaac and Jack, along with Tobe and Will were resting in the shade of Jack's waggon, Squire Fewster approached, he said to Jack, *"Go rouse that scoundrel Archer and bring him forth to me"*. The Squire settled himself upon a barrel, whilst Jack, assisted by Isaac and Tobe clambered aboard the waggon to carry out the Squire's instructions. In the meantime Will went to his own waggon and returned with a small barrel of salt.

The prisoner was bundled forward and held before Squire Fewster, who with a penetrating gaze was assessing the man, who had little hair upon his crown, the few teeth he had were rotten, he looked to be some three score years old, but the Squire judged he was probably only two score years old, he was bedraggled and scruffy and his eyes were sunken and dull. After observing Archer, the Squire addressed him, "*Well fellow, what have you to say*", the miscreant looked sullenly at the Squire and the muttered, "*Twern't I Sire*", Squire Fewster turned to Jack and said, "*Where was he*", Jack replied, "*Squire, 'e was atside o't 'ogshead an 'e wa' drunk an 'e still 'ad tankard in 'is 'and*". His master mused for a few moments in judgement and then said, "*Six lashes for you scoundrel*", turning to Jack he said, "*Bind him to yonder tree, then bring Chester to me*". Isaac knew Chester very well, he was a huge man, he was as strong as an ox.

Whilst Isaac and Tobe were securing the prisoner to the tree, Jack moved toward one of the fires, where he saw Chester towering above a throng of the Squire's men. He told Chester the Squire had summoned his presence, the big man grunted and strode off toward the Squire. When he saw Chester, the Squire said to him, "*Chester, take this waggoner's horse whip and give that felon over at yonder tree six of your hardest lashes*". Taking the long whip Chester stroked the handle and end fronds, smiling as though he had just met a long lost friend, he looked at the Squire and said, "*I'll mek im scream Squire*". He then turned and strode over to the tree, cracking the whip as he did so. Upon reaching the forlorn figure at the tree, Chester, took hold of the man's collar, he roughly pulled the man's head upwards, grinning at his victim, he held the whip up against the man's face and said, "*Kiss the leather*". He then took great care to measure the distance he needed to ensure each stroke was totally effective.

Whilst Chester was carrying out his preparations, members of the column began quietly to move forward and formed a large circle around the tree. When the Squire saw Chester was ready to commence, he shouted, *"Commence the punishment"*. Chester drew back his arm and then whipped it forward with great speed, the leather fronds smote into the soft skin of the victim's back and he screamed out in extreme pain. There was total silence among the gathered onlookers, broken only by the pitiful moaning of the victim Archer.

With each successive stroke, Archer screamed for mercy, after the fifth stroke he collapsed into unconsciousness, but Chester proceeded to deliver the sixth and final stroke. This impacted with a loud thwack upon the victim's open wounds and blood spattered onto the bark of the tree, some splashing onto Chester's forearm. The Squire shouted, *"Cut him down, treat his wounds and throw him onto a waggon"*. Will Thornton moved forward as Jack cut Archer down, he then liberally rubbed salt into the man's wounds, then with help from others they carried him to Minton's waggon's. and threw him onto the back of one of them. Before leaving Archer, who was lying in a heap on the waggon floor, Jack turned and looking across toward the man, he muttered to himself, *"Well tha's payd ah 'evvy price for yah crime, but, like as not, ya won't ah lernt any lesson from it"*.

CHAPTER XI

Injuries to Rose

Rose stirred and opened her eyes, daylight was filtering into the room through the small window, she was in bed, she could feel pain in her left ankle, she felt pain across her temple. She cried out for the children, a shadowy figure came towards her, she recognised him as Duncan, the elder of the visitors. Rose again spoke the names of the children, the man nodded and smiled re-assuringly at her, he turned and left the room, he returned with both children. Willie and Ann were excited to see her awake, they eagerly explained the games they had been playing with Rory and that they were going with him to show the way to the Manor House. Having seen their mother was still alive, they soon decided they must return outside to seek further excitement. When the children had gone, Duncan by speaking slowly was able to explain to Rose the events after the fracas with the troopers. He told her that he thought her ankle was broken and would take some time to mend, the troopers, Duncan told her, the troopers were both dead and their bodies had been burned in a nearby wood and bone fragments and tissue not consumed by the fire had then been buried.

The horses would need fodder, there was none on the farm and the little pasture would not suffice their needs for more than a day or so. He told Rose that anyone enquiring to know why the horses were there, should be told they had been found grazing down the track a little distance from the cottage, of the riders there had been no signs. Duncan went on to say that Willie had mentioned there were a lot of stables at the Manor House and he had asked Willie to take Ann and show Rory the way to the Manor House and they were already on there way. He asked Rose if she was hungry, she nodded, he left her and after a short while he returned with food and goat's milk. After she had eaten her fill, Duncan told her to try to sleep and he left the room.

With Rory leading the two horses and Willie and Ann skipping ahead showing the way, they had set off for the Manor House, as they were approaching Tobe's house the children saw their Aunt Nan, she was in the garden busy cutting some flowers, they ran forward excitedly. Nan was pleased to see them and she enquired where their mother was, the boy told her she was in bed. This puzzled her and with difficulty Rory explained the events of the previous day, but he omitted the details of the killings. Upon hearing of Rose's injuries Nan became worried, Rory calmed her and re-assured her that he and his uncle would take care of Rose and the children for the present. Nan thanked Rory and told him she would visit the following day after checking on Tobe's parents at the cottage. As Nan returned back inside the cottage, Rory and the children continued onto the Manor House.

When they reached the Manor House, Rory entered the stable yard and halted, he looked about him and saw a gentleman sitting astride his horse, he was talking to an elderly groom. Rory asked Willie who the man was and Willie told him he was the Squire's Estate Bailiff (Mr. Strong), leading the horses, Rory approached the man, he explained the circumstances of (how the animals had been found grazing along the track and the lack of identity of the owners), he went on to say that that due to lack of forage and stabling Rose was unable to see to the animals' welfare. The bailiff told him that stabling would be arranged at the Manor until the Squire returned and told the groom to take the animals into the stables.

As they were crossing the courtyard of the Manor, Lady Fewster came from within, she called the children over to her, as the children walked over to her, Rory accompanied them. She said, *"Willie Stackpole, what are you doing here, has your Mother sent you"*? Once more Rory stepped forward and explained how Rose was incapacitated by her injuries and the need to find stabling and fodder for the horses had prompted their visit. Lady Fewster listened attentively, she expressed her concerns for Rose's welfare and stated she would send her housekeeper on the morrow to check out the situation. Rory assured her that between them he and his uncle would care for the family.

Leaving the Manor House, Willie indicated the track home and he and Ann looked for flowers in the hedgerows to take home for their mother. Upon arriving back at the cottage, the children rushed to tell Rose of their meeting with their Aunt Nan and Lady Fewster and of the impending visit's of both their Aunt and the housekeeper from the Manor House on the morrow. Taking the flowers Ann went into the kitchen, where Rory was telling Duncan of how the horses were stabled at the Manor House. Duncan and Rory had watched Ann as she took great care to arrange the flowers in a tankard of water, they all returned to the bedroom where Duncan placed before Rose a platter of bread and a wooden pot containing honey. He told how he had discovered a nest of wild bees and had removed the honey from it, they all ate heartily and Rose in spite of the pain she was suffering from her ankle smiled as she saw the happiness and contentment upon the faces of the children.

At Duncan's behest Rory shepherded the children from the room telling them they must help him check and fodder the sheep. Duncan meanwhile pushed the heavy coffer around to the side of the bed, he then left the room and returned with a large bowl and a jug of hot water. These he placed on the coffer along with a large hessian drying sheet, then with great care he assisted Rose to sit on the side of the bed. Upon his return he brought to her a bundle of clean clothing, he told her to call if she needed help and then he left her in privacy. With extreme difficulty and much pain, Rose was eventually able to remove the remnants of her torn clothing and then tenderly wash and bathe her bruised body. Feeling much fresher, she commenced once again with much difficulty and pain to dress herself and then made herself as comfortable as she could on the bed.

Her thoughts at this time were of Isaac and the danger she felt he would meet, this made her a little sad and caused her to be tearful. She was startled when her thoughts were interrupted by a knocking at the door, when she called out the door opened and Duncan once again entered the room. He was carrying a leather riding boot, he told Rose it had belonged to one of the roundheads and he was going to cut it down and strap it round her leg and ankle he thought it might help ease pain when she moved her leg in bed. Taking his knife from his belt, he cut away the top of the boot below the knee, he the cut away the sole and the heel, he then cut along the stitching at the back of the boot from top to bottom. After inspecting what remained of his handiwork, he stooped on one knee and gently folded the leather around Rose's leg and ankle. He found there was an overlap of leather in some places, he marked certain areas with the point of his knife and taking the leather cast of Rose's leg he skilfully trimmed away edges of the leather. After scrutinising the cast, he grunted and again placed the cast in position around Roses leg, taking thin strips of leather which had been hanging from his belt he securely fastened the cast around her leg. He asked Rose to carefully move her leg, she did so and found that her discomfort was greatly eased.

When she awoke next morning, Rose found her leg was not as painful when she raised herself up and sat on the side of the bed, she heard voices through in the kitchen, she called out and Duncan accompanied by the children came into the room. The children were carrying a platter containing food for her to break her fast, Duncan was carrying a bowl and a jug of water. Duncan smiling and gesturing gave her assurance that the children were no problem and that Rory was taking them into Thirsk with him, after he had finished breaking his fast and that would allow Rose to have a quiet morning to adjust to the problems caused by her ankle. When Rory called, the children dashed off shouting their goodbyes to Rose as they ran into the kitchen. After the children had gone, she refreshed herself by washing and then she managed, by hopping and hobbling to get round the bed and get to the press where the blankets and clothes were stored. With difficulty she changed the blankets on the bed and then hobbled and hopped to the door into the kitchen.

As Rose entered into the kitchen through the bedroom door, Duncan entered from the outside yard, he was carrying two pieces of newly cut tree branch and some strips of leather (about four fingers wide), he was not pleased she had left the bedroom and he assisted her to sit on a sturdy chair at the side of the fire. She watched as he heated the heavy metal poker in the fire, when the poker was bright red he took it from the fire and with great care burned a hole through the centre of the smaller piece of tree branch. Then taking the longer of the saplings he placed the top edge against the hole in the small piece of wood and with great care tapped the smaller piece onto the larger sapling. He frequently stopped and examined his work, finally he placed the crosspiece of the implement under his arm and lifting his corresponding leg he leaned heavily upon the implement and took a step forward with his other leg and then a step with the prop implement, this took the weight from his leg.

He then helped Rose to stand and bade her place the 'arm' of the prop under her armpit, he decided the prop was too long. He sat Rose down again and then with his sharp throwing knife he proceeded to cut a small piece off the branch (about three fingers deep). When he had satisfied himself with the tidiness of the recent cut, he then took the strips of leather and tightly wrapped them around the arm of the prop and secured them firmly to the long shaft. Again he helped Rose to stand and then smiled broadly as she was able to 'walk' across the room with the prop taking the place of the injured leg. Rose smiled and said, "*Luk ah can walk agen*".

She spent some time practising with the 'prop' and she found if she took care and tried not to rush, she could get about quite well. Duncan entered the cottage from the outside yard, he told her she must not try too hard, they heard the happy shouts of the children returning and Rose had to show them how she could get about using her new 'prop'. They were all in a happy mood as they enjoyed their supper together and Rose was pleased she was able to put the children to bed.

After Duncan and Rory had withdrawn to the barn to sleep, Rose also felt tired and went to bed, she could not sleep immediately, her thoughts wandered as she worried about the dangers Isaac was about to face. She prayed he would be safe and soon be back with her, she was thankful for the help Duncan and Rory had given and pondered who they really were and how long would they stay.

She fell into a restless, uncomfortable sleep, she awoke suddenly at daybreak, she was worried and uncertain, she had so wished Isaac was there, he would have dealt with all her worries.

CHAPTER XII

Overnight at Aldwark

When the columns reformed and set off for the river crossing just beyond Aldwark, all the men in the columns were solemn and subdued, there was little chatter amongst the men. The recent 'whipping' which they had witnessed caused many of them to ponder upon the punishment meted out to Archer, villain though he was, he had many friends in the columns. Minton led them along secluded tracks, which enabled them not only to skirt by Aldwark, but also greatly reduced the prospect of encountering Parliamentarian troopers. Their arrival at Oliver Calvert's farm was achieved without incident and Minton along with Sir George rode forward toward the rambling farmhouse to seek advice from Oliver Calvert.

They dismounted outside the impressive front door (it was a large oak door which had been strengthened by having iron straps bolted onto to it) as a young groom led their horses away to the stables, Oliver Calvert opened the door. He was a tall, thin, bewigged man, some three score years old, he had a fresh, healthy complexion, after a hearty welcome, they followed his bidding and entered the house. Before taking them into a large withdrawing room at the front of the house, Calvert paused and turning in the doorway bellowed down the hall for victuals to be brought. The room felt 'homely' and comfortable and it was furnished with a number of sturdy oak armchairs whose comfort was improved by many soft cushions, the fabric of which was enhanced by an adornment of bright floral pattern stitching. After making themselves comfortable, a steward entered the room he was bearing a large tray (made of basketry) upon which was placed a large jug of ale and three pewter tankards, after serving the drinks the steward withdrew and they each partook of their refreshment in quiet contemplation.

Sir George, after quaffing his ale, explained at some length to Oliver Calvert, the need of their large party to cross the river and questioned whether Calvert's raft would be suitable for that purpose. The man was enthusiastic and explained that the equipment had been in use for over ten years and no problems had ever been encountered. He did however stress that the equipment was strongly made and was safe. It was not put to use at times when the river was liable to flood, which was usually in wintertime. Calvert assured them, that he would feel honoured if his raft was used in the King's cause, Sir George accepted the offer with gratitude.

Turning to his visitor's, Calvert said, *"Gentlemen, if you would please follow me"*, he led them down the Hallway and through the kitchen, from where they exited into the stable yard. Whilst Sir George and Walter Minton were mounting their horses, Calvert assisted by his grooms brought out eight heavy horses. When Calvert was satisfied that he had the right horses, he mounted the lead horse himself and instructed two of the grooms to mount the rear two horses. As the heavy horses moved forward at Calvert's bidding,

Sir George and Minton, reined their horses in on each side of Calvert.

Squire Fewster immediately, ordered the column's to move forward when he saw his brother accompanying the heavy horses from out of the stable yard and take a track away from the farm buildings. After progressing some four furlong's the ground slowly sloped down toward the river, the area of sloping ground extended for some two chains alongside the river. A wide gravelled track stretched down the slope to the river on the opposite bank and upon that bank, a short way from the water's edge, was standing a sturdy oak tree trunk. It was bereft of branches and was shoulder high from the ground, a hole (about a hand wide) had been bored through the trunk. Moored on the nearside of the river was a large raft, it was constructed from tree trunks which were bolted together, it looked very sturdy and was of a size upon which a waggon and team could easily stand.

Looking at the scene in front of him, Isaac turned to Jack and said, *"Ow wi gonna get ower t'uther side"*, Jack replied, *"We'd best we't an' see"*. In order to ease the stiffness in their legs they got down from the cart and moved forward to join Will and Tobe. Isaac saw that Tobe was standing in the middle of the cart at the side of the hogshead of ale, he was busy filling some leather bottles with ale. On completing his task, he picked up the three bottles, he clambered over the side of the wagon and got down. He said to Jack, *"I 'ave ta tek these t' Squire, you an' Isaac can tek a swig fromt' leather bottle under mi seat"*. Jack took a long drink from the bottle which he had taken from under Tobe's seat and then he passed it over to Isaac, who found the ale quite refreshing. Tobe said to them both, *"Will sez it'll tek two owers' ta get us all across"*. They sat down in the shade at the side of the waggon, they were at the end of the column, they all watched the preparations with great interest.

After tethering their horses, Oliver Calvert, accompanied by two of his men, walked forward and boarded the raft. A third man had walked toward a small jetty standing in the water to the left of the raft. He got into a small boat which had been tied to the jetty and he rowed it slowly toward the raft. Coiled on the raft was a thick rope, the end was secured to the rowing boat and the oarsman rowed across the river. Upon reaching the other side the oarsman untied the rope and walked to the oak tree stump, he passed the rope through the hole and then took the rope back to his boat. After securing the end of the rope to his boat, he rowed back across the river the end of the rope was then firmly hauled onto the bank. It was then fastened to the harness traces of the waiting team of eight heavy horses.

Meanwhile under Calvert's supervision, the remaining end of the rope coil had been made fast to the front of the raft. The end of a smaller coil of rope set back on the bank was attached to the rear of the raft and the remainder of the rope was laid out on the bank alongside the first rope and would be used to haul the raft back when required. Calvert satisfied himself that all was safe and then called for the first team and waggon to be led onto the raft.

The first of Sir George's waggon's was drawn forward to the raft, the younger of the two horses stopped just short of the raft and despite the efforts of drivers and ostlers refused to move onto the raft. Wil said, "*That young 'oss needs a talking to*", he got up went to his own waggon and took hold of a piece of hessian sacking, he folded it under his arm and walked off toward the raft. When he got to the raft Jake Bowyer was patting the animal's neck and trying to coax her forward, the horse took a couple of nervous steps backwards and Jake had to take a firm hold of the bridle to steady her. Will said, *"D'ya want me ta fettle her Jake"*, the man nodded his assent and stepped back to let Will take over.

Taking the bridle, Will gently pulled the head of the horse downwards, he put his own face against it's ear and started talking in a whisper to the animal, the calming effect was almost immediate. Whilst still whispering, he took the hessian cloth from under his arm and placed it on the horse's neck behind it's ears, the rear part of the cloth he secured by tucking the ends behind the bridle straps. Still whispering re-assuringly he slowly pulled the front of the cloth over the top of the animals head and let it slide down over the eyes, these actions did not distract the horse in any way and it stayed perfectly calm.

Taking hold of the ends of the cloth, Jack again tucked behind the bridle strap, taking a firm hold of the bridle Jake bade both horses to move forward, in unison both animals calmly pulled the waggon forward onto the raft. Turning, whilst still holding the bridle and continuing to whisper re-assurance, Will waved to Jake for the raft to be pulled across the river. Jake went across and spoke to the ostler holding the reins of the team eight attached to raft, the man nodded in response to Jake's instructions and then set his team slowly forward. Upon reaching the far bank Will was still whispering and he swiftly led the horse, which still had it's eyes covered from the raft.

The transfer of the remaining waggons continued and half were across the river, when a horseman galloped forward down the sloping banking, a troop of Cavalier Cavalry remained at the top of the steep banking. The horseman approached and reined in alongside Sir George, who was sitting astride his horse observing the proceedings.

The rider bowed and taking his large colourfully plumed felt hat from his head, he swept it graciously sideways in greeting towards Sir George.

He then said,"*Sire, I am Captain Langley and I ride with Prince Rupert's Army in support of His Majesty King Charles*". Beaming and sitting straighter in his saddle, Sir George responded, "*I am Sir George Fewster and I lead these men and supplies to York to support His Majesty King Charles*". Both men commenced to dismount and ostlers ran forward to take their horses and tether them in the shade of adjacent trees. After they had walked away from the area of the raft landing, Sir George suggested to his companion that they move out of the bright sunshine and take advantage of the shade provided a by a nearby willow tree.

After looking around, Langley, having satisfied himself that they were clear of eavesdroppers turned to Sir George and said, "*Sire, you will not be successful if you attempt to approach York along the route you have chosen, the Parliamentarians have large troops of Cavalry and Infantry in position along the roads from Knaresborough and from Wetherby.*" Sir George said, "*Can you Sire, explain your purpose to me*". Langley explained to Sir George that Prince Rupert had moved at speed from Knaresborough and had completed a flanking movement by crossing the river Ure at Boroughbridge, to allow his Army to move toward York along the road from the north. Langley himself had been part of the force sent by Prince Rupert toward the Skip bridge to mislead the Parliamentarians in thinking that they were the advance force of the Royalist Army approaching from Knaresborough.

The ploy had succeeded and Prince Rupert and his Army were even now approaching toward York un-opposed. After the success of the plan, the advance troops were stood down and fell back to Boroughbridge to follow Prince Rupert's main army, Langley had been despatched to ensure this raft crossing was denied to the Parliamentarians.

Throughout Langley's discourse on the military events of the day, Sir George listened intently and even when Langley concluded, he remained in a pensive pose after several minutes he turned to him and said, *"Captain Langley, I thank God for the information you have given me, we must return across the river and follow Prince Rupert to York"*. Returning to the raft landing point just as the vessel was being made secure, both men boarded and the situation was explained to Oliver Calvert.

Urgent instructions were shouted by Calvert to his men, that they were to make ready to return all the waggon's back across the river, Sir George passed similar orders to the drivers and ostlers who were just leading a waggon off the raft. The team and waggon were led quickly off the craft, turned round immediately and just as quickly led back on board.

The return of the waggon's across the river went smoothly, all involved worked calmly and non of the heavy horses re-acted to the situation. As Langley prepared to move off to gallop on to York, Sir George went across to him and said, *"Your information has probably saved many lives from within our group, I thank you and wish yougood luck, god Save King Charles"*. Langley, bowed forward in his saddle and saluted Sir George with a flamboyant sweep of his brightly plumed hat, he wheeled his horse and galloped off toward York.

Sir George conferred with his brother and Walter Minton, they were all agreed they must make good speed in order to arrive in York to help the King's cause in the forthcoming battle, orders were given, the men and waggon's were quickly drawn up in their respective column's.

Walter Minton led the group forward, he took the cart tracks along the fields that formed the riverside flood plains, they made good progress and by early evening were within sight of Newton, which was but a short distance from whence they thought the bridge of boats crossed the River Ouse at Poppleton, Minton halted his mount and Sir George rode forward and joined him, they agreed they should bypass the village and make camp for the night a mile or so beyond. After rounding a bend in the river, Minton saw the ideal location to make camp, when he reached the large copse of trees which was some two chains in distance from the river bank, he halted the column's and amid much activity, but very little noise, a fairly safe camp was established.

After feeding, grooming down and picketing the two horses after their toils of the day. Isaac and Jack both made up their straw and blanket beds under the waggon. Whilst Isaac went to the river to fill two leather buckets with water, Jack set about making their own small fire, by the time Isaac returned the fire was blazing brightly. Jack was sitting upon a large slab like stone alongside the fire at his feet was a cauldron, he filled the cauldron with some of the water which Isaac had brought from the river and placed it on the fire. From a small hessian sack at his side Jack took out a skinned rabbit, he cut the animal into portions and put them into the pot.

After enjoying their tasty meal, both men sat at the fire in quiet thought, both men considered how the events of the following day would affect their lives. Some time had elapsed, when Jack Grainger turned to Isaac and after two or three nervous coughs said, "*Wu'dst tha do summat fo' me.*" Isaac was surprised by the question, but said, "*Aye Jack, tha no's ah will,*" Jack seemed to be quite emotional, but then said, "*Well, if out 'appens ta me ter morrow, will ya mek sure, that* both o' me 'osses an't waggon get back home agin safe." Trying to re-assure his friend Isaac said, *"Tha's nowt gonna 'appen ta thee, but ya no I'll si that 'osses an't get cart back."*

Isaac felt his friend had been re-assured and continuing their conversation had become difficult for both of them, relief was felt by both men when Jake Bowyer walked into view from round the back of the waggon. He said to them, *"Sir George 'as told Squire that we all as't ta be ready ta move off just after daybreak tomorrow"*. They thanked Jake and they both set themselves to preparing for sleep under the waggon and had little to say unto each other.

Within a short time, there was quiet around the campsite, as each man gave thought to his own feelings of what fate could have in store for him on the following day. Few slept soundly through the night, most slept fitfully and awoke frequently, most although tired, were glad when daylight began to break. Within a short time, as men arose the campsite became a hive of activity, fires were fuelled as water was boiled to prepare porridge for breakfast. Waggon's were loaded, prior to the horse teams being put into the shafts and eventually the wagon drivers took their places on their waggon seats.

Having mounted his horse and spent some time shuffling about on the saddle to make himself comfortable, Sir George looked around the scene and saw that all was set for him to give the signal to move off. With his arm outstretched a he gave a wide arching wave to signal the columns to move off, there was little or no banter or chattering amongst the men. When they reached the high road, they turned right heading towards York, Jack turned to Isaac and said,, *"Av ya sin 'osses then, they can sense a bad day"*. In reply to his friend Isaac just nodded his head,

Shortly after they had set off along the York Road, Walter Minton, who had been riding with Sir George, set his horse into a trot and went on ahead of them. Isaac, being of a curious nature, turned to Jack and said, *"Wer'st ya think he's off ta"*. Jack thought for a little while, before saying, *"Appen Sir George 'as sent 'im on ta see if''t road is clear ah roundheads"*.

As the waggon's moved on at a fair walking pace, both Isaac and Jack, withdrew into their own thoughts. Looking across at the fields they were passing, Isaac saw farmers, who with help from their families and their neighbours were busy making hay, loading the tall haywain's with the hay from the last few fields and getting it stored before any heavy rain could wreak it's vengeance upon it. Why is it, Isaac thought, the countryside is so quiet and peaceful and when needed neighbour helps neighbour. Yet throughout our land, countrymen are fighting each other and most of us don't know why. We who are poor don't have a choice, we either do as we are told, or we are punished by starvation or pain and threats, Why, does our Lord allow this.

Isaac's thoughts were interrupted, when Jack shouted out, *"Wat's Minton wavin 'is arms about fa now"*. Walter Minton bade his horse forward and reined in alongside Sir George. Not knowing the cause of the wait, Squire Fewster rode forward along the line of waggons and took his place alongside his brother and Walter Minton. After engaging in deep conversation for some minutes, they appeared to have reached agreement and there were many nods of heads made, before the group broke up, Minton wheeling his horse and trotting back towards Poppleton, Sir George backed his horse to the roadside and signalled his Squire to join him, Squire Fewster rode along the line toward the rear waggon.

Shortly afterwards a meesenger sent by Squire Fewster came forward to tell each waggon driver to pull their waggons into the roadside. Most men dismounted from the waggon's and stretched their limbs and chatted with their various friends who were riding on other waggon's, From the numerous pieces of gossip which was passed up and down the line, it generally became accepted that the reason for their wait was that Prince Rupert's Army were not yet all across the river. It was expected another hour would pass before Sir George led his group forward toward Poppleton. Eventually messages were received from both Squire Fewster and his brother Sir George, ordering all the men to return to and board their various waggon's.

Following a sweeping wave of his arm from Sir George at the front of the column the waggons moved forward, as the column entered Skelton, Jack Grainger was busy passing on his knowledge of the area to Isaac, who was sitting disinterestedly at his side. Approaching the village Church, Jack nudged Isaac and said, "*Si yon Church it's St. Giles, an it wer built fra stone left ower fra building York Minster, ah nos, cos Squire Fewster teld mi.*" In a short while, the column left the road and took a track on the right leading away from the road, the track was sheltered by trees growing on either side for some distance. After leaving the cover of the trees, Isaac looking ahead, said to Jack, "*Look ah can see bridge o' boats*". Isaac could see waggon's not from their column crossing the River, Jack said, "*It's River Ooze, Squire Fewster teld mi that as well*". At the bridge the column halted and Sir George rode over and engaged in conversation with the Captain of a Troop of Royalist Cavalry who were in position to protect the bridge.

Sir George walked his mount back to join Walter Minton, both then steadily rode their mounts across. The first waggon followed them a short distance behind them, each of the remaining waggon's followed in turn. When all waggons had safely crossed the River, the column moved off along field tracks, these were now clearly marked, worn grass caused by the passage of Prince Rupert's Army clearly stood out.

Once again as was his wont Jack Grainger was busy taking note of the surrounding countryside and when he turned his attention skywards, he turned to Isaac and said, *"Luk at yon sky, ah don't like luk o't colour ah them black clouds, tha's rain on it's way, you mark mi werds, it'll be here afore dark"*. Isaac in turn cast his gaze skywards, he nodded in agreement with his friend and said, *"Aye, ah think tha's reet"*. Isaac saw after they had got some distance from the river, the ground was rising and to his left he saw the pinnacles of a building which stood out on the sky line, it seemed much larger, than other buildings around it. Isaac concluded it must be York Minster, he was surprised by the size of the building.

Some distance further on, the thoughts of both Isaac and Jack were interrupted, by excited shouts from men in the waggon's ahead of them, rising from his seat, Isaac could see in the distance, ranked along the top of a hill which was sloping down towards them, groups of Cavalry and lines of foot Solgers, Standards and Banners fluttering in the breeze could be seen interspersed between the various groups. There was was some cannon at intervals and Isaac could see great bellows of white smoke which was followed almost immediately by the roar as the weapon's propelled their deadly missiles on their way. Isaac saw immediately in front of them the Royalist Army led by Prince Rupert drawn up in ranks stretching across the moor. Cannon fire was being returned into the Parliament Armies lines and he saw mounted Solgers trying to calm and restrain their mounts. A number of coaches and a large number of waggon's loaded with provisions, food, weaponry, powder, shot and heavy shot for the Cannons were drawn up in small squares over to his right.

Both Isaac and Jack had been shocked at what they beheld and neither of the men could know what carnage and fear would unfold on that battlefield before that day ended. As their Column moved forward once again Jack flicked the reins to urge his charges to "walk on". When they moved onto the Battlefield, Jack allowed his horses to follow the waggon in front of them and each driver eventually stopped his waggon so that the column formed a rough square similar to the waggons which had arrived before them.

After dismounting, Squire Fewster accompanied his brother Sir George and Walter Minton, as they led their horses across to where they saw the officers were assembled. Meanwhile their men after feeding and watering the horse teams, tethered them close by the camp. They then set about unloading the waggons and making camp. A space allowing access and egress from the small compound between two of the waggon's, Jack Grainger's was one of these waggon's. Jack said to Isaac, *"Ah thout these stakes an t' straw 'ud cum in 'andy, wen ah brout em"*. He then commenced to drive the stakes into the ground in a criss cross formation across the entrance space, about two paces away from the waggon's.

When he had satisfied himself that the sharp stakes would deter even the bravest of Cavalry horses Jack placed his straw bales on the ground along the length of the hurdles and broke them open and spread the straw about to enable him to set it alight when he needed to.. Satisfied with his handiwork, Jack returned within the their small compound and said to Isaac, *"Aye, ah think tha 'll fettle yon rownd 'eds"*. Isaac looked toward the newly erected barricade and then nodded his agreement to his friend. Cannon were still being fired by both sides and cheers and jeers usually rang out when cannon shot was occasionally landed close enough to cause quite a few of the Roundhead Cavalry horses to rear up and despatch their riders to the ground.

Looking about their own compound of waggon's Isaac could see that most of their group were standing around their own small fires, talking and waiting. Rain had started to fall but not too heavily, the clouds though looked very black and threatening that worse was to follow. He saw in the far side of their lines, Generals and officers of the Royalist Army had to started to make their way back to their Coaches at the rear of the field. He saw Sir George, Squire Fewster and Walter Minton were heading toward Sir George's coach and he said to Jack, "*It luks as tho' t' Battle won't start til' termorrow*". Jack was thoughtful and then said, "*Ah don't think tha'll be much sleepin dun ternite*". Isaac nodded his agreement and they started to cook themselves some supper. As the rain got heavier, Isaac using canvas and stake fixed it to the side of the waggon, making an awning under which he and Jack could shelter and eat their meal. When he had finished, he saw that similar shelters had been built onto the other waggons by their occupants.

CHAPTER XIII

Siege Raised

The trained bands of Citizens who had spent the night patrolling their section of Wall, saw as the Sun started to rise that there was a ground mist drifting over the distant open ground. Most mornings, smoke and shouts could be seen and heard coming from the leager camps at Heworth and on Fulford Moor, which was hidden behind the Cannon batteries, on Lamel Hill. Strangely this morning, all was quiet and smoke was absent.

Sgt. Josh Hogg had been on duty throughout the night at Clifford's Tower, he was calling the Roll and checking Garrison solgers who had been chosen to patrol the Wall's that morning. His attention was drawn toward raised voices coming from without the gateway into the Tower Keep. He quickly called the patrol he was addressing to order and marched them toward that Gateway and then through it, for them to continue onto the Wall to take up their positions and relieve the nightime patrols of solgers and trained band citizens from their duty.

Turning, Josh approached a small group of solgers and citizens who were gathered at the gate around the Garrison Sgt. They were all talking excitedly and the Garrison Sgt. was trying with much difficulty to get them to be quiet. Finally after he had roared at the top of his voice, *"Quiet"*, the group, as if they were one person, stopped their jabbering. Then after listening to the story of each man, a story emerged that they all were claiming that at each of their sections of the Wall, there was no activity from, or sight of the leagers.

After listening to stories given by solgers and citizens alike, the Garrison Sgt. instructed them to return to their homes or quarters to rest and then dismissed them. He then sought out Sir John Glenham, the governor of the Citie, to whom he gave all information passed to him by the members of the night patrols of the Walls. Whilst the Garrison Sergeant was awaiting instruction from the Governor, loud voices could be heard from without. Then suddenly, all was silent and this was followed by an urgent knocking upon the Governor's door and a spoken request from the Governor's Clerk requesting permission to enter.

Sir John called out to his Clerk to enter, slowly and with much creaking, the great oak door swung inwards. Entering and after pausing to close the door, the Clerk then stepped forward, saying to his Master, *"This urgent letter has been received by messenger from Sir James Dudley at Walmgate Bar"*. Taking a very slender bladed knife from the large and ornately carved inkstand, he carefully slit open the envelope. He took out the parchment letter and started to read, after reading the letter, he took from the drawer of his large table a clean sheet of parchment and an envelope. He sat musing, stroking his chin with his left hand and after a few moments of thought he commenced writing.

When he had finished writing, he sealed the parchment within an envelope and after affixing his own personal seal upon it, he passed it to his Clerk, saying to him *"Please pass this to the waiting messenger and instruct him to deliver it personally to his Master Sir James Dudley"*. Taking the letter from his Master the Clerk bowed his head slightly in deference and withdrew from the Chamber.

When they were alone, he said to the Garrison Sgt., *"That message I have just received from Sir James Dudley supports everything you have told me concerning the leagers, all around the Walls, they appear to have vanished"*. He stood up from the table and walked slowly over to the fireplace, he appeared to be deep in thought. At the fireplace he turned and stood for a few moments, before saying, *"Sgt. I have detailed Sir James to send out a Troop of Cavalry and a platoon of Foot Solgers, they are to go out toward Fulford to seek out what trickery the leagers may be planning"*. From outside, occasional Musket shots could be heard and there was the sound of much cheering, shouting and laughter.

Retuning to the table the Governor sat down and turning to the Garrison Sergeant, he said, *"You must go back to your post and check what all the commotion is about, but please inform me immediately when any further Messages arrive from Sir James Dudley"*.

Drawing himself to attention the Garrison Sgt. bowed his head to Sir John, turned and marched smartly from the room. When he got to the main entrance of the Keep, he saw his friend Sgt. Josh Hogg standing, he was talking to a Cavalier Officer on horseback, he saw Sgt. Hogg move his hand to take the animal's bridle and took a firm hold until the Officer dismounted. A short distance away a further six Cavalier Officers were similarly dismounting from their horses. Passing the reins of their mounts into the hands of attendant ostlers, he noticed the animals were well lathered and must have been hard ridden, the group then followed closely behind Josh as he led them forward. When they reached the Garrison Sgt. the Officer asked to be shown with some urgency into the presence of the Earl of Newcastle. Asking the group to follow him, the Sgt. enterd into the building and espied the Governor's Clerk stepping toward the main staircase, calling out he caught the man's attention. He bade him to take the officers and present them to his master the Governor of York.

Returning to the Keep, he noticed Sgt. Hogg was absent and he heard some way distant, from the direction of Fulford, frequent muttled musket fire. From without Clifford's Tower, much shouting, laughter and singing, could be heard from all parts of the Citie. At this time (mid morning) the Earl of Newcastle, accompanied by General King and other Royalist officers arrived, they were followed some little time later by Sir Edmund Cooper, the Lord Mayor and a number of Aldermen and Gild Masters.

Shortly afterwards, amid some commotion, Sir James Dudley arrived with his Major and Sergeant. In company with his Major he hurried inside. They left their Sergeant to hand control of their horses to the ostlers. Turning the sergeant, who was holding his left arm across his body and supporting it with his right arm, he walked very slowly across to join the Garrison Sergeant. It could be seen that the man was ashen faced, upon the tunic of his left upper arm there was widespread saturation of blood, he became unsteady upon his feet, he suddenly staggered forward and fell heavily upon the ground. Stepping forward quickly to give aid to the man, the Garrison Sergeant knelt at his side, he gently turned the man onto his back and cradled his head. The man looked very shaken, but he was still conscious.

Turning to some Whitecoat solgers who had gathered around him after the man fell, the Garrison Sergeant instructed them to help him to lift the man. He was carried inside and taken into the Guardhouse and he was placed upon a large but uncomfortable looking wooden Settle. A large horse blanket was placed over the man's body and the Garrison Sergeant detailed a Whitecoat solger to seek out the Barber Surgeon and bid him to come urgently to treat injuries which the man had sustained.

Upon once again checking the health of the injured man, the Garrison Sergeant found the man to be unconscious and his breathing was very shallow, he was still bleeding heavily from the wound to his chest. A few minutes later the Barber Surgeon arrived, he bent over the man and commenced to examine him. After he very brief examination he stood up straight and turned to the Garrison Sergeant, he said, "There is nothing more I can do, this man is dead, he has lost too much blood".

– o0o –

Meanwhile in the centre of the Citie, Luke Watts was in his workshop in Trinity Passage, he usually started his work early every Friday, his practice was to quickly clear up and complete his orders for that week. Then he had plenty of time check his stock of leather and estimate the amount of leather he would need to buy in when he later that day visited the Tannery of Ike Owens which was just without the Walls near to Lendal Ferry. As he worked, Luke heard the resonant toll of Big Peter indicating eight hours of the clock.

As Great Peter became silent, Luke became aware of loud cries of laughter, singing and shouting, being curious, he opened the door of his workshop and stepped outside into Trinity Passage. The noise appeared to be coming from the direction of Gudramgate. it got louder as it came closer, amongst the noise Luke could also discern a clip clop of horses hooves. In the distance Luke heard the occasional sound of Musket pistols being fired. Becoming ever curious Luke stepped over toward the Butcher Shoppe of his neighbour Will Wright.

Luke stepped into the shoppe and called out Will's name, entering the shoppe from the backyard and beaming a smile right across his face, Will said, *"Wat gud news wi 'ave got terday, round'eads 'ave gon"*. Luke, *much to his own* surprise, as well as how surprised Will looked, stepped forward and threw his arms around the shoulders of his friend embraced him in a huge hug of relief. Both men then stood back, amid much laughter and joy. The two men discussed how this recent development would affect their lives and businesses in the following months. Luke then took his leave and returned to his own workshop.

Crossing Trinity Passage, he entered his workshop and went straight into the kitchen, Ann was at the fireplace stirring a cauldron. She turned towards him and he grasped her in his arms in a firm embrace. He then said, *"Leagers 'ave left, Prince Rupert 'as brought his Army"*, Ann in turn clapsed her arms around Luke and started weeping with joy.

Sgt. Josh Hogg left Cliffords Tower and went out into the Citie streets, as he passed by the Taverns and Alehouses he saw throngs of Newcastle's Whitecoats and solgers from other regiments standing in large groups outside the various hostelries. They were drinking and singing and there was great excitement all around. Moving on and entering Gudramgate, similar scenes met his gaze, normal passage along the causeways was not possible, he saw crowds were so dense in number it had made passage through extremely difficult.

As Josh pushed slowly through, he heard from some groups of solgers arguing amongst themselves and uttering complaints about the time that had passed since their last pay. Josh knew that since arriving in the Citie in April, few Solgers had received any Pay. Josh could understand the discontent of the Solgers and the anger shown by some of them.

Throughout the Siege most of the Gates into the Citie had been blocked on the inside within their Barbican's, by broken old waggons and heavy blocks of stone, with intention to prevent leagers access if they had succeeded in smashing the Citie Gates. As he approached Monk Bar, Josh saw this type of work being carried out. Heavy horses were being used to pull out carts and heavy stonework, the men working here, were, as throughout the Citie, in a happy and joyful mood, the sound of the many Church bells rang out across the Citie.

As Josh entered through the Gates of the Kings Manor, he heard the Great Peter the Minster Bell resounding over the Citie tolling the midday hour. Going around the building to the rear Courtyard he entered Kings Manor by the Kitchen door and made his way to the Servants Hall which had been used from the start of the Siege by the Sergeants of the Garrison to meet and arrange the Duties of men under their Command. Josh took a seat at a table occupied by several of his friends, they were soon worriedly discussing the drunken and mutinous threats that were being uttered by a great many of the solgers concerning their reluctance to fight until they had received all of the pay due to them. They all agreed that these problems would be very difficult to settle their men into going to Battle

Chatter of the many voices in this small hall, suddenly quietened, there was much shouting and noise, from the sound of many booted footsteps clattering on stone flooring, this commotion was coming from the Main Entrance area. Noise from the chattering and raised voices of the newly arrived group faded as footfalls of the group appeared to be mounting the main staircase to the upper floor. Shortly afterwards Josh and those others gathered within the Kitchen Hall heard the sound of footsteps coming from the passage which led from the main entrance. Whoever the persons approaching were, could not be guessed, but, their voices indicated they were engaged in carefree conversation.

Three male figures appeared in the entrance doorway of the Kitchen Hall. Josh recognised immediately that they were Sergeants of Cavalry from Prince Rupert's Army. Many others in the Hall recognised them also and many shouts of welcome to them went echoing around the room. Space was quickly made for the trio and they seated themselves at the table at which Josh was sitting, tankards of Ale appeared in front of the visitors with which they could quench their thirst, each man gratefully accepted the Ale and together each quaffed the contents of their tankards

After satisfying their thirsts, the newcomers announced to all around the table the purpose of their visit, Prince Rupert's Army was approaching the Citie from Boroughbridge and were to make overnight camp at the edge of Galtres Forest near to Skelton. Prince Rupert had sent General George Goring accompanied by some Cavalry Colonels to deliver a letter to the Earl of Newcastle. The Sergeants along with a troop of Cavalry were there as a defensive shield for General Goring and his officers. It was intended they said, that they would be setting off to rejoin Prince Rupert and his Army within the hour.

– oOo –

At this time out in the Citie, Luke was making his way to the Moorings close by Ouse Bridge, he had been told that a ship had made it's way up river from Selby to pick up the

Venetian Ambassador and his entourage. It was known that the vessel had arrived in Selby from Venice almost a month previously. Ye ship was carrying cargo from Venice which had been ordered by various Merchants and Tradesmen. Several of the Cordwainers in York had been awaiting parcels of Leather which were originally shipped from Spain.

Luke was the Senior Searcher of the Company of Cordwainers of the Citie and he was tasked to examine all Leather entering the Citie by the Port of York. He had to check all the various parcels of leather for quality and suitability before any was offloaded from the vessel. There was much activity on the wharf around a vessel which was being unloaded. Luke saw the tide was on the ebb, water markings on the wharf showed that the hide tide at been had been one of four feet but was now nearly at low tide level. Seeing an imposing looking man, who was dressed in a smart bright blue colour tailcoat and white britches who was closely watching these events, Luke felt quite sure he was the Captain and upon speaking to the man, Luke was directed onto the deck to speak to the Quartermaster who was supervising the unloading of Cargo.

Following instructions he was given by the Quartermaster, Luke went below deck and found his way to the hold at the bow of the vessel. He found the rolled up parcels of leather, of which there three in total. After checking each parcel and found they were all of good quality, Luke happily marked each label by making his mark upon each parcel label. He asked a deckhand to help him to carry the goods off the boat. As they stepped onto the wharf, Luke saw his friend Keit pushing his cart along the wharf away from the moored vessel, Luke shouted and caught his friends attention.

Keit stopped and leaving his cart he walked back to speak to Luke. When Keit saw the parcels of leather he said to Luke, *"Dus'tha want thim the'r on't cart, we'l gi's a' lift wi' em"*. Keit's cart was only half full with goods he had picked from the boat and there was ample room for the parcels of leather Luke had collected, they quickly lifted the leather onto the cart and then made their way from the wharf. Luke asked Keit, if was going any where near Layerthorpe Postern, because he wanted to deliver the parcels of leather to the Cordwainers Hall, in Pavers Lane.

After some minutes of thought Keit said to Luke,*"I a'st ta go ta George Blades Mill tha's t'oo brac'its in't cart fa' im, but, wi cu'd go t' Hall fust if tha likes"*. Streets were still crowded with citizens and solgers alike still revelling with pleasure because the Siege was lifted. With Luke helping his friend to push the cart they made steady progress and as they got to St. Saviour's Lane, they saw Constable John Cundill, who was struggling to restrain a drunken Whitecoat solger.

Both Luke and Keit left the cart and went to give assistance to John Cundill, they both took hold of the solger, who was so drunk, he could not stand and slumped to the floor, Keit said to Luke, *"Thu' keep,'ur eye on'im til ah get som binding an we'll truss im up an mek im fast ta yon railin."* Keit went to his cart and came back with some lengths of strong binding and they fastened him to the railing as Keit had suggested.

Thanking them, John Cundill told them he would get some of the Citie trained band who were drinking in the Black Swan Inn, in Peasholme Green to help him carry the Whitecoat sol;ger to the Kidcote prison on Ouse Bridge. As the Constable moved away to head to the Black Swan, Luke said to Keit, *"Aye John's as likely to 'ave just left that thee'r Tavern 'isself"*. Both men laughed at the remark and turned their attention back to pushing the cart.

At the bottom of St. Saviours Lane, they turned into Hundgate and thence along Havers Lane to Cordwainers Hall. Luke thanked his friend for his help and watched as Keit set off to continue his journey to George Blade's Mill. When Luke went into his Company Hall, he found Moses Akombe, who was in company of the Lord Mayor, Sir Edward Cowper, they were discussing the needs to enable the Hall to be used as a Hospital, to care for the injured from the expected battle at Marston Moor. Without disturbing the two men, Luke put his parcels into a store cupboard and then left the Hall.

To return to his workshop, he walked by way of Aldwark, outside St. Anthony's Hall at the corner of that street, there was a large cart with two heavy horses in the shafts, standing outside the Hall. Members of the Citie trained bands were unloading large planks and trestles from the cart, Luke guessed that Hall also would be used as a Hospital. When he got back to his workshop in Trinity Passage, the Great Bell of St. Peter was booming out five of the clock. He saw the door to the workshop was closed, he pressed the handle down, to ensure it was locked and then walked round to enter the kitchen from the rear yard.

As he stepped inside, Luke saw Uncle Josh was sitting at the table and appeared to be just finishing a meal, on the Settle behind were a canvass bag (which Luke had made for him) and laying alongside it were pair of Musket pistols and a Musket Rifle. Luke went over to the table and seated himself upon a chair opposite Josh, pausing in his eating, Josh said, "*I have to leave with ye Garrison to go to ye battle early in ye morning.*"

Luke was surprised how quickly they were going to leave the Citie, he said to Josh, "*When I was out, many of the solgers, were so drunk, ah'd a thou't it'd tek day's for 'em ta gerit* out of 'em". Again pausing in his eating, Josh said, *"We've got orders to round 'em all up and take 'em to Clifford's Tower ta try ta get the drink out of 'em"*. Having finished eating his meal, Josh was drinking some nettle wine from a leather tankard, placing his tankard back on the table Josh went on to say, *"It won't be easy and even if we succeed we have to deal with the threat of Mutiny, none of them have been paid since the Siege started"*. Luke then said to Josh, *"Will they get their pay then"*, once again after placing his tankard on the table, Josh went on to say, *"After this Battle, we will all get paid, the King is sending sacks of it by ship an' it's due at Scarbro' within days"*.

Pushing back his chair, Josh rose from his seat, he turned and went across to the Settle, he picked up his belt and slung it across his shoulder. It was quite heavy, caused the weight of his musket pistol and the two soft leather bags, one containing his black powder and the other his musket shot, he turned and took his cape from a hook hanging from the kitchen door. Throughout this period of conversation between Luke and Josh, Ann had been sitting in nook at the side of the fireplace, where she had been sewing.

At this point Luke could see she looked very upset and the redness about her eyes indicated to him she had been weeping. Josh came forward and she embraced him tightly and again she began weeping, as Josh gave her calm re-assurances that he would return safe and well from the impending Battle. She stepped back and Josh turned to Luke for a moment and both men looked at each other and then firmly grasped each other by the hand and patted each other on the shoulder, at the same as they wished each other well.

Josh then turned and stepped forward to the Kitchen door he paused for a moment, gave cheery wave of his hand and went through the doorway into the rear yard. Immediately Josh had closed the door behind him, Ann threw her hands around Luke and started sobbing uncontrollably. Try as he may, Luke had great difficulty to calm and re-assure his wife. He took her over to the Settle, they both sat down and Luke hugged her lovingly and he spoke softly to her. After some minutes, Ann started to calm down and her husband could sense she was starting to relax.

Feeling the warmth of her husband's embrace and she sat quietly, he could see she was in deep thought. Presently she stirred and she took a kerchief from the pocket of her apron, she sat up straight. Using the kerchief she wiped her tear stained face, she experienced a number of slight shudders as she recovered control of her emotions. Then with a deep sigh Ann turned to face Luke and she said, *"He'll b' killed ya know 'e won't cum off that Battlefield alive"*. Luke to re-assure her said, *"Josh no's wats wat, 'es bin in battles afore"*. Turning, Ann went to the kitchen table and upon pulling open the drawer, she took out a bulky canvas bag, she had to use both hands to carry the bag to the Settle

She sat down and passed the bag to Luke, taking it from her Luke realised how heavy it was. Ann said to him, *"Ya'd best ave a look inside"*, upon opening the draw strings of the bag, Luke gave a gasp of surprise, the bag was full of Gold Sovereigns. Placing his hand inside the bag, Luke took out a handful of the coins and sorted through them with his other hand. Most of them had been minted in King Charles reign, but, there were others minted in the reign of King James. Whilst Luke was sitting stunned beyond belief, Ann went on to say, *" Uncle Josh, wen 'e gev me t' bag, he said ta mi, look after this money and if he was unlucky, that he wanted us to 'ave it and ta name fust son we have after 'im"*.

Ann was again overcome by emotion and Luke put his arm around her and pulled her toward him. They sat in this position for quite some time and when she could shed no more tears, Luke said to her, *"Well lass, am sure he'll be back, we'll hide bag in here until after battle and the we'll see how things are then"*. After having a quick bite to eat and having made sure Ann was in control of her emotions, Luke had to leave to go to Cordwainers Hall, the Court of Assistants were meeting to make plans.

When he got to the Hall in Hundegate, the Court members were chatting in two or three small groups, entering with the Master Moses Akombe, the Chamberlain, led the members into the Court Meeting in the Annexe of the Hall.. Master Akombe took charge of the Meeting and he told the members they had to discuss what arrangements which the Company should take, if after the Battle it became necessary to turn the Hall into a Hospital for the wounded Solgers. Most members made suggestions, to enable the smooth creation of the facilities and volunteers to assist the wounded.

– oOo –

All Junior Officers, along with the Sergeants of the Earl of Newcastle's Whitecoat Army, spent many hours clearing solgers from Inns, Taverns and Alehouses across the Citie and escorting them to quarters within Clifford's Tower. There was much anger amongst the solgers and talk of Mutiny unless they received their pay, was quite commonplace. The general mood and anger of the men was made known to the Earl of Newcastle, who along with his most Senior Officers discussed how they deal with the problem until well past the midnight hour.

Came daybreak, whilst most of the Solgers were no longer drunk, many of them were feeling ill and still being awkward and not co-operating in preparing to march to Marston Moor to battle with the Parliamentarian Army.

Promises, that a money waggon was on it's way from the King were still not believed by many.

Mid-morning came, pleas, threats, cajoling and further promises, were still not wholly believed, but, a lot of waverers were starting to weaken in their protests. The Royalist Lieutenants and Sergeants, were bade to get amongst their men and rally them to the King's cause. Their efforts started to reap rich rewards, attitudes amongst the Solger's changed and by mid-day, the majority were accepting and carrying out orders and by one of the clock, some Regiments, mostly cavalry, were leaving the Citie heading to Marston Moor.

CHAPTER XIV

The Battle of Marston Moor

July 2nd, 1644

By the mid afternoon, the Earl of Newcastle was able to lead the bulk of his Army out of the Citie to join up with Prince Rupert and his Army at Marston Moor. Their departure from the Citie at Micklegate Bar, was greeted with much cheering and waving banners of support from the Citizen's and Garrison Solgers alike. As the column's passed by the Sconce on London Road, defending Garrison Solgers, shouted cries of good luck and waved their support, a few fired Musket shots up into the sky.

After marching by way of Holgate and Poppleton, Newcastle's Army finally started to take up it's position on the Battlefield by about five of the clock. Spasmodic Canon fire was being used by the Parliamentarian Army which was drawn up across rising ground some distance from the much lower ground, which was being held by the Army of Prince Rupert, whose cannon were firing defiant salvo's back up the hill. Stretching across the Moor between the two combatant Armies, there was a thick gorse which was bordering in many parts along it's banks, a ditch which meandered it's way across the battle line between the two armies.

The presence of this ditch and the gorse. was likely in battle to present a serious hazard to the Cavalry of both armies. Opposing General's would have had taken note of the consequences these could cause in the impending Battle and made their plans accordingly.

At the rear of the fighting lines, the Earl of Newcastle alighted from his coach. His Squire helped him to dress for Battle, assisting him with his cuirass and chain armour around his lower body and legs. After handing his Master his heavy Cavalry sword, the Squire moved across to where the Earl's heavy horse was tethered. He brought the animal over, and after handing the reins to an ostler, he assisted his Master to mount the animal. After mounting, the Earl looked about the scene, he saw most of the Royalist officers were mounted and similarly surveying the activity taking place about them.

Looking skywards Newcastle could see sinister black clouds forming above the Battlefield, their presence suggested to him that heavy rain would quickly follow and would likely mean that no battle was likely to take place that evening. He walked his horse along the battle line toward where he could see Prince Rupert's Standard fluttering limply in the drizzly conditions. As he drew closer, Newcastle saw that his Royal Highness was mounting his charger and his favourite dog a large white Poodle who Newcastle recalled was named "Boy", began barking loudly.

As Rupert wheeled his mount around, he saw Newcastle approaching, he was but twenty paces away. Rupert steadied his horse and waited until the Earl had joined him. The two men exchanged greetings and then walked their Mounts away toward the rear of the field of Battle. When they reached Prince Rupert's enclosure where his coach and Tents were located, the two men dismounted and entered Rupert's Dining Tent to partake of Supper.

When they had seated themselves Prince Rupert displayed his annoyance with the Earl and demanded an explanation of why he and his Army of Whitecoats had not arrived at the Battlefield early that morning as he, Prince Rupert had been expecting. The two men, whilst seldom had they liked each other, because of their status in the eyes of King Charles, they tolerated each other. Forcefully the Earl made known to Prince Rupert the problems faced by an Army during and after being under siege for ten weeks. Whilst being surprised by the passion and annoyance displayed by the Earl, Prince Rupert listened and whence the Earl concluded his outburst the Prince very politely suggested they eat Supper.

At the conclusion of their meal, they discussed tactics for the morrow, for they both had agreed the Battle would take place this eve because of the weather storm, which even as they spoke was worsening. They parted each to their own quarters.

– o0o –

As they sat under their makeshift shelter, Jack and Isaac could see the rain was much heavier and Jack began struggling with the small canvas satchel which he was wearing around his waist. He was trying to cover it over by pushing it under his working smock. Seeing his friend was having difficulty, he said, "*Jack, ah don't see it matters if tha' satchel get's wet*", his friend after a deep sigh, replied, "*Squire geh mee some match sa ah cou'd set lite ta yon straw quicker, ah don't want match gerrin' wet*". Finally, he satisfied himself the match would keep dry and sat back into his former sitting posture.

There were suddenly many loud bangs and they could see large plumes of white smoke billowing from Parliament Cavalry cannon and rising skywards from the dark grey skyline, the plumes stretched right across the width of the Parliament battle line. The first shots were quickly followed by more shots and Isaac and Jack could see that whilst the first shots fell short of the Royalist line the second and others which followed fell amongst the front ranks of musketeers and some beyond the musketeers ranks causing havoc in the Cavalry lines behind them. After a dozen or more of such salvos, Isaac saw lines of Cavalry ride out from behind the canon, there were troops right across the skyline and were interspersed with ranks of Musketeers.

The Cavalry moved forward at a slow trot in close order, similarly the ranks of Musketeers moved with them at a similar speed and the front line firing ahead and then over taken by the lines behind them, who then fired off their shots their. Isaac saw this tactic did have some effect, he saw some Musketeers in Royalist lines fall after being hit, he also saw a few horses in the advancing Calvary fall, causing their riders to be thrown onto the ground.

As the advancing line arrived at the bottom of the hill, they had to stop. The thick gorse and thorn bushes at the side of the beck crossing the hillside, forced both Cavalry and Musketeers to spread out and try to force their way through to the beckside. Mounted or on foot, the attackers had great difficulty keeping a footing on the thick, slippery mud alongside the beck. Musketeers on both sides were discharging their weapons with great rapidity in spite of poor weather and ground conditions. At the end of the line, a group of cavalry, maybe a dozen or more had jumped the ditch, they quickly broke through the line of Royalist Musketeers.

The men had drawn their swords and galloped forward amongst the foot solgers who stood in their way. Many of the musketeers lost limbs after receiving fearsome blows to the neck, shoulders or arms from Cavalry swords arcing down upon them as they struggled to reload their weapons. Others were crushed and trampled into the ground as gallopping horses collided with them.

Jack was bending forward alongside the stakes he had set in position, try as he may, he was finding it impossible to light the straw, which had become too wet. He decided to return into their small compound of waggons, he stood upright and as he was turning, he shouted out in terror as he saw a Cavalry horse was right upon him and the sword caught him across his neck. Isaac turned as he heard the terror stricken yell as his friend called out, he saw the sword strike into his friends neck and then he crumpled and fall sideways onto the ground and lay there, so still.

Isaac dashed over to where Jack lay, he was face downwards he turned Jack onto his side and saw the lifeblood of his friend was pumping from his neck, Isaac vainly tried to stem the bleeding by pressing his hand across the wound, but still the blood oozed from it. He was powerless as he watched life ebb away from Jack, he saw the stakes still standing like sentinels and Isaac realised that this war had not been sought by the Common people, it was for a cause which would have little benefit to simple country folk, who were most affected by it. Isaac stood and dragged his friend back into the compound, he laid the body onto the waggon and covered it with a canvas sheet.

Picking up a makeshift wooden "pike" from a bundle on the waggon. Isaac was overcome by the shock of the death of his friend, he crept forward to the entrance to their small compound of waggons and he crouched between the shafts of Jack's waggon. He still had his "pike" in his hand, his body suddenly shook about, he could not control his shuddering.

He forced his mind back to reality, looking around the Battlefield, to his left, he saw groups of Royalist Cavaliers persuing Roundhead Cavalry, whilst to his right he saw, Royalist Cavalry making a hasty retreat from troops of Roundhead Horse, who were close up behind them. Isaac saw a number of the persuing horses fall throwing their riders to the ground as they were hit by musket shot fired at them as they passed the position of Royalist Musketeers close by.

As the dust settled, Isaac saw four horses were down, he saw a dozen or more White coated solgers run from the Royalist line toward the fallen horses. Two of the horses had regained their feet as the solgers reached them, three of the riders were also struggling to stand up and were trying to find swords they had lost in the fall. Musket shots rang out and they fell to the ground, their horses took fright and galloped off. The White coated solgers after picking up the swords and pistols of the fallen men then dashed back to their own lines.

Turning his attention toward the Battlefield ahead of him, Isaac saw many, many bodies stretched right across his field of vision. Musket fire was predominant in all areas of the Battlefield, yelling voices were constantly ringing out, shouts by men charging forward in attack, interspersed with the pitifully painful pleas and cries for help from the injured and dying. Riderless horses were running in all directions, they were in panic and fear. Isaac saw a horse plodding toward him, it was a chain or so away from him. A body was hanging across the saddle in front of the rider, who was a solger and he appeared to be having difficulty staying on the saddle. He was leaning forward over the body, but, he kept slipping to his left side and clutching desperately onto the saddle pommel to prevent himself from falling to the ground. Rising to his feet, Isaac moved forward and took hold of the horse by the bridle and led it carefully around the line of stakes Jack had erected near the entrance.

Isaac took hold of the outstretched arm of the rider and supported him as he dismounted, as his feet reached the ground the solger collapsed in a heap. Grasping the man under his shoulders, Isaac helped him toward the waggon and seated him, resting his back against the wheel. Returning to the horse, Isaac similarly carried and dragged the other body over to the side of the waggon and after laying the man in a comfortable position and as he turned the man's head, Isaac was shocked, the man looking more dead than alive was Squire Fewster.

Bending close to his body, Isaac saw that Squire Fewster was still breathing, he took a cloth and wiped away the mud which had been caked around the Squires face and mouth, this enabled him to breathe much more easily. Ye Squire's right arm was heavily bloodstained between the top of his shoulder down to his elbow. Material from the arm of his tunic was torn and tattered and hung in strands. Isaac could see bone sticking out through the flesh, he knew his Master needed urgent attention from a Barber/Surgeon.

Knowing that in the carnage and chaos of the Battlefield which he saw before him, the task of finding a Barber/Surgeon would be nigh impossible, he must, he decided get his Master to York. He covered the injured limb by taking a kerchief from his neck and fastening it firmly over and around the wound, he went to Jack's body and removed a larger kerchief similarly tying it over the wounded area. Then, with great difficulty, (the Squire was quite a portly gentleman) he lifted him onto the waggon at the front end, so as to keep an eye upon him during the journey to York.

As he turned to give attention to the wounded solger, he saw far to his right a large number of Whitecoated solgers, Jack, had told him they were the Earl of Newcastle's men. He saw they were surrounded by a large circle of bodies of their comrades who were lying dead or wounded on the ground, the screams and shouts were pitiful as they echoed across the field. Parliamentary Cavalry and Musketeers had surrounded the group and the Whitecoats were falling in large numbers as they fought bravely to hold their ground, it was murderous to see, Isaac turned his head from the view.

Crouching beside the injured solger, Isaac spoke to him, asking him where he was hurt. Struggling to catch his breath and speaking with difficulty, the man said, "*Musket shots here,*" he once again struggled to place his arm over his chest on his right hand side. Isaac reached for his water bottle at his belt and placed it to the man's lips, he gratefully took several drinks from the vessel and then motioned his hand, indicating he had finished. Undoing the solger's tunic, Isaac saw there was much blood congealing around several wounds to the man's chest.

Realising the man was badly injured, Isaac spoke to him saying, "*I am going to try to lift you onto the waggon, can put your arm around my neck and I will lift you at the same time*". With much grunting from Isaac and groans of pain from the solger, Isaac was finally able to lift the man's legs onto the cart and help him to get into a comfortable position. Looking over to the line of tethered horses, Isaac saw both of Jack's horses, in spite all the noise were standing in line and quite calm.

Crossing over to the animals Isaac, led both of them back to the waggon by their bridles, both animals were used to Isaac being around them, but, conscious of Jack's absence, Isaac spoke to them quietly and calmly, just as he had heard for so long how Jack talked to them. Isaac thinking back could remember the pride Jack displayed when the Squire gave him charge of them shortly after they had been foaled, followed by the many months of training and patience his friend had given to his charges. Tethering the horses to the waggon, Isaac took the gear, harness, reins and all leathers and buckles he needed to dress the horses ready for the cart.

When he had made the horses ready, he backed them into the shafts and fastened the necessary gear to the shafts and the waggon. He checked on the condition of the Squire and the solger, Squire Fewster did not respond to his questions, but he was still breathing. When he spoke to the Solger, the man started mumbling, but Isaac could not understand what he said. Urging the horses forward, Isaac was able to manouvre the waggon slowly from it's position in the circle of waggon's to set off on his journey to York. Looking around the Battlefield he saw the heavy rain had lessoned considerably, having all but stopped.

The fighting and noise were still intense, he saw there were but just a handful of Whitecoat Solgers still fighting valiantly, their fallen comrades were lying on the ground, in an ever enlarging circle of death. As he turned the waggon to make his way from the field of battle Isaac saw ahead of him, lying close to a number of dead and injured horses a large white dog, it was long coated and was heavily splattered with blood, it was obviously dead. The waggon made slow progress as it left the battlefield, Isaac struggled at times to avoid debris and cannon craters, the unyielding mud also made steering the waggon difficult.

After leaving the battlefield and Marston Moor, Isaac entered a bean field and started to follow a track at the edge of the field. To get a better view of the track ahead of him, Isaac stood up on the footboards in front of the driving seat, something which he had seen Jack do many times. As he did so, he saw at intervals lone solgers, vainly trying to hide themselves amongst the beans. In another field he a saw a small group of Royalist Cavalry spread out across the field and fleeing from the Parliament Cavalry which was pursuing them. Though his progress along field tracks was slow, Isaac eventually came to the York Road.

Not knowing if the bridge of boats at Poppleton was still open, Isaac decided to stay on the road to York and not take a track signposted to Poppleton. As he continued his journey he saw, at intervals along the side of the road, injured solgers were sitting and lying, they were crying out for help and assistance that he was not able to give them. He continued on toward York and as he arrived at the village of Houlgate, a number of coaches came up behind him at a furious gallop. He was not able to see who were the passengers, but from the attire of some of them they were in Cavalier dress. He pulled his waggon to the side to let the coaches go by him, before he re-commenced his journey he turned his head when he heard a voice coming from behind him within the waggon.

He stepped over the seat into the back of the waggon and saw the solger struggling to get to his feet, Isaac said to him, "*Yer won't do thissen much use trying ter get on yer feet,*" but struggling to catch his breath the solger, finally managed to say, "*I as't to get bet back onto the field, my men need me*". The effort had drained most of his strength and his head fell forward and then he slumped over to one side, he was breathing with great difficulty. Kneeling at the side of the solger, Isaac tried to place him into a more comfortable position and decided he must continue with all speed to York and a Surgeon's help.

As he got near to the Citie Walls, the road was blocked by waggon's, cart's, bedraggled solgers on foot and horsemen and many peasants carrying their meagre possessions, wrapped in tattered blanket cloth, no one was able to move forward because of the denseness of the crowd. Isaac pulled his cart onto a narrow foot track at the left side of the road whilst he pondered what he could do. Isaac noticed just near where he had stopped a small track turned off to his left, Isaac set his charges forward and he turned the waggon into the entrance. He had to call his horses to halt almost immediately after turning. At the side of the track just ahead of him a man was trying vainly to push a handcart, but because of the length of the grass and the weight of the goods piled high upon his cart, the man was finding it an impossible task. Seeing that Isaac was watching what he was doing, the man lowered the shafts to the ground and started to walk slowly back toward Isaac. He patted the horse nearest to him as he walked by, when he got to Isaac he stopped and he said, *"Ist tha tryin' ta get int' Citie"*, Isaac nodded and said, *"Aye"*, thinking thoughtfully to himself, the man grinned and said, *"Ah, can get thee in"*.

Isaac, showing interest replied, *"How can thee, get this waggon thru' yon crush, an anyow who ah thee"*. Smiling broadly the man said, *"My name is Keil Slarky an' I'm a Master Plaisterer, ya see't Trained Bands ah checking to see if any roundheads are trying ta ger in, but ah can get ya in at Lendal Postern"*. Isaac was wary of the suggestion and said to Keit, *" 'Ow will ya do that then"*, again grinning broadly, Keit replied, *"Aye, John Cundill is't Constable and he let mi out, i've bin stocking up wi' food, ya nivver can tell what'll 'appen next"*. Nodding his head Isaac said, *"Aye reet then"*, Walking back to his cart, Kiet shouted, *"Giv' mi 'elp, to load sum ah stuff onto your waggon, an then i'll be able to push mi cart"*. Working quickly they soon moved enough of Keit's goods from the cart and onto the waggon, Keit checked and found he was then able to easily push the cart.

As they moved off, with Keit pushing his cart ahead of the waggon, he shouted to Isaac, *"Follow me"*, it had stopped raining and even in the half light Isaac was able, by keeping his horses close up to Keit to follow him. In a short while, Isaac could see a river ahead of them and to his right close to the river, he could see from the light of the lanterns they were holding, that there were three or four figures upon the Wall, as they got closer Isaac heard Keit shout out to the figures. As Keit got close to the Wall, he stopped and Isaac saw they were standing outside a gate which was just about wide enough for his waggon to pass through.

Keit banged loudly on the gate with his fist, the door creaked, as it opened very slowly and not fully, a frail figure wearing a dark cloak and carrying a lantern in one hand, a wooden staff in his other hand and in his waist belt (was what Isaac was told later, was a wooden rattle), the figure stepped out and stood in front of Keit. As they conversed, Isaac saw the man was using the staff as a prop, he had placed the implement behind his right buttock and allowing himself to lean upon it, he looked quite old. Their conversation ended and the old man turned and shouted to someone within, to open the gate. Once again the gate opened, this time fully, Keit started pushing his cart forward, as he did so he turned his head and he raised his arm, bidding Isaac to follow him.

After they had passed through the gate, Keit stopped and walked the few paces back to the waggon and said to Isaac, *"Reet, do'st tha no, weer tha wants to be"*, Isaac told him of his two injured passengers and his need to find a Barber/ Surgeon. Keit said, *"Reet, foller me"*, they followed the River and then came to a bridge, which they started to cross. They then passed through a variety of narrow streets and alley's until Keit brought them to halt, they were standing outside a fairly large building of stone structure.

CHAPTER XV

A Citie in Turmoil

As Isaac dismouted from the waggon and said to Keit, *"Ah wi 'ere then"*, Keit stepping onto the causeway, said, *"Foller me, this is St. Anthony's Hall, an its bin used as't Hospital sin seege began"*, they walked forward and entered the building, the hallway was deserted, but as they got partway along the main corridor, they could hear the murmur of voices as they came to a sideroom, a lady was sitting at a table near the door, she was cutting strips of linen from a sheet which was lying on the table and thence rolling the strips up tightly. She saw Keit and smiling cheerfully, she said, *"Mr. Starkey, can I help you"*, Keit replied, *"Ello Mrs. Akombe"*, and then he explained to her that Isaac had two injured people from the battle, on the waggon outside.

The good lady stopped her work immediately and joined Keit and Isaac in the corridor, as she did so, she turned and called out to someone still in the room, *"Come, Mrs. Watts, we have more important work to do now"*. Keit was surprised when the person appeared in the doorway, it was Ann Watts, the wife of his friend Luke. Ann smiled and said, *"Ello Keit, ah didn't think it wa' you Mrs Akombe wa' tawkin' ta"*, pointing to a small cart which had a flat top and was standing just across the Hallway, Mrs. Akombe said, *"You can use that cart to wheel the injured solgers in"*.

Isaac and Keit took the cart out to the waggon, Isaac decided the Squire would be first, with some difficulty, the two of them lifted the Squire from the waggon and onto the cart and re-entered the building, Mrs. Akombe was waiting in the doorway of a room further down the corridor and she said, "Come this way please". Keit and Isaac pushing the cart, followed Mrs. Akombe into the room, Isaac saw there were beds placed low to the floor on both sides of the room, but, there was a corner to the left side of the door which was curtained off. More than half of the beds were emtpy, Mrs. Acombe went to the far end of the room near to the window, she pulled back the covers of the bed on the right side of the window. Turning to Keit, she said, "Now Mr. Starky if you and your friend could very carefully lift the patient onto the bed, it would be most helpful". As they took hold of the Squire he groaned quite noisily until they settled him upon the bed.

As Mrs. Akombe and Ann then moved to the bed and made the Squire as comfortable as they could, Keit and Isaac left to return outside to bring the wounded solger in for treatment. As they were walking down the corridor and approaching the front door, the door burst open and hit the wall with a loud crack, two men entered, each carrying large leather bags, which were too full to be closed and exposing to view what Isaac took to be medical instruments. In their haste, a saw like tool fell from the bag of one the men, Isaac stooped and picked up the implement and handed to its owner who nodded his thanks to Isaac as they continued their dash down the corridor. Keit turned to Isacc and said, *"Th'er in a rush, ah 'ope tha get the'er in time"*, Isaac nodded and said, *"Aye, who ah they"*, Keit said, said, *"Theer both*

Barber/Su'geons, but, 'ave 'eard it sed, yon who dropped 'is saw is more of a bu'cher than out else". They went through the door and Keit placed the cart close to the waggon as Isaac had climbed onto it. Bending over the solger, Isaac spoke to him. but he got no response, dragging the Solger over to the side of the waggon, he was able with Keit's help to place the patient onto the cart.

Whilst they had been busy with the solger, a coach had drawn up behind the waggon, and the coachman and with the help of a servant were struggling to carry their Master a Cavalier Colonel through the door into the Hall. Two members of the Citie Trained Bands were passing along the street and they dashed forward to give help. Whilst they waited outside the door, Isaac saw a group of ladies approaching the doorway. They were all wearing shawls pulled over and around their heads and shoulders, which gave them protection from the heavy drizzle which was falling and each was clutching either a wickerwork basket or a large hessian bag. They each spoke cheerfully to Keit as they passed through the door, generally enquiring of his reason for being present at the Hall, Keit in a good hearted way explained his presence to them. After they had all entered the building Keit explained to Isaac that the ladies were the wives of craftsmen who were members of the Citie's Craft Gilds. They had all come to help the Barber Surgeons and nurse the injured solgers.

After getting their cart through the doorway Keit and Isaac pushed it down the corridor entered the room where they had taken Squire Fewster, they could see Ann Watts at the end the room tending to Squire Fewster, as she turned she saw them and moved forward to them, half way up the room she stooped at an empty bed waved to them to push the cart to that bed, Isaac and Keit took hold of the solger and lifted him onto the bed. Ann then stepped forward to make the patient comfortable, she suddenly stepped back and with a shocked look upon her face she exclaimed loudly *"Oh no, it's Uncle Josh"*, she then started to sob uncontrollably. Isaac moved to her side and placing his arm around her shoulder he started to walk her toward the door, he glanced over his shoulder at Keit and with a shake of his head gestured him to follow with the cart. As they got to the doorway into the corridor Mrs Akombe met them and immediately stepped and clasped her arms around Ann in a comforting embrace.

Looking at Isaac over Ann's shoulder, with an enquiring look in her eyes and mouthing the question *"What is the matter"*, Isaac advised her what had taken place, the wise older lady nodded and started speaking soothingly to Ann and led her gently across the corridor into the room they had been in when Keit and Isaac first arrived at the Hall. Leading the heartbroken Ann over to the table she pulled out a chair and gently got her charge to sit down. Turning to Keit, Mrs. Akombe asked him to go to a room further down the corridor, where the wives of the Craftsmens Gilds were helping and for him to seek out the Butchers wife Mrs. Wright, saying to Keit, *"She is a good friend and neighbour, she is down the hall cutting bandages"*. He nodded he knew her and her husband, their shop was opposite Luke's workshop. Keit found Mrs. Wright and advised her what had taken place and the good lady gladly accompanied him back to the room where her friend was in need of comfort.

When they had returned outside to the waggon Keit said, *"If ya foller me, an can let ya put waggon under a shelter I ave in me yard, an ya can sleep sleep in t' waggon"*, Isaac thanked his new found friend for his offer and gratefully accepted it. They turned into a street and Isaac saw from the sign at the end, that it was called Hundgate, at the far end of the street they turned left and some way down that street on the opposite side of the road, they turned right and went through an archway and they stopped in a large courtyard. Keit went back to the waggon and pointing across to a large barn standing in the far corner he, said,"*Ya si yon barn, well ya can put waggon in them stalls in t' corner of it shud be alreet for t' 'osses*". Isaac nodded and said, "*Reet, thanks*" and then just like his poor friend Jack, he clicked his tongue and urged his charges forward toward the barn. In the barn he halted the horses and jumping down he commenced taking off their tack by the light of a lantern he had found and lit it with one of Jack's precious matches

As Isaac finished his tasks and his two charges were in their respective stalls, Keit re-appeared, he was pushing his cart and upon it a few sheaves of hay each carefully bound with twine he had also brought a hessian sack, he handed it to Isaac and said ,"*It's corn, ah feed 'ens wi it, this 'ill see t'osses til termorrow, an then we'll get summat fixed up*". In each of the stalls the horses were eating the hay which Isaac had put in the racks fastened to the wall and he filled each of the nose bags with corn and when each horse had finished it's hay, he fastened a nose bag around it's head. He went to the waggon and got some bread and cheese from his back pack and sat on the waggon seat whilst he ate it. His thoughts turned to all the events he had seen and heard and with sadness he thought of happier times he had spent with Jack and realised how much he would miss his friend in the days to come. After he had finished his own food, he saw the horses were no longer chomping the corn in their nose bags, he went across and removed the bag from each animal and after giving each animal a quick rub down with straw, he took some blankets made a comfortable bed for himself under the waggon.

Isaac was awakened next morning by the cheerful voice of Keit calling out to him, he blinked his eyes and rolled from under the waggon, he saw Keit standing by his handcart close by the waggon, he was smiling broadly and he said, *"Ah thout' tha must ah a stopt breethin or summat, dost tha n how long it's bin since cocks stopt crowin"*, Isaac rose to his feet and busied himself brushing his hands down his clothing trying without much success to remove the bits of straw which clung lovingly to him. Keit said, as he pointed to his cart, *"Ave brout thee two barrels of ah watter, one of 'em fa t' 'osses ta drink and one fa thee ta wash 'osses down wi"*. Isaac, finally gathering his thoughts, smiled at the thoroughness of his new found friend and said, *"Thanks, tha thinks about wat's needed don't ya Keit"*. His friend smiled, nodded and said, *"Reet, ahs got a big plaistering job on terday, so ahs of ta work"*.

When Keit had gone, Isaac firstly broke his fast and then groomed each of the horses in turn, after which he the took hold of the horses by their bridles one in each hand. He led the animals out into the courtyard, intending to exercise them by walking them around it, before returning them to their stalls. When he got to the far corner of the courtyard, he saw, standing at the side of a shed which was in an advanced state of dis-repair, a gate, which was open and gave access to a grass paddock. There were a few chickens scratching and clucking in an area to the left of the gate and towards the centre of the paddock there was a nanni goat grazing and close by to her, gazing contentedly around her surroundings was her kid. As Isaac led his charges around the paddock, he checked the hedges around the paddock, he was delighted to find the hedges were in good order and would safely keep his horses secure. He stopped, unbridled the horses and went to the gate and passed through it, closing it after him.

Isaac spent a few moments leaning on the gate, to check the horses were settled and turning he set off to find the St, Anthony's Hall, to enquire after the health of Squire Fewster. He then intended to seek out a Parson to enquire for advice to arrange a Funeral for his friend Jack, who was still lying in the waggon in the barn. From his memory of the route they had taken from the Hall the previous eve, Isaac soon found his way to the Hall, he entered and as he walked down the corridor, he encountered Mrs. Akombe, the good lady recognised him immediately and enquired if she could offer any help to him. Isaac explained his concern about the present health of Squire Fewster, she smiled and said to him, *"Come follow me"*, they passed down the corridor and entered the room whence Isaac had last seen his Master. Isaac was staggered by the numbers of injured that now were lying upon every inch of floorspace and leaving scarce room to enable a person to walk amongst them. When they got to Squire's bed, Isaac was staggered at his Master's appearance, he thought he was dead, he turned and looking at Mrs. Akombe he whispered, *"He is not dead is he"*.

The good lady stepped by Isaac and as she knelt to the floor she pulled a small mirror from her apron pocket, she held the implement toward the Squire's face just about a hand's width away from his face. Isaac stood watching her carry out the task, she slowly rose and turned to face Isaac, she turned the mirror into Isaac's sight and said, *"No, your Squire is not dead, you can see your Master's breath upon the mirror"*, Isaac nodded and looking upwards whispered, *"Praise the Lord"*. Mrs Akombe rearranged the covers of her patient and as she turned she beckoned Isaac to follow her. When they got into the corridor she seated herself upon a bench and bade Isaac to seat himself beside her. She turned toward Isaac and said, *"Your Master's Life, is in our Lord's hands, he is very gravely ill, the Surgeon had to remove his arm and he has lost a lot of blood, his body is seriously shocked, we must pray for his recovery".*

Isaac sat with head bowed, he felt bereft of plans to deal with the situation in which he found himself. He turned to Mrs. Akombe and said, *"My friend died on the field yesterday, but ave still got 'im in't waggon, can ya 'elp mi".* Patting Isaac's hand very gently, Mrs. Akombe said, *"Don't worry I can and will help you, just sit here a for a short time, gather your thoughts together and I will be back, then we can decide what you must do".* A short while later she returned and after seating herself on the bench at the side of Isaac, she said, *"I have made enquiry and found that arrangements have been made for two solgers, who passed away to join Our Lord during the night are to be buried tomorrow, you must visit the Church of the Holy Trinity in Gudramgate and speak to Parson Atkin, he will help you".* She then went on to give Isaac directions to find his way to Gudramgate, nodding his thanks to the lady as he rose to his feet, he said *"Thank you, Mrs. Akombe, you 'ave gin me strength",* he then walked down the corridor to leave the Hall.

As he set foot onto the causeway outside the Hall, he stopped and looked in bewilderment, the throng of people walking in all directions avoiding, coaches, waggons, carts and horse riders, everyone appeared to be in a hurry. Isaac had never seen nor had he ever been in scenes of activity like this before, even on a Market Day in Thirsk. He set off and apart from dodging careless horse riders and people bumping into him he found his way to the Church which Isaac thought, looked to be very old. As he walked up the pathway to the Porch, he heard a voice calling to him, Isaac stopped and looked around, he was not able to see anyone and was about to resume his walk up the path, when he heard a voice call, *"What do you want"*, Isaac again looked about and still could not see anyone. He then he heard the voice call again, this time the caller said, *"I am up here on the tower, wait I will come down"*. In but a few minutes a figure emerged from the doorway, Isaac saw immediately the male person was a Vicar or Parson.

When the man came up to Isaac, he said, *"Good morning, I am Parson Atkin, how may I help you"*, Isaac, stammered a little and then gathered his thoughts and said, *"Mi friend got killed in't Battle yestaday, Mrs. Akombe sent me, ah need to get 'im buried"*. Taking Isaac by his arm, Parson Atkin led him to a seat placed to the side of the Church door, he sat down and bade Isaac to do the same, he then said, *"Where is the body of your friend lying now"*, Isaac thought to himself for a moment before answering and then he said, *"Ah brout 'im in on't back o' waggon from t' battlefield, an' ah brout two fair wunded men as well, but the'er in't 'ospital an' Jack Grainger's on't back o' waggon in Keit Starkey's stable"*. Parson Atkins face brightened up when he heard this news and he said, *"You must get hold of yor friend Keit and between you make a shroud, in which to put the body and then make sure you are here in the morning before ten of the clock, then we will have a Burial Service in a corner of the Churchyard for your friend Jack Grainger an two Solgers, who also died in the Battle"*.

Isaac left the Churchyard and as he stepped into Gudramgate, he saw the street was even more crowded than it had been, Citizens and solgers were struggling to avoid being trampled or kicked by horses rearing, as their riders tried to control them, caused, as Isaac witnessed himself, by passers by, citizens and solgers angrily slapping or even kicking animals as they passed. Noise from the clattering of hooves upon the cobbles and shouts and screams and oaths being exchanged from all directions. To avoid the noise and as Isaac felt, for his own safety, he turned off into a lane to the left, there were fewer people there and it was much quieter. Drivers and shopkeepers were unloading carts and taking goods and wares into premises. As he was passing a waggon with a pair of heavy horses in the shafts, which was waiting outside a Gunsmiths workshop, Isaac saw Keit's cart, it had (Plaisterer) painted on the side. It was standing opposite a workshop, which had a swinging sign above the door indicating WATTS Cordwainer.

Isaac walked back toward where Keit was working and as he was doing so, Keit came out of the door. Isaac told him of his visit to Parson Atkin and what that good Cleric had agreed to do. Keit thought for a moment and then said, *"We'll go back inside an' see if Luke 'as any canvas or owt like that, ta mek a shrowd from"*, as they entered the workshop Luke came in from the kitchen. After telling Luke of their needs to make a shroud, he replied, *"Ast' tha no's, wi 'ave ta bury Anne's Uncle Josh, well 'ave just med a shroud for 'im an' laid 'im out int storeroom at back"*, turning he beckoned Isaac and Keit to follow him. They went through the Kitchen and across a small courtyard, from which they accessed a building where hides of leather and various animal pelts were hanging on brackets protruding from the walls. A trestle table was placed centrally in the store, upon which was lying, enclosed in a shroud the body of Josh Hogg. Luke went across to the right hand corner of the store, where a number of rolls of various materials, were standing upright upon the floor, he picked up the smallest of the rolls it was the same material (hessian) from which the shroud was made.

After unrolling the hessian and holding it high above his head to estimate it's length, Luke turned to his two companions and said, *"Tha's plenty 'ere to mek another shrowd"*. Isaac nodded his thanks and Keit said, *"Luke, can'st tha giv' us a hand ta mek it, cos tha' med a good job on't one for Josh"*. Luke paused before answering, he then waited until Great Peter the loudest bell in the Minster tolled the hour of ten of the clock, he then said, *"Go back ta Keit's yard, an ah will be theer when Great Peter tolls eleven of the clock."* Keit said, *"Ah think ah'd best cum as well an' bring some trestles and boards ta lay im out on"*, Isaac thanked both men for their kindness and he said to Luke, *"How can ah ever repay thee"*, Luk waved him away and said, *"Isaac, we liv' in 'ard tymes an' Our Lord tells us, wi must giv' our 'elp ta them as needs it"*. Isaac, stepped forward and clasped Luke by the hand and gave it a very firm shake, he then turned and left the storeroom to find his way back to Keit's yard.

Upon stepping into the street, he had to stop at the edge of the causeway to allow two carriages accompanied by outriders and travelling at a fast trot clatter by, the wheels were bouncing upon the street cobbles. After passing Isaac, the outriders shouted oaths at a group of small boys who were playing on the cobbles, they darted to safety in all directions. As Isaac got to the end of the street he found himself once more at the Hall of St. Anthony, on their visit the previous evening Keit had told him the Hall was in Aldwalk, another street crossed the end of Aldwark and looking across to the other side of that street Isaac could see an Inn, from the wall of which was swinging the sign of a Black Swan. Recognising where he was, Isaac crossed over the cobbles and set off to walk up the street to his right. After walking a short distance he came to the corner which he knew was Hundegate. As he turned to his left into the street, Isaac stopped in surprise, on the causeway on the other side of that street was Will Thornton, He was walking slowly, his head was down and he did not seem to be aware of anything going on around him.

Despite calling out loudly to his friend, Will appeared not to hear him, Isaac stood at the kerb and awaited the passing of horse riders trotting in single file, as they passed him, Isaac dashed across the causeway and had to stop abruptly, as a Cavalier officer riding his mount at a fast trot approached from the opposite direction, he shouted oaths at Isaac and berated him, the man had to pull harshly on the reins and he was nearly unseated as his mount swerved and missed Isaac. Shaking his fist in anger toward Isaac, the rider trotted on his way. Somewhat ruffled by his experience, Isaac finally, crossed the street and saw that as a result of the noise and commotion, Will had turned and he was staring toward Isaac with a look of surprise on his face. The two men greeted each other warmly with much handshaking and laughter, Isaac suggested that Will accompany him back to Keit's yard, Will agreed to do so.

As they walked along Isaac listened as Will explained his experiences on the Battlefield, after the Parliamentarian Cavalry had broken through the Royalist Lines. Will had wandered about looking for the Squire but he had to seek shelter, when the Roundhead cannon again started pounding the Royalist lines. When he got to the Royalist compound where he had left his waggon, he found that it had been struck and was smashed beyond repair. He then made his way to the rear of the battle lines where the horses had been picketed for their safety, he told Isaac that many of the horses were dead or lying about badly injured. He went to the baggage area, further to the rear and was delighted when he found his team wandering close by, each animal grazing, with it's length of tether rope trailing along behind it, Cannon fire was still roaring from the hillside. Because of their strength those heavy horses had managed in their panic, to rive their iron tether rods out of the ground and moved away from the blasts they had encountered.

Will then went on to say, that as he was leaving the Battlefield, a weary looking man walking at the side of the track pleaded to Will that he may agree, to his riding Will's second animal to York. He told Will that he knew the safest tracks to take. On their journey, he explained that he was Coachman to the Lord Mayor of, York, Sir Edmund Cooper, he said his horse team had bolted as the Cavalry had charged down the hillside, he had later found the coach smashed beyond repair in a Cannon crater, one horse was dead still harnessed in the shafts and the other was standing near the wreckage with a badly injured foreleg and it looked as though it too would die, the animal could not walk. The man left the field to return to York, but, after a short walk he had to stop and sit under a tree to rest, he had stumbled and injured his back. He expressed his thanks and gratitude to Will, the route he guided Will, was mostly across fields and little known tracks, at no time did they encounter solgers from either side on their journey to York.

Upon reaching the Citie, Will was guided by his new found friend through the winding streets of the Citie to a stable yard where the Lord Mayor's coach and his horse team were usually stabled, Will's horses had been fed and watered and then Will had slept the rest of the night in the stable. As they approached Keit's yard, Isaac said, *"This is w'ere t'osses an't waggon is bin kept"*, both men entered the yard and crossed toward the barn, where Isaac had left the waggon and Jack's body. At this point, Isaac thought it best to acquaint Will of Jack's death and the circumstances surrounding it. As he told the story, Isaac could see that his friend was both shocked and saddened upon hearing the story. Isaac pointed to the waggon and said,*"Ave' laid 'im out on't waggon fa now, wi ave ta put 'im in a shroud ready for 'is burial termorrer"*.

Whilst the two men were talking, they heard a loud squeaking noise, looking round they saw Keit entering the Barn, he was pushing his cart and he was whistling cheerfully. Isaac said to him, "*Ah think tha awt get sum grease on yon wheels*", smiling broadly, Keith went on to say,"*Ah will, wen ah gets sum time, ave brout som trestles and 'essian, as welll as a needle an' sum strong thred that Luke gev mi*". They then set about setting up the trestle bench, which took but a few minutes. Keit then said, "*Luke can't cum, but he showd mi 'ow ta do it*", he then unrolled the hessian upon the trestle, he secured it from rolling off the trestle by placing a heavy wooden mallet at one end and a solid stave of oak at the other end, these were articles he had taken from his cart. Ever the practical one, Keit then said, "*Reet, ah ya gonna bury 'im in 'is clothes or not*", Isaac and Will spent a few minutes considering this matter and they both agreed that Jack would remained clothed within his shroud.

Thus decided, Isaac and Will went to the waggon to bring Jack's body, they both climbed onto the waggon and between them carried it to the edge, Will jumped down and held the head and shoulders until Isaac alighted and he took hold of the legs. When they reached the trestles they laid the body upon it. Keit then took hold of the roll of hessian which was lying on the floor and unrolled it back along the body to the head. After checking he had sufficient material to join with the other end he cut through it. Then starting at the feet and using the bodkin and thread which Luke had given to him, he carefully sewed the two together along one side and then similarly sewed the edges on the other side, then carefully gathering the two top edges together, he sewed the top edges of the hessian and with a little pulling and adjustment he was able to fasten the top edges along the shoulders at the back. All three men surveyed Keit's handiwork and agreed he had done a tidy job.

Keit told Isaac that he had a job to do at the Common Hall, which would take him the rest of the day. Before leaving he said,*"Be redy 'ere in't morning as clocks strike nine of t' clock, a'll be 'ere by then wi 't cart, an wi can push 'im ta church on that"*. Then with a cheerful wave of his hands, he took hold of the cart handles and pushed it, wheels still squeaking out of the barn. Isaac then related to Will the details concerning the injuries sustained on the Battlefield by Squire Fewster and how unwell he was this day, in St. Anthonies Hall as a result of those injuries. As he was finishing the story the hour of one of the clock boomed out across the Citie from the Minster Belltower. Isaac then said to his friend, *"Ah must go ta visit 'im"*, Will said, *"Ah'll cum wi thee"*. Both men left the Barn and set off to make their way to the Hall to see their Master.

There was still much activity in the streets, there was much bustle amongst people walking and various small groups of horsemen, who were mainly solgers clattering by. Often clusters of chicken were scattered away, with much squawking and flapping of wings as some errant horse went to close to them. When Isaac and Will reached Aldwalk, they saw a waggon standing at the side gates of St. Anthony's Hall and they saw shrouded bodies being carried from the rear of the Hall and placed on the waggon, they counted eight in all. Isaac looked at his friend Will and said, *"Wat a waste, more 'onest and God fearing men slawterd"*.

They made their way into the hallway, Isaac espied Mrs. Akombe further down the hallway, she was speaking to a man whom Isaac had seen on his last visit and he knew him to be a Barber/Surgeon, the apron he was wearing was badly bespattered with blood. As Isaac and Will approached, the man turned away from Mrs. Akombe and entered a room on the other side of the Hallway. Mrs. Akombe smiled when she saw them, she then said, *"Our Lord, never ceases his wonders to work, your Master has surprised us all"*. She pointed into the room whence Isaac had left his Master and she said , *"Go in to see him, but he is weak, don't stay too long"*. Isaac entered the room, with Will closely behind him, there was little room between each bed space and both men threaded their way carefully between the narrow aisles, until Isaac stopped at the bed of Squire Fewster. He looked comfortable, he was breathing normally, but his eyes were closed, he was placed in a near sitting position supported by many pillows.

As they stood observing their Master, he appeared to become aware of their presence and his eyes slowly opened, he tried to move his body and he winced as he felt the pain caused by his movement, he relaxed and with a sigh, sank back into his former position. With the trace of a smile forming around his lips, he turned his head slightly, he looked intently at his servants. He caught his breath for a moment and after starting to cough very weakly, he stopped and held his breath for a moment, he said, *"Isaac and Will, it is good to see you both, it gives me great pleasure and can you pray tell me which day is this and where am I lodged"* he asked them and he spoke very slowly, his eyes looking despairingly around his surroundings. In but a few words, Isaac informed his Master of his rescue by Josh Hogg and the subsequent events which had involved Isaac bringing them both to York for treatment of their wounds.

Squire Fewster shook his head sadly and then said, *"Have either of you any knowledge of Jack Grainger"*, Isaac gave his Master the brief details of Jack Grainger's sad death. The old man was quite visibly saddened by the news, he did not speak for some minutes and then said in a very soft voice, *"Was he left on the Battlefield"*, Isaac again briefly, explained the circumstances and the Funeral arrangements that had been made. After spending several minutes pondering all he had been told, *"I am deeply sorry at the news you have given to me, I fear I must rest now, but are my riding boots in your view"*. Will saw the boots against the wall at the head of the bed, reaching out and picking them up, he said, *"They are here Master"*. Squire Fewster's countenance brightened up and he went on to say, *"Take one of the boots each, one heel will screw off"*. Looking at each other with puzzled looks, both men started to unscrew the heel of the boot they were holding, Isaac found the heel of the boot he was holding, began to unscrew from the boot. Holding the heel in his hand he placed the boot on floor and said, *"Squire, I have your boot heel in my hand"*. Squire Fewster then said, *"Lift up the lid at the top and take out two of the Gold Sovereigns which are within"*, Isaac did so and the Squire then said, *"I want you both to take one coin each and then take Lodging in the Citie and obtain provender for the horses, also ask the parson who buries Jack to visit me"*.

Both men glanced at each other, with looks of surprise on their faces, Squire Fewster went on to say, *"I know both of you are loyal and trustworthy men and I can rely upon both of you to carry out my wishes, please go now, I wish to rest"*. Humbly, Isaac and Will murmured their thanks and withdrew from the bedside and left the room. In the Hallway they found Mrs. Akombe sitting at a side table, writing in a leather bound journal. They stopped near to her and when she became aware of their presence, she stopped writing, looked up at them with a pleasant smile upon her face and said, *"How may I help you"*. Isaac enquired of her if she could advise them of somewhere they could obtain suitable lodging. She told them of her friend Widow Cuthbert, who kept a small tavern, the Fat Friar which was in Little Shambles, she told them it was clean and homely and Widow Cuthbert would welcome them warmly, she added, her frailty was a great difficulty to her in running the tavern, Mrs. Akombe concluded by giving them clear instructions to follow to the Fat Friar.

Leaving the Hall they crossed the end of St. Saviourgate and made their way forward toward St. Andrew's Church, after passing the church, the pair walked along St. Andrewgate. As they reached the end of this street, they entered a Square where standing before them was the King's Church, after skirting round the left of the small graveyard of the Church, they entered a passage way at the rear end of the Church. Ahead of them was the Shambles and after walking but a few paces they turned into Little Shambles on their right hand side. As they approached the end of Little Shambles on their left side, they saw a much faded sign depicting a Friar of a very large stature, the figure was smiling as if in welcome to all who passed. The sign, was hanging lazily on only one very rusty chain and swung slowly in the light breeze and emitted loud squeaking noises. At the side of the building was a rickety wooden stair which led up the side of the gable end of the building to a doorway which was set in the roof space, upon each side of the doorway was a small window.

Approaching the door, Will took hold of the sneck handle and as he pushed open the door, it creaked and tilted alarmingly, upon entering, they saw the room was small, a fire place was opposite the door and against wall at the left side of the door was a heavy wooden gantry upon which were standing barrels of differing sizes, an assortment of chairs, four small benches and a settle were set around three solid tables. It was a dark room and despite there being two windows, little daylight filtered into the room due mainly, to the dirt and grime on the window glass. As they stood taking stock of their surroundings, Isaac called out a loud, *"Hello"*, they heard a croaking call come from a doorway to their right, they watched with curiosity as they heard a shuffling and coughing, accompanied by what sounded like the scraping of wood across stone slabs. A stooped and elderly old woman came slowly into view, she moved toward the fireplace and with great difficulty settled herself into a well cushioned chair with wooden arms, which was placed at the side of the fireplace.

After much puffing and gasping and readjusting the various cushions and shuffling her frail body into different positions, she took a deep breath and looking at Isaac and Will she said, *"Gentlemen, what are your needs"*, Isaac explained their circumstances and their need of lodging and sustenance until Squire Fewster would be fit to return home. When Isaac had finished explaining their needs, she nodded slowly, she then appeared to go into deep thought, after a few minutes she again looked at them and went on to say", *"I can meet your needs, I have two garret rooms at the top of the wooden stair outside, I have not cleaned them because I can't climb the stair, if you could clean and tidy them and if you could do some jobs to help me, I would charge you a very fair rent, go have a look and see what you think"*.

Both men nodded in agreement and turning went out of the front door, care had to be taken mounting the stair, the handrail was rotting in many places. Upon entering the Garret rooms, it could be seen the last occupants had left them in a mess and bed covers were filthy. In each room there was an overpowering stench, which caused both men to step onto the stair outside. As they recovered their breath, Will said, pointing to the buckets, *"Them buckets are full of piss and shit"*. Isaac nodded his head in agreement, before he turned and set off down the stair closely followed by Will.

Before re-entering the Tavern, Will said to Isaac, *"Well dus t' think wi can clean it up"*, after pondering the question for a minute or so, Isaac replied, *"Well if both got stuck into it, wi cud brek it's back in a cuppel of hours"*. After pondering nodding in agreement, Will replied, *"Wi'd best go tell Widow woman then"*.

They re-entered the Tavern and told Widow Cuthbert of their decision, she smiled and looked pleased and then said, *"Ah'll feed thi and we'll see how it goes"*, she then discussed with them the cost of their lodging. After much discussion, Will and Isaac, each paid the Widow Cuthbert for two weeks board, the widow promising them, she would lower her rate when she had seen how much work they had done. Both men thought about the offer and nodded their agreement and thence the three of them in great solemnity shook hands to seal their arrangement. Thinking they should make an immediate start on cleaning their rooms, Isaac asked Widow Cuthbert, where her buckets and brushes were stored. Following her instructions Isaac and Will went outside into the shed in the yard at the rear and from an array of leather and metal buckets and many different sizes of brushes, they chose items suitable for their needs.

After some two hours of cleaning and many ascents and descents of the rickety stairways, both men stood and admired the finished result of their labours. Each room smelled and looked fresh and clean. They were pleased with the result of their labours. Will said, *"Well now, ah think ah'd best go and bring mi 'osses 'ere, if I can find mi way"*, Isaac told his friend he would go with him. They made their way once more through the busy streets and as they passed the Church of St. Sampson they saw a large crowd surrounding a horseman, a Herald, who was reading loudly from his scroll to the assembled audience. Citizens and Solgers alike listened, as they were advised the Gates of the Citie would be closed and barred at sunset on the Orders of Sir John Glenham, the Governor of the Citie. After rolling up his Scroll the Herald gave a loud cry of *"God Save King Charles"*, turning his horse, the Herald rode slowly from the Square. The sombre silence of the assembled audience, starkly contradicted the euphoria of the previous day.

Will and Isaac left the Square in silence and walked down the street from the Market and turned into the street of Spurriers (or Spur makers), at the end of this street they followed the crowd and saw ahead of them a bridge over the River Ouse. As they entered upon the Bridge, Isaac was surprised to see Workshops and bigger buildings built on the bridge. Through the shutterless window spaces, examples of the products being made by the craftsmen working within, could be seen. As they passed over the bridge, they came upon a Chapel with a Clock tower. Beyond this, Isaac espied the Common Hall on his right hand side and then on his left side he saw the Sheriff's Prison, which had many broken windows, through which some inmates looked forlornly out at passer's by, whilst others with outstretched arms, had baskets and bowls, hanging through the holes and calling out and shouting as they begged for food.

Leaving the bridge, two men walked into Micklegate, they proceeded up the hill and as they passed the Church, they turned left into a narrow cobbled lane, after a few paces Will turned into a courtyard, a barn and a stable stood to one side. Crossing to the stable, Isaac saw, as they entered that Will's team were standing shaking their heads contentedly. As Will set about grooming one animal, Isaac lent a hand grooming the second horse, after completing the grooming, Will gave both animals water from large size buckets. As Will turned from taking the empty buckets away from his charges, he saw his friend from the battlefield, the Lord Mayor's Coachman was standing just without the doorway. Will waved and called out cheerfully to him, the man advanced into the stable and Isaac saw the man was walking lamely, his gait was shuffling and his skeletal frame seemed to be leaning heavily to one side. He grimaced with each step he took and he was quite out of breath.

As the man reached Will, he took hold of Will's outstretched arm and after gripping it firmly and shaking it vigorously, he seated his rump upon top of the sacks of oats standing against the wall and then commenced shuffling his body to make himself comfortable, after which he took several large intakes of breath. He then smiled broadly at Will and Isaac and said, *"Amh better now, ah think"*. Will still puzzled said, *"Wat's tha dun"*, before answering the man took several sharp intakes of breath and then said, *"When ah fell owt' o't of t' coach last night, wen t' cannon ball hit it, ah 'ert mi ribs, an t' Barber sez ave cracked em and ah ave ta get a tite 'oss girth put roun em"*. Looking around the stable Will saw bridles hanging from a rail attached to the wall opposite the stalls. Stepping across to the rail, he selected the broadest girth on the rail and walked across to where the coachman was sitting on the sacks of oats, he said, *"Reet, we'll get thi trussed up then, we'll fassen it rund under ya gansey, so we'll ave ta tek that off* .

Will ignored the protestations of the coachman, and with help from Isaac, they managed, with difficulty to draw the garment over the coachman's head, the man grumbled and groaned and was being totally unhelpful. Taking the bridle Will told the man to lift his arms, painfully and grudgingly the man struggled to comply with Will's request. With Will standing at one side and Isaac at the other, the bridle was pulled and tightened around the man's body, amid constant oaths and complaint, directed toward them by their patient. Completing that task Will said, *"Wen we'v got ya gansey back on, ya'll feel a lot better"*, the gansey was replaced with more complaints and oaths. Looking at them the coachman after taking several deep breaths, commenced trying to breath normally, his distress appeared minimal. Looking pleased with himself he said, *"Tha' nos. it dus feel better, thanks"*. Will gathered together his few belongings, a few oddments of extra clothing and the horse blankets, which he rolled up, before he placed all of the articles into a large hessian sack, which had a rope drawstring at the top.

After a few sweeping glances around the barn, to check he had not overlooked anything, he turned to the coachman, who was still sitting on top of the bags of oats, Will went over to him and thanked him, the man struggled to rise and stumbled and Will caught him before he fell to the ground. His breathing was laboured, he was gasping for air, Will supported the man as he began attempting to again seat himself upon the sacks of oats. Regaining his seat and after several minutes of gasping for breath, he was able to say, *"A'll sit 'ere til ah get's mi breath back, you two 'ad best get on yer way "*. Will picked up his sack and hung it around one of his horse's neck and took hold of the halter rope, looking round, he saw Isaac had similarly taken hold of the halter of the other horse. Again shouting his thanks and goodbyes to the coachman, Will accompanied by Isaac walked their charges through the stable door and into ye courtyard.

They left the stable yard and turning right into the cobbled lane, the pair retraced their route back over Ouse Bridge and into the Pavement passing the Church of St. Crux as they turned into Whip-ma-Whop-ma-gate and made their way into St. Saviourgate. After passing along this street, they then turned right into a narrow cobbled lane at the side of a Church and very soon after they entered Hundegate and at the end of the street, they turned right opposite another Church and entered Keit's yard. Whilst Will was settling his two charges into their stalls, Isaac went to the paddock and brought in his own two charges, which he to led into adjoining stalls. All the animals were fed and fresh straw placed into the stalls, before both men left the building to return to the Fat Friar, where they were hoping Widow Cuthbert would have Supper prepared for them.

As they made their way through the streets toward Little Shambles, a dishevelled group of about twelve white coated solgers bespattered with blood, either walking lamely because of their own injuries or trying to support the more seriously injured members of the group, they looked so pitiful and weary, Isaac felt sorry for them and the plight they were in, he turned to Will and said, *"Tha won't be many ah them left fra t' battle, tha wer' slawter'd like animals, an no body cares, weer's t' officers now"*. Will nodded his agreement and the pair continued on their way from near King's Church, they soon found their way into Ye Shambles and thence into Little Shambles, the sign of the Fat Friar, was still hanging from it's one rusty chain and squeaked as it swung slowly in the slight breeze.

They approached the door, Will lifted the sneck and they started to walk in, both men stopped and smiled at each other, as they savoured the smell of roasting meat which drifted in from the kitchen and was permeating around the room in which they were standing. At this juncture Widow Cuthbert appeared she was smiling broadly as she shuffled in through the doorway, she directed them to take a seat at the table. Isaac saw three large wooden platters had been laid on the table in front of three heavy chairs, still smiling Widow Cuthbert said, *"Sit the down and we'll take a bite, I got a haunch of beef nicely roasted"*. Before Isaac and Will could comply with her request, Widow Cuthbert, who was turning to go into the kitchen said, *"Maybe you can help me bring in the food"*. Both men followed her into the kitchen and both were startled to behold what they saw, everywhere was sparkling clean, jugs, pots and pans, all neatly stored on shelves and the fire ovens and hobs gleamed, there were no grease, soot or smoke marks to be seen. Smiling at the surprise shown by her guests, Widow Cuthbert said, *"I 'appen can't cope wi t' rest o't house, but I 'ave ta keep mi kitchen clean"*.

All the food was carried through and placed on the table and they all seated themselves at the table, Widow Cuthbert placed the palms of her hands together and said a small prayer of thanks for the food and Isaac and Will with due reverence and in unison said, *"Wi, Thank you thee Lord"*. Skilfully carving the haunch of beef Widow Cuthbert placed generous portions onto the plate of each man and then invited them both to help themselves to boiled cabbage, roast carrot and turnip. A large plate of newly baked bread spread with butter was also available, as they were eating their meal, both men were assailed by questions from their host, they were usually able to answer with a polite yea or nae. After they had finished eating, Widow Cuthbert bade both men to help themselves to a tankard of ale from the casks on the nearby gantry. Isaac and Will did as they had been bidden and after taking a large quaff each from their tankards they both nodded their approval and complimented her on the pleasing flavour of the brew.

After the meal both Isaac and Will assisted Widow Cuthbert, by checking the casks on the gantry, replacing those that were empty and tilting with chocks those whose contents were in the lower half of the barrel, making drawing off the ale from the cask easier. When they had completed the task she had set, she expressed her gratitude to them for their labours. Knowing they would have to rise early on the morrow in order to allow them to prepare for Jack's burial, Isaac and Will wished their host a good night. After taking their leave they left through the front door and they made their way warily up the rickety stair to their garret rooms.

Awaking and sitting up in his bed, Isaac was unsure of his surroundings, until he gathered his thoughts, sunlight was shining through the small garret window, the foul smell of yesterday had gone. He got out of bed and dressed, he went down the rickety stair and entered the small rear yard, he saw a large rainwater butt and after examining it, he saw it was full of water, he sniffed and there was no odour from it, he stuck his finger into the water and tasted it. It tasted good, he espied a wooden bucket standing alongside the door, he went over to it and picked it up and went back to the butt, where he drew of a quantity of wate into the bucket and then placed it onto a trestle table. After taking off his upper garments and his heavy boots, he commenced to wash off the grime of the previous two days. He felt refreshed as he made his way back up to the garret room, where he checked to see if Will had awakened and found to his surprise, his friend was not present in the room.

Returning back down the stair, Isaac entered through the front door of the Fat Friar and saw his friend was sitting at the table, he was breaking his fast and Isaac noted the he had a full platter of food before him. As Isaac was wishing his friend a hearty good morning, Widow Cuthbert shuffled into the room from the kitchen, she cheerfully wished Isaac a good morn and bade him to take a seat at the table. Turning she took from ye oven, which was set in ye fireplace, a large platter and placed it down in front of Isaac. Looking down at ye 'feast' set in front of him, Isaac saw there were slices of thick bacon, several slices of braun (which was made from ye flesh of pigs heads) and two slices of of thick rough baked bread which had been fried in ye fat of the cooking meat. He started to eat with zest and little or no conversation took place between the two men.

After their hearty meal and when they had brushed their clothes and cleaned their boots, Isaac and Will were ready to attend the funeral of their friend Jack Grainger, as they left the Fat Friar the bell of Great Peter, boomed out the hour of nine of the clock from the Minster. They made their way to Keit's yard and they arrived just a few minutes before Keit. Paying respect to their purpose of the morning, his wishes to them to have a "good morn" were short and sombre, they saw Keit had washed down his cart and had removed all traces of plaister splashes from the cart. They carried Jack's body over and placed it on the cart and Keit checked the stitching of the shroud to ensure their were no unsightly gaps. Satisfied all was in order, Will and Isaac took hold of the shafts and set off pushing the cart, with Keit following a respectful two paces behind them as they made their way through the Citie streets to the Church of the Holy Trinity, in Gudramgate. Citizens going about their daily work or chores stopped and bowed their heads in sympathy and respect.

As they arrived at the Church, Garrison solgers were carrying the bodies of the two solgers from a waggon and into the Church, Parson Atkin was standing very solemnly waiting to accompany the deceased solgers and Jack Grainger into his Church. Parson Atkin solemnly led the group up the aisle and the three shrouded bodies were placed on trestles in front of the Altar. Both Isaac and Will throughout the short service were recalling and thinking of the events and occasions, both sad and happy which they had both shared with Jack Grainger. Parson Atkin then led the way out of the Church into the Churchyard where all three deceased were laid to rest in separate graves adjacent to each other. After the Burial Service, Parson Atkin expressed to both Will and Isaac his condolences and prior to leaving the Churchyard, Isaac passed on to him the request Squire Fewster had made for the Parson to visit him.

After leaving the Churchyard, Keit told them he would take his cart to Layerthorpe Postern, work was being done quickly to strengthen the walls, it was feared the leagers would return to renew the siege in two or three days. He left them and they made their way along Gudramgate towards Monk Bar. They noticed that horse drawn carts and waggon's were entering into the Citie, many were laden with goods for the Citie's craftsmen and others carrying food products. Children ran excitedly alongside the waggon's. The carter's, were not slow to scold the children, berating them with oaths and gestures and fiercely waving their arms. When the figure of the Constable (John Cundill)was seen approaching, the errant children moved very quickly away. Though he walked with difficulty and at times, swayed alarmingly, to the children, he was a force to be reckoned with and a visit by him to see their parent's was to be avoided at all costs.

At Monk Bar, Isaac enquired of a passing Citizen the whereabouts of the Hall of St. Anthony, he was directed to turn right into Aldwark, as they passed along the street, a platoon of Garrison solgers marched toward them heading up to Monk Bar. Upon reaching the end of Aldwark, Will pointed out St. Anthony's Hall and the pair entered through the front door into the now familiar passage leading from the entrance Hall. Mrs. Akombe was approaching them, Isaac thought to himself she was looking quite weary on this morn, she said to them, *"I think it best, for your Master not to be disturbed at present, he has a fever and I must see that he rests as much as he possibly can".* Both men looked enquiringly at each other and Isaac then said, *"Is he dying"*, gently as she always was, Mrs. Akombe said, *"If the fever can be controlled, he will improve"*. Patting Isaac on the shoulder, Will turned and said to Mrs. Akombe, *"Tha nos wat's best for 'im, can wi cum back tomorrer"*, Mrs. Akombe half-smiled and nodded her head in approval.

Leaving the Hall, the men stood outside talking and after a few minutes, with both men nodding to each other Isaac said, *"Reet, we'll go an giv' The Fat Friar, a gud cleen up"*. When they got back to the 'Fat Friar' they spent most of the afternoon cleaning and carrying out small repairs. Widow Cuthbert was delighted when she saw the result of their efforts and as she thanked them, she shed a few tears of joy. For Supper that evening, she served them salmon, she told them a 'neighbour' had trapped two that very afternoon at the weir at Na'burn. They all went to their beds that evening in a very happy state of mind, helped by freshly brewed ale.

CHAPTER XVI

A Citie in Turmoil

The next morning after a hearty breaking of their fast, Isaac and Will went to Keit's yard to feed, groom and exercise the horses, as they finished their tasks and they were making themselves ready to again visit Squire Fewster, Keit arrived, as ever he was pushing his cart, it was loaded with bundles of hay, which Keit said he had found when he had visited the Leager's camp, they had left it in their haste to leave when they heard of the arrival of Prince Rupert. So, Luke said, "*Ah thout ti mi'sen, waste nowt, want nowt*", Isaac and Will laughed and Will said to Keit, "*Tha's not got a 'oss 'ave ya*"? Smiling as usual Keit said, "*No, but you two 'ave, them 'osses 'ill eat it, won't tha,*" Isaac said, "*Keit, 'ave thout about all tha's done for us and ah want tha ta no we'll si thee's not owt a pocket wen wi leave 'ere*", Will nodded in agreement. With a thoughtful look on his face, Keit said, "*If ah can 'elp a body ah does, so don't worry*".

After unloading the hay, Keit said, "*Work at Poste'n at Layerthorp ast' to be dun ter day, leagers ah gerrin back into theer camps owtside ot' Walls, so i'll go do mi bit*". On their walk to the Hall of St. Anthony, although it was mid-afternoon

Isaac remarked to Will how quiet the Citie had become, there were very few people on the streets and no solgers were to be seen, it looked as if everyone had sought the shelter of their homes. Upon their arrival at the Hall, they entered and made their way down the passage from the from the entrance hall. They saw no sign of Mrs. Akombe, but approaching them was Mrs. Wright (the butcher's wife), whom Isaac remembered had assisted so well, to look after Luke's wife Ann at the time of the death of her Uncle Josh. They asked Mrs. Wright of the whereabouts of Mrs. Akombe, she looked at them sadly and then said, *"Ye poor lady has worked so hard in here, a Fever as tekken 'old of her, she's very poorly"*, both Isaac and Will expressed their sadness and told Mrs. Wright they they would pray for her friend.

After nodding her head in agreement, Mrs. Wright smoothed down her apron and then with a friendly smile, she said, *"Now, ow can ah 'elp you"*, Will explained to the good lady who they were and then said, *"Can we see our Master"*. She nodded and gestured with her hand that they follow her, they entered the room they had left, but a day ago. As they approached where Squire Fewster was lying abed, Mrs. Wright turned to them and whispered, *"He is sleeping, it is best if he is not awoken"*, she then stepped aside and gestured to them to approach the bed, with a re-assuring smile and in a very soft voice, she said, *"It is best if you do not stay too long"*, she turned and then left them to return to her duties and both men nodded their thanks. Looking at the Squire, Luke said to his friend, *"Ee's got ah bit o' colour in 'is face 'an 'is breathin' betta"*, Will nodded and said, *"Aye ah think 'e luks better tha 'e did"*. They stayed at the bedside, for but a few minutes, before leaving their Master and then speak to Mrs. Wright. As they got into the corridor they saw the good lady walking toward them, they asked her when they could return, thinking carefully she said,"*T'would be best if ya left it until ye morrow*". They nodded and agreed they would return on the morrow.

After leaving the Hall they decided to walk around in the Citie, in order to learn their way around the streets, they headed passed Hundegate and sauntered up St, Saviour's Lane. There was much activity along many sections of the Citie Wall and around the Gates, much of the damaged stonework was being replaced and remedial work was being done hastily. From the Monk Bar they approached the Great Minster, both men were struck in awe by the Towers and huge buttresses of that building. After leaving the Minster they made their way down Stonegate and eventually came to (the street of the furriers) Coney Street, they progressed the length of that street until they came to Ousegate. It was from here they could see the great bridge stretching across to the far side of the river, standing on the bridge they were able to look down at the staithes and wharves, they could see large boats were being unloaded as quick as possible in order they could sail south on the high tide which was due in but a few hours. Everyone was working to make the Citie safe before it it was fully besieged once again, all the Citizens going about their daily lives in the Citie, looked to be concerned and worried about how the outcome of the forthcoming weeks would affect their daily lives. They could only wait and hope.

By mid-afternoon Isaac and Will decided to return to the Fat Friar, planning to make repairs to the rickety wooden stair which led up to their garret rooms. Before they got to the Fat friar they met Keit, he was pushing his cart and Isaac was quite surprised to see the cart was empty. He told them he was going to the sawmill to get some oak joists to help strengthen the gates at Layerthorpe Posten, Isaac asked if they would be able to get timber from there to repair the

Garret stair. Keit said, *"Cum wi me, an they'll sort thee owt"*. Accompanying Keit, he took them through ginnel's and snicket's until they came to a woodyard, which was off Walmgate just behind St. Deny's Church.

Isaac and Will had discussed what they would need and knew the number and lengths they would need, the Sawyer cut the lengths of wood they required and they paid for it from the money the Squire had given them. It was all roped together and they decided it was too heavy to carry manually and would have to use the cart and team of horses, the sawyer suggested they place it in his barn until they were able to return. They decided to immediately go to Keit's yard and return to complete the task that day, they told the sawyer of their intention. They returned to the sawmill within the hour and quickly loaded the new timber onto the waggon, when they arrived outside the Fat Friar, they saw Widow Cuthbert emerging from the front door, she looked at them in bewilderment and when they explained what they intended to do, her emotions overtook her and she wept tears of joy.

Will took a large canvas sheet into the rear yard and found two trestles within the shed, he set them up and then he and Will carried the long joists (there were over a score of them) into the yard and placed them on the trestles. When that task was done they covered the wood with the waggon sheet and made it all secure. Widow Cuthbert came to the kitchen door to call them in for their evening meal. Will said, *"Well, wi'd best eat now then and tek t'osses ant' cart back wen we'v finished"*. Isaac nodded his agreement and tethered the horses to a large metal ring set in the wall. After finishing their meal, they took the horse team and cart back to Keit's yard, there they groomed, fed and watered both teams of horses and settled them into their stables for the night.

Leaving Keit's yard they set off to return to the Fat Friar, as they strolled along Hundegate, Isaac saw Keit's friend Luke Watt's, who after hearing Isaac call out his name stopped and waited until they caught up with him. He told them he was just leaving Cordwainers Hall, where he had attended a Meeting to discuss how members of the Cordwainers Guild felt concerning the relaying of the siege of the Citie . All the Craft guilds in the Citie were having Meetings and most fellow craftsmen Luke had spoken to favoured seeking terms to yield the Citie to Lord Fairfax. Whom they and most other citizens, thought was a very fair man, who could be trusted to uphold the ancient rights of the citizens. As they spoke, they suddenly heard cannon fire, Luke said, *"Aye, some say, the'd sin t' Leagers on Lamel Hill, now the'v let us no the'v set theer cannon's back up"*. Both Isaac and Will nodded and Isaac said, *"Ah think them shots was ta let us 'ear they wer' back"*, shaking his head slightly Luke said, *"Aye ya reet theer"*. The three men said their goodbye's and Luke moved on toward Aldwark,.

There was no more cannon fire as Isaac and Will continued their walk back to the 'Fat Friar', but just as they were entering the Hostelry further shots were heard, the sound came from the same direction as the previous shots. The two friends opened the door and they stepped inside. They saw Widow Cuthbert sitting in her favourite chair at the side of the fireplace and four members of the Citie trained bands were sitting at a table to the left of the door, their Muskets were standing against the wall in the corner behind them, their conversation was hushed, their faces solemn.

Crossing the room Isaac and Will went to the table at the fireplace and seated themselves in the company of the good lady, who smiled them a welcome and bade them both to partake of a tankard of ale, thanking her, they went across to the gantry and filled a tankard from a cask of their chosen brew. As they returned to their seats they could hear nine of the clock tolling out from Great Peter at the Minster. As if prompted by the tolling, the Trained Bands members rose and each man picked up his musket and re-arranged his bags of powder and shot, before they headed to the door and left the building, they faced a night on the Wall guarding the Citie. Their thoughts would like most of the other citizens, were the leagers were likely to attack before terms of surrender were discussed. When they were alone, Widow Cuthbert told Will and Isaac, that she had heard that Sir John Glenham had told the Lord Mayor that he would ensure the Citie was held to the last man and she had also heard that Sir John in his capacity as Governor of the Citie had sent a message to King Charles, assuring him the Citie would be held. The Lord Mayor, had advised Sir John, that the Craftsmen and Citizens alike, were against another long Siege.

When they took their leave, to retire to bed, both Isaac and Will had heavy hearts and were concerned about events that may happen in the ensuing days and weeks. The next morning following the breaking of their fast, Will and Isaac set out to visit the Hall of St. Anthony, to seek news of the health of their Master, Squire Fewster. Upon entering the Hall, they sought out Mrs. Wright and they finally found her in a small kitchen, set back from the main corridor. She was filling a number of large pitchers with water from a large wooden rain water butt, which was standing on a gantry at the side of the sink. Isaac called out, *"Mrs. Wright, 'ello"*. As she turned to face them both men could see she had been weeping heavily and grief was showing on her face.

She took a kerchief from the pocket of her apron and slowly dabbed tears away from her eyes, then she moved across toward a table and seated herself upon one of the chairs, she gestured the two men to sit also. The lady looked somewhat bewildered and said, *"I am sorry I am so upset, Mrs. Akombe, passed into the hands of our dear Lord, during the night"*. Isaac was saddened to hear the news, the lady had been so helpful and kind to him for the few days he had known her. He expressed his sadness to Mrs. Wright, he said, *"I am sorry to 'ear thi news, she wah a kind an' gentel woman"*, tearfully Mrs. Wright nodded her agreement. After again using her kerchief, she turned to Isaac, she said, *"I am pleased to tell you that your Master is much stronger today and you can go si im', 'es in the same bed, Parson Atkin 'as bin ta see 'im, he left jus' afore you got 'ere"*.

Taking their leave from Mrs. Wright, Isaac and Will made their way to see their Master, as they moved toward his bed they could see he was in a sitting position on the bed, he was supported by many pillows and bolsters. When they reached his bedside, he smiled broadly at them and bade them closer to him. He told them he was feeling much stronger and his wounds were not as painful, he then asked them if they heard from or any information regarding his brother Sir George, both men shook their heads dolefully. He went on to tell them, that his Surgeon had told him, that if he continued to regain his strength, he may in a few days be fit enough to move out into private Lodging of his own choice, he then said, *"The cleric you saw, has visited me and I have asked him to seek out suitable Lodging for me"*. The two servants were surprised, but pleased at the news their Master had given to them, they both nodded and smiled at him.

The Squire appeared to be deep in thought and Isaac and Will stood watching him and they waited, not wanting to distract him. After a few minutes he turned to them and said, *"I wish you to come to see me each day, the good Cleric will return and advise me, whence he is able to find somewhere that will be suitable for my needs"*. After pausing for a minute or so, he went on to say, *"As you go about the Citie, please make enquiry for news of my brother, Sir George"*. After enquiring about the horses, the Squire told both men, *"Whilst we are sheltering in the Citie, if you can, you should try to make use of them and yourselves to help in defending York"*. Nodding their heads in agreement with their Master's instruction, Isaac and Will left the bedside and withdrew back to the Hallway and after saying their goodbyes to Mrs. Wright, they left the Hall.

In the course of the next few days, Will and Isaac were able to use the waggon and horses to help in work of repairing and strengthening the Citie walls, each day they helped Keit in the area of the Postern at Layerthorpe and shoring up work near the Castle Mills. Many waggon loads of rock and rubble were carted to those sites and set in place as directed by the Stonemason's at each site. As they made their journeys back and forth across the Citie they saw each day right across the Citie, Garrison solgers carrying their fallen comrades from the Battle into different Churches across the Citie. Other funerals were taking place on the day when long with Keit, both Isaac and Will attended the funeral Service of Mrs. Akombe which took place in the Church of St. Crux, Isaac realised what a popular and well loved woman she must have been, the Church was crowded, Craftsmen and their wives from so many of the Citie Guilds filled the Church. As they left the Church amongst the throng of mourners, Isaac saw amongst the Citizens that Keit was in deep conversation with Luke Watts.

When they stepped from the Church gates into Gudramgate, they made their way toward Adwark, as they were turning into that street, Keit caught up with them, he was quite breathless due to dashing to catch up with them. Upon regaining his breath he said, *"Luke, as told me, Lord Halifax an' t' other Parliament Generals 'ad teld t' Governor ta tu'n Citie ovver to 'em an' t' that Lord Mayor an' t Governor 'ave asked leager General's ta parley wi 'em"*. Both Will and Isaac looked at him in surprise and Keit went on to say, *"They's agreed to it"*, Isaac was pleased with the news he had just been given and smilingly, he said to Keit, *"Ah 'ope they end this bloodshed"*, his two companions nodded their heads in agreement. Throughout that week the topic of conversation amongst all sections of the Citizens had been about sightings that the Parliamentarians had been seen raising Batteries around the Citie and rumours were now widespread that the roundheads had been making many ladders with which to climb the Walls when they stormed the Citie.

At the end of the following week, on the day before the Sabbath, three gentlemen who were men of honour and rank, volunteered to present themselves to the Parliamentary Generals as Hostages, in a gesture to display that the safety of the Parliament Officers would not be at risk whilst Parleying was taking place in the Citie with the Governor, the Lord Mayor and other prominent Citizens. The discussions were hard and unrelenting between the two sides and went on throughout the day and carried on until nearly nightfall. At this time the Parliament Officers left the Citie and returned to report their progress to their Commanders and to seek permission to allow the Parley to continue the following day, despite it being the Sabbath Day. Approval was given and the Parleying continued throughout the Sabbath Day, until finally during the morning of the following day full agreement was reached and at the noon hour, the Parliament representatives left the Citie, taking the Articles for their Generals to subscribe to.

After the Parliamentarians had left the Citie, Citizens were upon the streets, standing on corners in small groups, there was hope that the Parley had been successful and that the Siege would be lifted. In the late afternoon four Heralds road forth from the garrison at Cliffords Tower, each to a different part of the Citie and within but a short space of time, word spread right through the Citie that the Siege was to end on the morrow. There was much cheering, excitement and looks of great relief showing on the faces of most of the people. Isaac and Will were just returning on the waggon to Keit's yard, when they heard the news, both men beamed, with broad smiles on their faces. The news on everyone's lips, was that Garrison Solgers and all Royalist followers who wanted to do so, would be be afforded Safe Passage from the Citie, pledges had been made that their departure out of the Citie, which would start at noontime on the morrow, would not be hindered by any Solgers from the Parliamentarian Armies.

Isaac and Luke decided they would visit Squire Fewster "poste haste" to inform him of the glad tidings. Upon arriving at the Hall of St. Anthonie and approaching their Master's bedside they saw he was sitting up in his bed and was looking very pleased, he told them had already been informed of the cessation of the Siege, but, then he went on to say, *"Parson Atkin has visited me and told me he has secured a Lodging for me with two devout Christian Ladies, who live in The Ogleforth, in the shadow of the Minster and he is arranging with them for me move, in but two days time"*. He paused and then went on to say, *"I need you to bring the waggon on the day I move and then both of you can assist in my removal"*. Both men nodded and Isaac said, *"W'at time of tha day, dost tha want us here Squire"*. Thinking for a moment, Squire Fewster said, *"I think it would be best if you came at ten of the clock"*. After nodding their heads, to indicate they understood, both men withdrew from the bedside and made their way out of the building.

Isaac and Will made little conversation to each other as they wended their way through the streets to return to the Fat Friar and as they approached the Church of St. Crux, both men stopped and bowed their heads in respect, as they saw two shrouded bodies which were laying upon stout planks on the bed of a cart outside the Church were pulled from the cart by Garrison Solders and carried solemnly into the Church. Several other bedraggled and weary looking Solgers followed their dead comrades into the Church. As they turned to continue their journey Isaac, said to his friend, *"Ah just 'ope wi niver 'ave ta si killing like this ever agin"*, Will nodded in agreement and said, *"Tha's reet theer, Isaac"*. They arrived back at the Fat Friar and went straight inside to the Parlour to seek out Widow Cuthbert. The good lady was over by the gantry, she was struggling unsuccessfully, to roll a small cask (a Firkin) onto the gantry. Both men stepped forward and took over from the frail old lady and under her supervision they restocked the gantry to her satisfaction.

After finishing their task and whilst Widow Cuthbert was in her kitchen fussing over the cooking of Supper, Will set about making repairs to some stools, which he had found when checking them some days previously. Isaac in the meantime was busy washing the grime from the glass of the window frames both inside and outside, as he was admiring his handiwork, Widow Cuthbert entered from the kitchen and told them to step up to the table as Supper was ready. Whilst they were having their meal, Widow Cuthbert espied the newly repaired stools and thanked Will for his handiwork She also remarked upon how much lighter the room was and complimented Isaac for his efforts.

At midday on the on the following morrow, it was a sad sight for many citizens of the ancient Citie, as they stood and watched as columns of weary and bedraggled solgers of the Royalist Army, trudged along the narrow streets toward, Micklegate Bar where they left the Citie, many would desert and return to their homes, they believed the Royalist cause was lost in the North. It was but a little time after the remnants of the Royalists had left, that the Army of Parliament headed by their Generals and followed by their cavalry, the breastplates and helmets of the riders glittering and shining in the sun light caught the shiny surfaces and then the bright colours of the banners of each regiment fluttering and rustling in the breeze, but throughout all of the columns there was order amongst the solgers, the watching citizens were mostly quiet, but at certain points there was some cheers of welcome as the columns passed by.

In the later hours of the afternoon, the Generals and Officers of the parliament Army accompanied by some of their Regiments attended a Service of Thanksgiving in the Minster, in order to give thanks for the deliverance of the Citie to them with so little blood shed. In the Citie meanwhile the common solgers of the Parliament Army with but few exceptions obeyed the Order which had been delivered to them by their Generals to respect the Citizens and their homes and personal property. In the few instances where the Order had been disobeyed, the culprits were heavily punished as an example to others in order to prevent similar future incidents.

Within a few days of the Citie having being rendered to the Armies of Parliament, two of the Armies left the Citie, leaving Lord Halifax as Governor of the Citie, his Lordship also dismissed some five hundred of his Cavalry from the Citie. Lord Halifax met with all sections of the Citizens to discuss all means which could be made to restore the extensive damage which had been caused throughout the Citie during the three months of besiegement. Much work would be needed to repair homes which had sustained damage, the River Ouse and it's wharves would need much attention to enable goods to be transported from and into the Citie. The Postmaster of the Citie was now receiving large quantities of Mail from all over the Country, much of which was dated from the time the Citie came under under Siege.

On the day following the departure from the Citie of the two Parliamentary Armies, Isaac and Will, assisted by Keit, arrived at the Hall of St. Anthony at ten o'the clock as they had been instructed by Squire Fewster. Upon their arrival they were met in the Hallway by Mrs. Wright, she bade them follow her into the kitchen, she said to them, *"I am sorry to tell you that your Master has received some very sad news. A messenger came to tell him that Sir George Fewster, your Masters' brother had sadly been killed in the battle. It was quite a shock to him and it upset him quite badly, he is presently sitting quietly in a small Ante room down the corridor"*. Isaac and Will thanked Mrs. Wright for her thoughtfullness and with a faint smile on her face, she bade them to follow her down the corridor. Toward the far end of the corridor she stopped outside a door, she knocked gently before she opened the door and stepped inside, gesturing the three men to follow her.

Isaac was shocked when he saw Squire Fewster, he saw before him a frail, stooped and weary looking old man, he looked at them sadly and said, *"My grief has overcome me, but I must seek to regain my strength, in order that I may return to my beloved wife"*. Isaac nodded his head in agreement and said, *"Master, we have come to take you to your Lodge in The*

Ogleforth, where rest and care by the two Gentle Ladies will speed your recovery". The Squire raised his head toward them, as if to speak, but then indicated his agreement with a nod of his head. Whilst Mrs. Wright fussed over the Squire straightening his bandages and draping a woollen blanket around his shoulders and upper body, Keit pointed out to Issaac and Will, a sturdy looking Armchair which had large castors, it was standing in a corner of the room.

They assisted the Squire to the armchair and they took good care he was sitting comfortably in the armchair and they found they could push it along the corridor without too much difficulty. After safely descending the steps at the front door, they stopped at the side of the waggon, Will let down the side of the waggon and with Isaac and Keit lifting the armchair, still with the Squire sitting in it upwards to the flatbed of the waggon, where Will who was standing was able to assist them to place the armchair onto the waggon. Isaac asked the Squire if he was comfortable and with a slight smile Squire Fewster nodded his approval. Keit suggested they leave the Squire in the chair for the journey and suggested he would go back to see Mrs. Wright and obtain her approval for them to return the chair after they had transported the Squire. Upon returning he told them the good lady approved of their request and thought the patient would have a more comfortable journey. As Great Peter tolled the midday hour from the top of the Minster, Isaac and Will left their Master comfortably ensconced in his new Lodging in Ogleforth the two gentlewomen still fussing around him.

As they stepped outside the house they espied Keit, he was sitting on the flatbed of the waggon with his feet dangling down, Will said to him, *"Where da ya want ta go now"*. After thinking for a moment, Keit turned and looking at Will he said, *"Ah 'ave a big job to do at Merchant's Hall, ah want sum clay from t' Bishop' Field's, an' sum straw an cowclap from t' farm jus' near Houlgate, ah won't gerrit all on mi cart, can'st ya bring this 'ere waggon ah yours and giv' mi a hand"*. Smiling broadly, Will said, *"Keit, after all thou's dun fa Isaac an' mi it'd 'elp us ta say thanks ta ya, let's get started"*. They all boarded the waggon and after crossing Ouse Bridge, they left the Citie after passing through Lendal Postern.

After which they followed a track about a furlong's width from the river and followed it's course for some distance, after they had gone about half a mile from the Citie Walls, Keit told Will to pull the cart off to the left onto bumpy land with very little grass, the area was littered with water filled pits, some much larger than others. Keit jumped down from the waggon and took a spade from the waggon he said Keit to Isaac and Will, *"Both of ya grab a spade and follow me"*, both men did as they had been bidden and then struggled on the uneven ground as they followed their friend, as he walked in front, Keit was half turning as he looked over his shoulder and he said, *"This is't Bishop's Field, an't Roman's med briks in't kilns on 'ere, an' I cum an' get clay off 'ere ta mek mi plaister wi"*.

He came to a sandy area and taking a bundle of hessian sacks which was hanging from his bel Keit picked up his shovel, he called out to Will and Isaac to similarly take a shovel and he walked a few paces, to where he saw a level piece of ground and thence started digging and removing the top surface, bidding his companions to do likewise. It was hard work, but after they had filled and loaded a score or so of the hessian sacks onto the waggon, Keit said to his companions, *"Reet lads, wi just 'ave ta go up track a bit and get sum cow pats owt ot' field"*. When they got to the field they found it much easier to fill hessian sack with cowpats, than it had been with the clay and in a very short time they had all climbed back onto the waggon and were making their way into the Citie, After they had passed through Lendal Postern, Keit directed Will the way to take to get back to his yard. When they got to the yard, they unloaded the hessian sacks in a corner of the paddock at the side of the barn, close to some large stone troughs.

Keit looked upto the sky and said, *"Yon sky luk's non ta safe ta mi, ah think tha'll be evvy rain inside of an 'our"*. Will and Isaac nodded their agreement and Will said, *"Aye, ah think Isaac, we'd best get waggon put away an' stable t' 'osses for neet"*. They quickly fed and watered all four horses and stabled them for the night and after saying their goodbyes to Keit they made their way to the 'Fat Friar'. Widow Cuthbert was pleased to see them and told them to each take a tankard of Ale and she would call them when she needed a hand to bring the food through from the kitchen, after they had filled their tankards, they were just sitting down at the table when she called to them, they went to help carry the food through .

They were part way through their meal, when they heard the front doorsneck rattle loudly, the door opened and Luke stepped over the threshold. After closing the door, he approached the table and said, *"Will, can ah ask a favour of thee,"* Will glanced toward Isaac and then turning to Luke he smiled and said, *"Luke wi ah in det ta ya, 'ow can wi 'elp ya"*. Luke took a stool and moved it closer to the table and seated himself upon it, slowly moved his hat round between his fingers, before saying, *"Ah ast ta start early in tha morn, ta collect about five score o' sheepskin's from my brother Matt's farm at Poppleton, an' ah thout if ya 'elpt mi wi ya waggon, wi cud move t' lot in one go"*. Both Will and Isaac smiled nodded their heads in agreement and Will said, *"We'll be up at crack o' dawn ta 'elp ya Luke"* and all three men shook each others hands vigorously. Luke then said, *"Canst wi start at seven o' the clock from mi workshop"*, Will said, *"We'll be theer wi t' osses an t' waggon"*. Mumbling his thanks Luke left them to finish their meal.

On the morrow Big Peter was tolling out the hour of seven o' the clock , just as the waggon with Will and Isaac aboard, stopped at the corner of Trinity Passage, they waved as they saw Luke standing outside his workshop, he saw them and began walking toward the waggon. He climbed onto the waggon and sat on the high seat with Will and Isaac, with Luke giving directions they passed through the narrow Citie streets and after crossing the river at Ouse Bridge they finally left the Citie at Lendal Postern.

The journey along the riverside tracks to Poppleton was uneventful and the sun was getting warmer as it rose higher into the sky. as they approached the end of what had been a particularly long track they saw the gate ahead of them was closed. Will let his horse team walk right up to the gate, where they stopped, Luke jumped down and opened the gate and the horses pulled the waggon through, Will halted the horses, until Luke clambered back onto the waggon and settled himself back onto his seat. After Luke had finished shuffling his rump about to make himself comfortable, he said, *"Reet Will, wi tu'n left 'ere an' foller this track reet up ta weer yon copse' is, an track bends round ta left theer, 'an ya can si Matts' Farm 'ouse in front thee"*.

They soon reached the Farmhouse and Luke directed Will to pass some stacks of Hay in the fold yard and then carry on into the stable yard, Will flicked the reins and stopped the horses in front of the barn door. They all jumped down from the waggon, after he had bent his back and knees, followed by arm stretches,, Luke stood upright he turned to Will and Isaac, he was about to speak when a man came round the corner of the barn and he called out a greeting and walked quickly toward Luke, whereupon both men shook each others hand warmly. Looking at the man, Isaac was surprised at how much the man looked like Luke, they were obviously brothers.

Turning to face his friends, Luke introduced his brother Abraham to them, they chatted together for a few minutes and then Abraham turned to his brother and said, *"Reet luke, ah'd best shew yu thee's skins"*, and turning he pushed open the large doors of the barn. Isaac saw within some neat lines of about half a score of trestles, the sheep hides were hanging along the length of each trestle. Luke walked amongst the lines and checked several hides. Finally, with a beaming smile across his face, he said to Abraham, *" Aye them 'ides ah sum o't best ah's sin in many a year"*. Abraham with a broad smile on his face said, *"Ah'm glad, ah'll let thee get on wi ladin 'em then, ah'll si thee afore tha go's"*.

After Abraham had disappeared round the corner of the barn, Luke said, *"Reet, let's get on wi it"*. Will climbed back onto the waggon and Luke and Isaac went into the barn, each hide had a small hole punched into the top left hand corner where strong binding thread had been passed through fastening the hides together in bundles of half a dozen. The three men worked well together and when they got to the last trestle, Luke paused and said to Isaac, *"If thou two ad not 'elped mi out, it wud ah tekken me weeks ta get em ta York, ah'd 'ave ta push ah few at a time on Keit's cart"*. Smiling to each other both men took a bundle of hides from the trestle. After they had put their final bundle onto the waggon, Will placed them into position and turning to Luke, he said, *"Tha's a score of bundles wi'v got on 'ere"*. Luke nodded and said, *"That's reet, an now wi can mek tracks for York"*.

At this point there was a shout from behind them, turning they saw Abraham had come round the corner of the barn and was walking toward them. Looking at his brother, he said, *"Tha's bin quick wi that job, tha's not bin but an 'our on't clock"*. Pointing at Will and Isaac, Luke replied, *"Tha's two good men 'ere"*. Abraham smiled and nodded his agreement, *"Now"*, said Luke to his brother, *"Ah ya still happy ah pays mi dues ta ya on Lammas Day"*. Nodding his head in agreement, Abraham held out his hand which Luke shook warmly. Luke turned and climbed onto the waggon, where he took his place on the high seat at the side of Isaac and Will. Having sat down, Luke started to shift his rump about on the seat in all manner of ways, before announcing to Isaac and Will, *"Reet, now I am seated, let us go to York"*. The return journey to York was uneventful and little was said by any of them until they were close to Lendal Postern, at which point Luke said to Will, *"As wi get throu't gate, tu'n ta t' reet an ya'll si Tannery Gate"*. Will acknowledged the instruction with a nod of his head. At the gates jumped down, he went forward and took hold of the bridle of the nearest horse and led them through the gate.

As he stopped the horses, Luke got down and walked to his side, he said, *"Tha'll' ave ta get waggon under yon hook"*, and he pointed upwards to the top of the nearest building, Will looked and right at the top of the building, he could see, set in the wall an open door which led onto a wooden platform, this was surrounded by a metal guardrail, protruding above the door was a large metal hook, it was secured by metal brackets to the wall of the building Will led his team round and brought them to a halt, the waggon was positioned directly under the hook, as he was giving each the horses a nosebag, there was a shout from above, a man was standing on the platform and Will saw the hook was being lowered, he waved acknowledgement up to the man and stepped back from the waggon.

Luke said, *"A'll go an find Tanner an settel mi bill wi 'im, mebbe ya can both mek a start loading"*, aye said Isaac, *"Will an' me a'll get on wi it"*. Luke entered the building through a nearby doorway and Isaac and Will got up onto the bed of the waggon, the hook was suspended above the flat bed of the waggon at about shoulder height. Hanging from the hook was a net, which was attached to the hook by a looped rope at each corner. Will unhooked the ropes and laid the net upon the flat bed of the waggon and he and Isaac gathered up one of the parcels of hides each and laid them upon the net. They then picked up two ropes each and attached the net back onto to the hook and when ready, they shouted to the man above who shouted to someone within the door and the net and skins were hauled upwards. The work went well and in but one hour of the clock, the last bale was rising steadily to the top of the building.

After the man at the top had dragged the last bale inside the building, he returned onto the platform and after a cheerful shout and a wave to them he returned inside the building and closed the door. Isaac and Will jumped down from the wagggon and Will went to the horses and removed nosebags and put them under his seat, they were both empty. Upon looking across the yard, Will noticed a large stone trough, he walked over to it and was pleased when he saw it contained water, he returned to the waggon he rummaged his hand into a recess which was built into the side of the waggon and took out two leather buckets, returning to the trough he filled both buckets with water and set off back to the waggon, he asked Isaac to hold one bucket up to one horse whilst he similarly dealt with the other. Both animals drank greedily and after taking their fill, they both tossed their heads about, almost as if offering their thanks.

As Will was replacing the buckets into the recess of the waggon, Luke appeared from out of the building, he said, *"Ah nivver thout it wud tek mi so long"*, Isaac and Will smiled and were shaking their heads, Luke, with a puzzled look on his face, said, *"Ah wud ah bin back ta gi thee a 'and, but,'old Silas Tanner, well e' ju' keeps on talking"*. Will said, *"An e' ju's stopped wen we got job dun?* Looking quite hurt, Luke said, *"Nay, tha can go an' ask if tha wants"*. Isaac and Will roared with laughter at Luke and Isaac said, *"Will's pullin thi leg, Luke"*, feeling a little silly at his own response, Luke too, started to laugh, along with his friends. When they had all calmed down, Will said,

"Well wi'd best be mekking a move, let's get 'osses ta stable, an a'll drop thee off at thi workshop Luke". Will and Isaac were already sitting and waiting and by the time Luke finally climbed aboard and after much shuffling and grunting, he finally managed to get his rump into a comfortable position on the seat. Luke then turned to Will and said, *"Well if tha's reet, let's get moving"*.

They dropped Luke off close to his workshop and set off to Keit's yard to stable the horses, they were just about to leave the yard, after feeding and watering the horses, when Keit himself came through the gate pushing his cart. He was as usual smiling broadly, he stopped and wiped his brow with his kerckief and said to them, *"Ast' tha seen Parson Atkin, he cem 'ere looking fa thee both."* Isaac said to Keit, *"Did 'e say w'at 'e wanted us fa,"* Kiet shook his head and said, *"No 'e went ta Fat Friar, ta si if yo'd gon' back theer"*. They both thanked Keit and set off for the Fat Friar, they walked faster than they normally would, they were both concerned why Parson Atkin was seeking them out and also they were feeling hungry and they were looking forward to another of Widow Cuthbert's tasty dinners.

As they entered the Fat Friar, both Isaac and Will were a little out of breath, Widow Cuthbert was sitting in her armchair at the side of the fireplace, Isaac saw there were still some glowing embers in the firegrate. She looked at them and said, *"I'st Constable chasin ya both, 'ave ya bin brekkin' t'law ?"* Both men protested their innocence, with a laugh she went on to say, *"Well, Parson Atkin, as bin after ya both, that Squire fellow on yorn, sez 'e want's ta si ya both"*.

Will said, *"Did I' Parson say why ? "*. With a shake of her head, the good lady said, *"Tha'd best go ta si 'im now and a'll ave ya Dinners ont' table for ya w'en ya get back"*. Nodding their heads in agreement and Isaac said, *"Reet, we'd best get on our way"*.

When they got outside, Will said, *"Wat's 'e want, da ya think"*, Isaac shook his head and said *"We'll soon no w'en wi get theer"*. Both men nodded and continued their walk, each having his own thoughts. Turning into Ogleforth they saw the street was deserted, they approached the home of the good ladies taking care of their Master. In answer to their knock on the door, a maid servant opened the door and took them to their Master's quarters. Squire Fewster was sitting reading a book and upon their entry into the room, he turned and placed it upon a small table at the side of his chair. As he turned back to face them, he was smiling broadly and he said, *"I have some very good news, my Surgeon came and examined me this morn, he has agreed that I am fit enough to make the journey home"*. Will said, *"Both me and Isaac are happy to 'ear that news Master, what do ya need us ta do"*. After spending some minutes, thinking deeply whilst stroking his chin with his hand, he looked up and said, *"It is, but two days to the Sabbath Day, on the following morn, Monday, can you have all packed onto the waggon and both horse teams ready to set off"*. Will and Isaac looked at each other and Will said, *"All will be ready on Monday morn Master"*. Squire Fewster, still smiling said, *"I thank you both, this day has indeed been uplifting for me"*. Nodding his head Will said, *"We will go now Master and make ready for Monday Morn"*.

After leaving the lodging of Squire Fewster, both Isaac and Will were silent for several minutes and then they both started chattering about the arrangements they needed to to make and make plans for the journey, It was Will's opinion that it would be better for their Master's health if they made their journey in just one day. He told Isaac that because they had the two teams of horses they could interchange the horse teams during the journey, he went on to say they would need to make an early start (6 o' the clock) and if the could get some wooden mounting steps, the Squire could ascend and descend from the waggon much more easily. Isaac said, *"Ah agree wi tha, we'll think it over t' neet"*. Will nodded his head and said, *"Aye"*. Little more was said until they arrived back at the Fat Friar".

They told Widow Cuthbert of their news, she told them she would sadly miss them both, they had been a good help to her, she uderstood they would want to get back home, but they would be most welcome if either of them returned to the Citie in the future. There was little conversation whilst they ate supper, whilst both Isaac and Will were pleased at the thought of going home, they were both also sad to be leaving behind this kind old lady, who had looked after them so well. Isaac, awoke as the sun was rising and he could hear Will whistling cheerfully in the adjacent room, as Isaac was dressing the aroma of frying Ham came drifting into his room, as it slowly drifted up the Garret stair from the kitchen below.

After breaking their fast, they made their way to Keit's yard, they hoped to speak to him before he set off after loading his cart to go to work. When they entered the yard they saw he was still there and as he turned round, he saw them and waved his arm in their direction. When they told him of their impending departure, at first he went quiet and he looked disappointed but after a few moments he brightened up and wanted to know when they were going and what plans they had. They told him of the plans they had started to make and when they mentioned how they were seeking some kind of mounting steps, to enable the Squire mount and discount from the waggon, he smiled broadly.

He said, *"Tha's no need ta wurry, ah'll si to that for ya"*. Isaac and Will thanked him warmly and after arranging to meet up with him later in the day, Keit set off to start his job for the day.

Upon Keit's departure, Will said, *"Well fust job I 'ave ta do, is check t' osses and giv' em all a gud scrub and groom em, then ya can walk em roun' paddock an I'll luk at em ta see if tha's any lameness"*. Putting on his smock, Isaac said, *"Aye reet, I'll mek a start on checking waggon out, until tha's reddy for mi ta walk 'em wi ya"*. They spent most of the morning at Keit's yard, carrying out all the tasks they felt were necessary to ensure that the waggon and both teams of horses would be ready for the journey back to Leake. As Great Peter at York Minster tolled the hour of four o' the clock, Will said, *"Ah think wi shud ah sum vittels, wat think ya on going back ta si Widow Cuthbert, an' eat wi 'er at Fat Friar"*, Isaac nodded in agreement and after turning the horses free into the paddock and securing the gate they made their way through the Citie to the hostelry.

Widow Cuthbert was pleased to see them and told them she had just cooked a sheep's head in the kitchen and if they had time to spare they could partake of sheep broth and newly baked bread rolls. Both men nodded and said they had time to spare. Whilst they waited they decided to re stock the casks on the gantry, a job which did not take them very long to complete. After finishing the job, they had just sat down on a bench alongside the large rough hewn oak table when Widow Cuthbert came shuffling through carrying platters and spoons, she said, *"Can one o' yah carry the cauldron of broth in from the kitchen"*, Will rose and soon returned carrying the steaming cauldron, he placed it upon a metal grid iron the middle of the table. The aroma from the steam arising from the cauldron, the smell of the herbs and meat wafted around the table, the good Widow passed generous helpings to both men and the meal continued as they each sampled and enjoyed their food.

On the following morning after they had broken their fast, Will and Isaac, made their way to Keit's yard. Upon their arrival, they were both surprised to find both Keit and Luke were already there. Smiling broadly, Keit said, *"Luke 'as cum ta giv mi 'and ta mek a Mounting Step ta get Squire Fewster ont' waggon wi' out brekkin 'is neck"*. Isaac replied, *"Ya such gud frends, 'ow can wi ever repay ya ?"* Luke slowly shook his head and gesturing his hand toward Kiet, said, *"It is we who ah in debt ta both on you"*. They all laughed together in merriment and then set about their varying tasks.

When Great Peter tolled out the mid day hour,. they all took a break for refreshment Luke had brought along a large wedge of cheese, Keit went to his cart and from it took a canvas bag from which he produced four loaves of rough baked bread. Isaac and Will exchanged questioning looks and Isaac said, *"Ta slek our thu'st, wi 'ave on't waggon, Ale in t' barell wi brout' wi us"*. Keit, smiling broadly said, *"Well, it luk's as if wi ah 'avin a feest"*. There was much chattering as the men partook of their meal, Luke said, *"Ah as no memory of us 'avin a feest as fillin a afor' us now, an' bin as'appi"*. His fellow diners all nodded their agreement, but strangely, no one thought to pause their eating to speak in response. Reluctantly, after having their *"Feest"*, they resumed their tasks, there was little banter as each man, gave thought to his own experiences as he examined his own personal trials, fears and sadness, which they had all endured whilst the Citie had been besieged and now it was over.

– o0o –

Upon awaking on Monday morn, Isaac was dazzled by the sunlight, after breaking their fast and saying their farewell to Widow Cuthbert, both Isaac and Will, left the "Fat Friar" and made their way to Keit's yard. Upon arrival they set about feeding and watering the horses, Will had on the previous day, already prepared and set out all the gear for the animals, harnesses, bridles, traces, reins, girth bands and nose bags, along with numerous other smaller pieces of equipment. They had started to prepare the team which Luke had selected for the first leg of the journey, when Kiet and Luke arrived. Keit said, *"Tell us wat wi can do ta 'elp"*, Will asked them to pull the waggon out of the barn and position it outside the door. A short while later, everything was neatly stacked on the waggon, Will had placed the first team onto the waggon shaft and the second team were fastened to the rear by their bridle rope. They were ready to set off, Kiet and Luke insisted they would accompany them to the Squire's lodging to assist with helping the Squire to board the waggon if they were needed.

After arriving at Squire Fewster's lodge, his personal baggage was quickly loaded and after their Master had expressed his thanks and said his goodbyes to the two sisters who had cared for him and to Parson Atkin, who was also waiting to wish him farewell, Squire Fewster attended by Isaac and Will left the house and went outside to the waggon. Keit and Luke had the Mounting Step in place and with little help needed from his attendants the Squire, safely boarded the waggon and made himself comfortable in the chair they had put in place for him. Isaac and Will sadly and with emotion said their goodbyes to Keet and Luke, as they turned to get on ther waggon, Keit took hold of Isaac's arm and said, *"Tek, this letter wi yah, Luke writ it fa mi, but, fra both on us, yur our frend"*, they then boarded the waggon, taking hold of the reins, Will clicked his tongue and the animals moved off, the waggon wheels rattling on the cobbles. They were on their way Home!

CHAPTER XVII

Returning Home

After leaving the Citie through Bootham Bar, Will took the road to Clifton and after passing through Clifton village they went straight on, following the sign to Skelton. After passing through Shipton, Squire Fewster asked Isaac to take a bottle of wine from a canvas bag in his baggage and prepare a drink of it in a suitable receptical for him. Isaac carried out his Master's bidding and gave him the wine in a small pewter vessel. The Squire took the vessel and the contents, he took a drink, he savoured the flavour and then swallowed it. Turning to Isaac, he said, *"Excellent, thank you Isaac"*, Isaac smiled at his Master and then returned to take his seat alongside Will.

Will looking up at the sky ahead of them and seeing quite a number of dark clouds coming their way, he said to Isaac, *"It luk's as if wi cud get a bit of a yon wet stuff dropping on us, ad wi best stop an put sum waggon cuvvers ower top of us"*, looking in the direction his friend was pointing, Isaac nodded his head in agreement and said, *"Aye tha's reet, wi shud"*. With a gentle pull on the reins Will guided his team of horses to the side of the track and the team stopped at his call. As Will placed the upright wooden beams into their different slots, Isaac placed corresponding cross pieces into the beams facing each other across the waggon, both men then draped the canvas awnings over the cross struts, when they had completed their task, Will said, *"That awning 'ill keep us dry fra most o't wet"*.

They resumed their journey and the rain was quite heavy for a few miles and then as suddenly as it had started, it ceased and the Sun broke through the cloud, Isaac said, *"Tha's no need ta stop, i'll tek awning off"*, Will nodded his head in agreement and Isaac got on with his task, he pulled the awning carefully down from it's supporting beams and neatly folded it placed it at the back of the waggon, it was easily accessible, should they need it ina hurry. Isaac left the spars and the supporting beams in place, in case they should be needed quickly.

Shortly after they had passed through Easingwold, Will pulled into the side of the track, turning to Isaac, *"Osses can 'ave a nosebag, wi can let 'em get sum water donw em in yon beck and then wi can 'ave sum vittals as well"*. Isaac glanced toward Squire Fewster and saw he was sleeping, at that moment he awakened, Isaac told him of their intention. The Squire nodded his and said, *"The godly matrons who have looked after me so well, have packed a cold meal for my journey, it is in my travelling bag, could you get it for me Isaac, I think also that another measure of that excellent wine would greatly compliment my food"*.

Isaac said, *"I will get it for you Master"*, he quickly found the food all nicely parcelled in a small basket and wrapped in a crisp white linen Napkin. Isaac gave the basket to Squire Fewster and then returned with the wine, to make things easier for the Squire, Isaac dragged over a heavy Coffer and placed it close to the side of his Master and placed the pewter vessel upon it.

Will and Isaac were quite surprised, when they examined the leather bag which Widow Cuthbert had given them for their journey. They found that along with a corked leather urn (which upon tasting, both men decided contained fruit Wine which the good Widow had brewed herself) there was also a number of small loaves of rough baked bread, legs of roast chicken and Rabbit and two small cheeses. They sat at the side of the waggon and they had a real "banquet".

Alas, their feast could not last forever and they set about changing the horse teams and making preparations to resume their journey. The afternoon was passing quite quickly, Isaac said to Will, "*Ah can't but wunder, ah mile or so and we'll bi in Thirsk*", Will smiled and said, "*Aye, ah nivver thout wi'd si this ere place ag'in*". As they looked ahead familiar sights grew closer and then they began to see people whom they knew and friendly shouts and banter were exchanged. Leaving Thirsk behind, both Isaac and Will were getting excited as they approached Little Leake and then Isaac and Will, quickly joined by Squire Fewster all shouted with delight when they saw Leake Church. After but a few yards Will twitched on the reins and the waggon turned and passed through the gates into the Manor House.

They all sensed how quiet it was, there was no one about, they turned into the kitchen courtyard and as the waggon pulled to a halt, outside the kitchen doorway, the housekeeper Mrs. Hopkin appeared on the threshold. She looked upset and the redness around her eyes showed she had been weeping, she just stood in the doorway and appeared bewildered. Will and Isaac got down from the waggon and after lifting down the wooden mounting step and placing it in position they assisted Squire Fewster to dismount. He was rather unsteady and both men supported him as he made his way to the doorway and Mrs. Hopkin looking more composed stepped forward and took charge as he entered through the doorway.

After unloading the Squire's bags from the waggon and placing them in the kitchen, Will and Isaac took the waggon and both teams of horses to the stables, where after halting outside, they unhitched the team from between the shafts and then along with the other two animals they led all four into the stables. Both men set to work and washing down and brushing each horse in turn and then fed and watered them all, upon completing their task, Isaac, said to his friend, *"Wid best si if Mrs. Hopkin, needs us ta move Squire's bags afore wi go 'ome"*.

Will replied, *"Aye ah think tha's reet"*, They crossed the kitchen yard and knocked upon the door, there was no immediate response, Will, again knocked upon the door, after what seemed to be an age, they heard a voice from within calling out, *"Wait I will be with you shortly"*. Both men recognised the voice of Mr. Strong, who was Squire Fewster's Bailiff, a few moments later he opened the door, Will asked him if he needed them to assist with Squire's baggage, to which he replied, *"No Will, that has been done, the Squire, has told me to send you home and that he will see you tomorrow, but he asked you, Isaac to come in, he needs Mrs. Hopkin and I to speak with you"*. Both men looked at each other questioningly, but, Will turned and walked slowly away, Mr. Strong, then stood to one side and bade Isaac to enter the kitchen, Mr. Strong gestured Isaac to take a seat at the large kitchen table and said, *"Mrs. Hopkin, will be joining us in but a few minutes"*, Mrs. Hopkin entered the kitchen.

Isaac noticed when she was sitting down opposite him, her face held a serious expression, after she had made herself comfortable, Mr. Strong, who coughed and cleared his throat, turned to Isaac and said, *"We have some very sad news to tell you"*. There was a pause of a few moments, before he went on to say, *"About two weeks ago, a fever struck down upon our small hamlet and it was so severe that several people died, I am so sorry to tell you that your wife Rose and your daughter Ann, were amongst those whom the Good Lord chose to take into his safe keeping"*. Isaac jumped to his feet, crying out, *"It's not tru, it's not tru, wi pray ta the Lord, ya ah wrong"*, he then slumped onto his chair, crying uncontrollably in his grief. Mrs. Hopkin rose from her chair and walking quickly round the table, she sat in the chair next to Isaac, she put her arm around his shoulders and he slumped against her breast and she spoke softly to him to console him, but, she knew her words were not being heard.

After while she felt the tension in his body ease a little, he stirred and moved into a sitting position, with his head bowed, with a nod of thanks he took the kerchief which Mrs. Hopkin proffered to him. His crying had stopped and he sat with his eyes closed Mrs. Hopkin and Mr. strong sat in silence allowing Isaac to gather his thoughts, as he contemplated the tragedy, which had come his way. In a but a short time, he turned to Mrs. Hopkin and gesturing with his arm, he said, *"Mrs. Hopkin, wat am I ta do"*, the good lady took hold of his hand and speaking very quietly, she said, *"Isaac, you have just had some shocking news given to you, take a little time to calm yourself, you know Mr Strong and myself will help you as much as we can"*. Isaac nodded his head and said, *"Ah thank ya fa that, can ya tell mi weer our Willi is"*. Mrs. Hopkin said, *"Willi is well and your sister Nan is looking after him at your cottage"*. With a weak smile, Isaac looked at her and said, *"Thank ya"*.

With a smile of re-assurance to Isaac, Mrs. Hopkin stood up and said, *"Whilst I am preparing us a drink, Mr. strong will have a little talk with you"*.

When she returned she was carrying a tray, upon which was some crockery, setting it down upon the table, she said, *"I am sure her Ladyship would in these circumstances approve of us taking a Pot of her Tea"*. Whilst they were having their tea both Mrs. Hopkin and Mr. Strong gave Isaac details of how the Fever had suddenly descended upon the Hamlet and how quickly so many people had been taken ill by it and were dead within two or three days, in all 17 people from their small hamlet had died all had been buried in a large communal grave at the side of the Churchyard, Lady Fewster had arranged all this with Parson Grimley. After finishing their tea, Mr. Strong rose and said to Isaac I will give you a ride back home to see to your son and sister.

When they reached Isaac's house Mr. Strong said, *"You must talk everything over with your sister and come to the Manor House after the midday hour tomorrow, I am sure the Squire will wish to see you"*. Isaac said, *"I will"*. He stepped down from the waggon and walked slowly toward his cottage door, as he reached the door, it opened, Willi was standing there and Nan was close behind him with her hands upon the boy's shoulders. No one spoke, but Willi started to sob, as he stepped forward and threw his arms around Isaac's waist, Isaac bent down and lifted his son from the floor and hugged him tightly to his chest, the boy nuzzled his head so that it lay comfortably between his fathers shoulder and neck, meanwhile Nan had stepped to Isaac's side, trying to clasp both Father and Son in her arms.

After a few minutes, Isaac stepped forward into the cottage and Nan followed, closing the door behind her. Isaac seated himself onto the settle, still clasping his son in his arms. Nan stood for a few moments looking down sadly at her brother and nephew, she then sat down gently at their side. Smoothing the boy's hair slowly with her hand, she said, *"Ee's bin askin' fa ya sin it 'appened, ee keeps shoutin' fa 'is mam, as well"*. Isaac just sat looking down at his son, who was now sleeping, Nan saw a number of tears falling down her brother's cheek, as she sat quietly watching. Isaac felt Willi stir in his sleep, he rose unsteadily and trying not to wake his son, he took him to his bunk, he placed him gently onto it and carefully covered him with a quilt. He stepped back and stood watching the boy closely.

When he saw he was sleeping peacefully he turned away and returned to join Nan in the kitchen. Brother and Sister spoke long into the night, neither of them knew how their futures may change and they were not really sure how they could deal with the coming months, Isaac knew, that Nan, like himself, could not read, he took the letter from his pocket and showed it to her, saying who had given it to him, he said, *"Keit gev it ta mi, e' said e' was mi frend, an' not ta forget im"*, Nan took the letter in her hand, after looking at it , she said, *"Wen ya go ta si tha Squire in tha morn, ask Mrs. Hopkin ta tell ya wat's in it, she can read buks"*. In the early hours of the new day, brother and sister were both weary for sleep, Isaac, insisted that Nan sleep in the bed and he took from within the settle a large eider feather Quilt and slept on the kitchen floor.

Isaac was awoken by his dog barking and scratching at the door, he quietened the animal and looked up at the sky, he was surprised, he realised it must be much later than when he usually rose to break his fast, it was much higher in the sky. He returned inside the cottage, Nan was in the kitchen, she was preparing food, in order to break their fast. Isaac told Nan of his fears that he may have overslept, as they spoke Will entered the kitchen and dashed across to his father and threw his arms around him, Isaac responded to him and reassured his Son that he would keep him safe.

After they had broken their fast, Isaac after reassuring Will I that he would be safe staying with Nan, he set off with a heavy heart to journey to the Manor House to see the Squire. On his journey as he passed Tobe's house, he felt quite sad, at the thought of his friend lying in a mass grave somewhere on or near to the field of Battle. He thought of Tobe's worries for his parents welfare, Nan had already told Isaac that Tobe's mother was amongst those who had died of the Fever which had taken such a terrible toll from amongst their small community. His thoughts brought back the shock of losing both Rose and their daughter Ann. He sat down on the grass banking whilst emotions took over his thoughts.

When he had calmed down and brought his mind back under control, he rose to his feet and resumed his journey. Keit's letter, he wondered what his friend would have to say in the letter and what did it all mean. As he approached Leake, Isaac thought to himself, how quiet it was, he listened intently there was very little bird song, the crows which usally created all the noise in the trees around the Church, their fighting and continual cawing appeared to be absent, Isaac felt it was not natural, he could not understand, were the animals and birds paying their respect to the dead.

Isaac entered the gates of the Manor House, he had been expecting the dogs to bark upon his approach, even they were quiet, he crossed the kitchen yard and knocked upon the kitchen door, after a few moments the door was opened by Mrs. Hopkin. She bade Isaac to enter, she took a seat at the kitchen table and gestured Isaac to join her, when they were comfortably seated she said, *"The Surgeon from Thirsk is dressing the Squires Injury, he should not be long now"*. Isaac nodded and then he said as he took the letter from the pocket in his smock *"Mi frend at York gev mi this 'ere letter, mi an' Nan can't reed it"*, the good lady and said, *"Would you like me to read it to you Isaac"*, Isaac nodded.

Opening the envelope, Mrs. Hopkin took out the letter, which she saw was written in a neat hand, before reading the contents to Isaac she glanced through the letter and said then said to him, *"Your friend Keit also cannot write, but he has put his mark to the letter, which was written by a person called Luke, who says he is a friend of both Keit and yourself"*. Isaac said, *"Aye, Mrs. Hopkin, Luke's bin a good frend ta mi as well"*. Mrs. Hopkin cleared her throat and started to read out the letter, *"Both on us want ya ta know, that if ever tha needs any 'elp, that both on us will allus be reddy ta 'elp tha, cum ta York if tha needs ta, we'll si tha reet"*. Mrs Hopkin paused and went on to say, *"Wi 'ope the good Lord teks care of you and yours, Good luck, your frends LUKE and KEIT"*.

Folding the letter and placing it in the envelope, as she passed it back to Isaac, Mrs. Hopkin said, *"Isaac, you seem to have formed a real friendship with these two men, who speak so highly of you"*. As Isaac was replacing the letter into the pocket of his smock, the door leading into the kitchen from the Hallway, opened and Mr. Strong entered into the kitchen and approached the table taking a seat opposite Mrs. Hopkin. He placed his small leather satchel upon the table and turning to Isaac, he said, *"The Surgeon has left and the Master and Lady Fewster are conversing at the moment, the Master was saddened when he was aware of your sad losses Isaac and I have discussed your circumstances with him"*.

At this moment, Mrs. Hopkin informed Mr Strong of the letter that Isaac had received from Keit, he turned to Isaac and said, *"May I read it please"*, Isaac reached into his pocket and passed the letter to Mr. Strong. After reading the letter he placed it back in to the envelope and whilst passing it back, he said, *"When you see the Squire, let him read your letter"*,

Isaac nodded and said, *"Aye"* As a bell started ringing on the wall of the kitchen, Mrs. Hopkin said, *"That is the bell for the drawing room, the Squire will see you now Isaac, Mr. Strong will take you through"*. Mr. Strong rose and said, *"Come follow me Isaac"*, he led Isaac into the Hallway and knocked upon a door on the right opposite the staircase

A voice bade them to enter, as they were passing through the doorway into the room, Isaac observed that both the Squire and Lady Fewster were sitting at the table. The Squire gestured to them to sit at the table opposite he and his wife, when they were seated, both Master and Mistress expressed their sadness and sympathy to Isaac and the Squire said, *"The blows you have been dealt, are most cruel for you, I need you to tell me what arrangements you may have discussed with your Sister concerning your future's and how you may be best able to move forward and adjust your life, are you able to"*. At this point Isaac's emotion and grief overtook him, he sobbed uncontrollably, his head slumped forward and rested upon his arms on the table, his body shuddered as the grief took hold of him. Lady Fewster pointing toward a cabinet on the opposite wall, she said, *Mr. Strong, could you please oblige me and bring a glass of Brandy over to help Isaac deal with the stress, from which he is suffering from at the moment"*,

The bailiff rose and crossed to the cabinet, he returned with a glass containing a goodly measureof Brandy. He resumed his seat at the side of Isaac and placing one hand on Isaac's shoulder, he said,*"Come now Isaac lad, take a sip of this, it will calm you a little"*, Isaac slowly lifted his head from the table, he sat himself up and took several sharp intakes of breath and after drying his eyes with a kerchief which Mr. Strong gave him, he took a drink from the glass handed to him by Mr. Strong. After taking a drink from the glass, Isaac could feel it burning as it went down his gullet, he replaced the glass on the table in front of him, he sat himself up straight upon the chair and took several more sharp intakes of air, He looked at the Squire and Lady Fewster and said, *"Ah can't 'elp it, am sorry"*, the Squire was shaking his head and said, *"Isaac, you have no need to apologise, we fully understand your sorrow and we wish to help you"*.

Mr. Strong gave a low sounding cough and said, *"If I may say a word Master"*, Squire Fewster nodded his approval and gestured to his Bailiff to continue, Mr. Strong, then said, *"Squire, I have informed Isaac of you and her Ladyship's desire to help him and he gave me a letter to read, which had been given to him by his friend in York on the day he left, I feel it may be of interest in your deliberations"*. Squire Fewster, expressed his thanks to his Bailiff and looking at Isaac, he said, *"May I see the letter"*, Isaac nodded and took the letter from his smock pocket and handed it to Mr. Strong, who rose from seat and took the letter walked around the table and passed it to the Squire.

After reading the letter, Squire Fewster passed it to his wife, she looked very thoughtful as she read the letter and nodded approvingly as she passed it back to her husband. Placing the letter on the table in front of him, Squire Fewster said, *"Isaac, would you care to tell us, what, if any plans, have you and your Sister have made"*. Isaac thought for a few moments and then said, *"Nan ses she'll stop wi us fa a few days, 'ill put mi 'ead down in barn on a night, but, she'll still cum ere ta work, ah still think nowt's 'append, an a'll wek up soon"*, Lady Fewster looked quite sad, as she turned and looking to her husband she said, *"I think you and I need a little time, to talk together, to find how best we can help Isaac"*, nodding his head, Squire Fewster said. *"I quite agree with you"*, he turned and looking across the table at his Bailiff, he said, *"Mr. Strong, would you kindly, return to the kitchen with Isaac and remain there until her*

Ladyship and I have discussed how best we may help, I will ring when we need you both to return".

The Bailiff rose and gestured Isaac to follow him, turning as he did so, he addressed Squire Fewster, saying, *"I will await your Summons Master"*, he turned and followed Isaac back to the Hallway, closing the door as they left the room. When they entered the kitchen, Mrs. Hopkin who was over by the fireplace turned and with a smile and addressed Mr. Strong, she said, *"I am just making up a tray of Tea, for the Master and Mistress, take a seat at the table and when I return, we also will have some tea"*. Mr. Strong and Isaac sat down at the table, Isaac was quietly gathering his thoughts, he felt he had little to look forward to in the future, Mr. Strong also was quiet, he took from the large sized pocket of his coat, a red coloured Notebook, he was still writing in the book when Mrs. Hopkin returned. She did not disturb the pair, she busied herself preparing a tray for the tea she had promised they would have.

After a minute or so she turned and carried the tray across, placing it up on the table saying, *"We will have our tea now, I am sure we will all feel a lot better for it."* As they were having their tea, Isaac told them how afraid he was of the future and that he was unsure if he could cope in the forthcoming weeks with all the problems that he may have to face. He went on to tell them that he still could not believe that he would never see Rose again, he felt sure he had seen her suddenly appear at the fireplace and then disappear just as suddenly. He said his world and happiness had crashed around him and he could not see a happy future ahead.

Mrs. Hopkin looked across at Mr Strong, she raised her eyebrows and then turning to Isaac said, *"Grief, when it enters our lives is very difficult for us to understand, whenever you need to talk, both myself and Mr. Strong are here to listen to you"*.

Isaac looked at them both in turn and said, *"Livin' 'ere on mi own meks mi feerful, but i'm stuck like a rat in a trap, 'ave no way ta get owt on it"*. Mr. Strong said, *"Let's see what the Squire and her Ladyship have to say to you, but don't worry, a way will be found to help you"*. As Mrs. Hopkin was placing the crockery onto her tray, a bell on the wall ringing out loudly, she said, *"The Master is ready to see you Isaac Mr. Strong will come with you"*.

The pair rose and made their way to the Hallway, when they reached the Drawing Room, Mr. Strong knocked upon the door and they both entered upon hearing the call from the Squire to do so. Squire Fewster bade that they be seated, when they had done so, he said, *"Isaac, I am very aware, that your actions on the Battlefield and afterwards, saved my life and I am indebted to you"*. He shuffled in his chair as he sought to ease the discomfort he felt from his previous posture, he then went on to say, *"You have been dealt a fearful blow, which has brought much sadness and grief into your life, we need to seek out the best solution and we will."*. He then told Isaac that Mr. Strong would take him home and they would talk again on the Morrow. When they got back to the kitchen, Mr. Strong told Mrs.Hopkin what had been said, she in turn stepped forward and hugging Isaac she said, *"All will be well"*.

During the journey to Isaac's home, there was, but little talk between the two men, each examining his own thoughts, when Isaac dismounted outside his home, Mr. Strong told him he would return to pick him up at the midday hour on the morrow. As Mr. Strong drove into the Kitchen Courtyard at the Manor House, he saw Will Thornton was walking toward him from the stable, Mr. Strong reined his horse back and dismounted from the cart. Passing the reins to Will he said, *"Will, can you give the horse a good brushing and turn it into the Paddock, the cart needs to go into the small*

Barn", taking the reins, Will said, "*Aye, Mr. Strong*", as he led the horse away toward the Stable, the two wheeled cart rattled and bounced upon the cobbled yard.

Mr. Strong crossed the Courtyard and entered the Manor House through the Kitchen door, Mrs. Hopkin was sitting at the table, she said, "*I will finish the menu's for her Ladyship and then we can speak*", after but a few minutes she put the quill upon the inkstand, she blew lightly over the last line or so of he page and closed the writing book. Turning to Mr. Strong, she said, "*I am worried about Isaac, he is so badly shocked*", Mr. Strong nodded in agreement and said, "*What do you suggest we opine to the Master and Mistress, to best help Isaac and his family*". Sadly and with a low sigh, Mrs. Hopkin replied, "*I do not feel, he will ever be able to overcome his grief, for as long as he continues to live amongst us, whilst all his happy memories from the past are continually in his head*". Mr. Strong thought for a moment and said, "*Mrs. Hopkin, I fully agree with you, like myself, are you also thinking, that making a fresh start in York, is the answer*".

The good lady, with a little smile playing across her lips, nodded her head, the Bailiff rose to his feet and stood in deep thought, he was stroking his chin as he slowly walked over to the window and stood looking out across the courtyard. He was thus positioned for several minutes, he then turned quite suddenly and walked back to the table, he resumed his seat, looking at Mrs. Hopkin, he said, "*The Master and Mistress, will I feel sure consider this option, if we put it to them, are you happy that we do that*". Mrs Hopkin, immediately said, "*I am, there is no other solution, that is providing Isaac wishes to do that*". Rising from her seat, Mrs. Hopkin said, "*When I took the tea tray in, Her Ladyship told me, they would wish to see us both upon your return, I will go to collect the tray and inform them of your return*", smoothing her apron down with the palm of her hand, she set off for the Drawing Room. When she returned, she placed the tray and cutlery adjacent to the sink and turning to Mr. Strong, she said, *"they wish to see us now"*.

Rising to his feet he smoothed down his waistcoat and adjusted the cuffs of his jacket, as he gave a slight pull upon his sleeve with his hand, Mrs. Hopkin remarked, *"You always look smart Mr. Strong"*, trying to hide his look of embarrassment, Mr. Strong turned and headed for the kitchen door, Mrs Hopkin followed close on his heel. After they had entered the drawing room, Lady Fewster bade them to be seated and then asked if they had discussed the welfare of Isaac and his family. They both nodded and then Mrs. Hopkin expressed her concern and fear for Isaac if he remained where all his haunting memories were. Mr. Strong explained how both he and Mrs. Hopkin had discussed what they had seen and what they heard whilst observing and listening to Isaac, seeing his deep grief, as he had opened his heart to them. Mr. Strong spoke, he said, *"Both Mrs. Hopkin and myself believe that Isaac would best come to terms with his grief if he lived elsewhere"*. Both the Squire and his wife had listened intently to what their servants were telling them.

When they had finished speaking, Squire Fewster thanked them for what they had said and then he looked questioningly at his wife, she in turn nodded her head. He sat quietly in thought for a few moments and then looking across the table at his two servants, he said, *"Both your Mistress and myself have thought long and hard of how we can best help Isaac"*. He paused briefly and went on to say, *"There is no doubt in our minds, that had Isaac, not acted as he did on that fateful day of the Battle, I would have been dead"*. He stopped speaking and looked very sad he as wiped his kerchief across his face, Lady Fewster leaned across and after squeezing his hand, she gently stroked it. He returned his kerchief to his pocket, he straightened his posture and after taking a number of deep breaths, looked at his servants and said *"I am Sorry, I was a little overcome"*. He then continued, *"I received help from my servant when I most needed it and in his time of need, Isaac needs my help"*, again pausing for a moment, he then went on to say, *"What you have told us, is also the conclusion that your Mistress and I have arrived at"*.

Lady Fewster rose and walked around the back of her husband's chair, she said, *"I sense that you are a little uncomfortable, your supporting cushions, appear to have slipped I will try to make them a little more comfortable for you"*. Her husband sat forward on his chair as she moved and patted the cushions into a more comfortable position, her husband leaned back as she bade him to, he nodded his head in approval as he sat backwards and he said, *"Thank you my dear, that is much more comfortable, now Mr. Strong, after I have talked it over with Isaac and he agrees, I want you to go to York with him and after talking to his friends and looked at all aspects, of which you feel are important, come back and inform me"*. He thought for a moment before going on to say, *"Bring him in to see me tomorrow at ten of the clock, if all goes well, you could both set off on your jouney the day after"*. Mr. Strong, after telling his Master he would carry out out his instructions, turned and withdrew from the room. Mr. Strong arrived at Isaac's house on the following Morn, he saw Isaac coming from within his small barn, he was carrying a small bucket of grain, as he approached he was throwing the grain so that it scattered upon the ground, noticing Mr. Strong was looking questioningly at him, Isaac said , *"Is is best ta mek em scrat rown' fa' it "*. Mr. Strong, smiled and then said, *"When you have finished can we go inside. I need to speak to both you and your Sister"*. Isaac nodded and said,*"Aye"*. In a but a few moments Isaac placed his bucket upon the ground outside the kitchen door and said, *"Yah'd best cum in"*.

Inside the kitchen, Nan was at the sink, Willi was standing beside her, she wiped her hands upon cloth and then turning to her nephew, she said, *"Willi go owt int' barn an' get t' eggs, i'll call ya weh ah want, ya back in"*. After Willie had closed the door, Nan joined her brother upon the Settle at the side of the fireplace, opposite where Mr. Strong was sitting, the Bailiff told them of the plans the Squire was suggesting, they were surprised. He rose and said *"I am going outside to help Willie look for the eggs, you must discuss, what I have told you, I will say to you both, that in my opinion, it is worth looking into, you can, if you wanted to, change your mind later"*, then with a little smile upon his face he turned and went outside.

Isaac and Nan as they spoke to each other, were both a little overwhelmed, at what was proposed, there were tears by both of them, though Nan was uncertain about how it would affect her, she told Isaac, that she felt, a new start would be a good way forward for Isaac and Willie. They discussed what Nan thought and then after further tears, they reached a decision, they both felt it was for the good of them all. Isaac went to the door and called out to Mr. Strong.

Following Isaac back into the kitchen, Mr. Strong again seated himself facing Isaac and Nan sitting upon the settle, he said to Isaac, *"Have you decided what you want to do "*? Turning to glance to Sister, Isaac nodded and then said, *"Aye, wi ave, Nan thinks it wud be gud fa me an' Willie, but she dunt no if it's gud fa 'er, but wi ave ta go ta York, ta si if it cud be fa us"*. Mr. Strong, thought for a moment and then said, *"I think Isaac, you have thought wisely, now I must take you to see Squire Fewster"*. Looking at Nan, he went on to say, *"Are you able to look after your Nephew Willie until your Brother and I return"*. Nan nodded and her face was brightened with a little smile playing across his face.

The journey to the Manor House was uneventful, when asked by his Master, Isaac told him he was was grateful for the opportunity to look at any different way to overcome his grief and the chance to build a future for his Son and possibly also his Sister Nan. The Squire listened to Isaac without interruption. When Isaac had finished speaking his Master sat quietly thinking for a few minutes and then went on to tell his servant, that the opportunity he was going to give to him should not be regarded as a reward in any way. He took a drink from the glass, before going on to tell Isaac, that in his mind, he felt fate had dealt Isaac an horrendous punishment and the Squire, wanted if he was able to soften his grief. He then spoke of the action Isaac had taken to protect his Master and subsequently saved his life and that he would be doing all he could to help Isaac. Squire Fewster then turned to Mr. Strong, saying to him *"Is it possible you can make arrangements, for you to accompany Isaac to York tomorrow, you can advise him where necessary and I will give you two letters of introduction and explanation of the purpose of your visit, the first on is to the two gracious Ladies, who cared so well for me at their home in Ogleforth and the second one to Parson Atkin, who has many contacts and will be able to offer advice".*

Mr. Strong thought for a few moments and then said to the Squire, *"Yes, I can give Will Thornton instructions for the job's that need to be done in my absence, he is a sensible fellow and I am confident he will see they are carried out, I will come back to speak to you this evening and collect the letters".* Squire Fewster readily agreed saying, *"Come at six o the clock".* Early the following morning, Mr. Strong arrived at Isaac's house to set off on their journey to York, Mr. Strong had chosen to use a small cart and one horse. Little was said by either man, Isaac had many thoughts of what the future might hold for him, but his heart was telling him that change was best for Willi and himself to overcome their grief and make a better life for themselves in York. Memories of Jack Grainger and Tobias Platt crossed his mind as he thought of the last journey he had made to York and how so much death and horror had taken place in such a short time. As he sat pondering, Isaac could only think to himself, what benefits had the battle and the slaughter brought to anyone, none thought Isaac. He then felt Guilty that he had left Rose to go fight, could he have stopped her falling ill if he had stayed at home. Sadness overcame him

After they had passed through Easingwold, the cloud cleared from the sky and the sun broke through spreading it's rays right across the countryside, they passed through Skelton and as they did so, Mr Strong said, *"Our journey has gone well, we should be in sight of York, within the hour"*. Isaac had not realised they were so near to York and his countenance brightened and he started to take an interest in his surroundings, he commented, *"Ah'd not thout wi wer' so close"*. Throughout their journey they had seen very few travellers, be they on horseback or waggon, now as they got nearer to the Citie, the number of waggon's and carts, approaching them from York increased, Isaac was surprised how many flocks of livestock, were being herded along the road, causing Mr. Strong to rein their horse in as a flock of animals walk by surrounding the small waggon. It must be Market day in York, I had not remembered, remarked Mr. Strong. Isaac's attention was suddenly drawn straight ahead, where he saw York Minster, it's stonework was glittering bright as the rays from the Sun made it sparkle and shimmer, Isaac was taken aback by the magnificence and beauty of the building, rising high above all the other buildings around it.

When they were passing through the village of Clifton, damage could be seen to many of the houses, beyond Clifton as they approached the Citie, much more damage could be seen to the houses. At they drew level with the Citie Wall, a round Tower which was part of the Wall, was very badly damaged and on one side the stonework was split from top to bottom. They entered the Citie through Botham Bar, Isaac could see on the stonework many holes where Musket shot had hit the stonework, Isaac gave Mr. Strong direction as they traversed the busy streets and very soon they passed the Hall of the Cordwainers in Hundgate and then ahead of them Isaac saw on the right the alley in which Keit's yard was located.

At Isaac's direction Mr. Strong turned and as they did so, Isaac saw his friend coming out of the Stable. Keit stopped and looked on in amazement when he saw Isaac get down from the cart, with much slapping of shoulders, the pair warmly shook hands amid a lot of laughter, Isaac saw Mr. Strong patiently standing holding the bridle of the horse. Isaac accompanied by Keit, went across to the cart and introduced his friend to Mr. Strong. Keit insisted that the horse be sheltered in his stable, for however long their stay would be, Mr. Strong expressed his thanks to Keit, but tried, unsuccessfully to explain that he could not impose himself upon such kindness.

Whilst Isaac was unhitching the horse before leading it into the Stable prior to stabling it, Mr. Strong explained to Keit the circumstances of the death of Rose and her daughter and advising him how the stress and strain were seriously affecting Isaac's ability to cope with his grief. He went on to tell of Squire Fewster's desire to help Isaac to overcome the trauma which had overtaken him, Keit nodded and said, *"Ah thank thee fa that, Luke an' me will 'elp 'im thro it"*. Both men looked round as they heard whistling, Isaac came out of the barn and he was whistling merrily. Keit looked at Mr. Strong and said, *"Lissen at that, 'es in a 'appy mood alreddy"*, Mr Strong nodded and smiled. When Isaac joined the pair, Mr. Strong, said to him, *"Can you suggest somewhere homely and comfortable where we can stay for the few days we are here"*. Isaac had no hesitation, he immediately said, *"Widow Cuthbert, will tek gud care on us in't Fat Friar, Mr. Strong"*.

After bidding farewell to Keit, Isaac accompanied by Mr. Strong set off, the streets were still quite crowded, as people made their way homeward from the Market, but they soon arrived at their destination. Mr. Strong stopped and for a few moments, he took stock of what stood before him, the sign portrayed a clerical man of large proportions, it was dangling on a solitary rusty chain and swung slowly in the slight breeze and various squeaks could clearly be heard as it did so.

Isaac stepped forward to the door, he pressed the sneck and pushing the door he entered over the threshold, closely followed by Mr. Strong. Widow Cuthbert, who was sitting in her chair by the fire, turned her head upon hearing their entry, when she saw Isaac, she gave a cry of delight and struggled as as she attempted to rise from her chair. When Isaac crossed the room and stood at her side she threw her arms around him and hugged him tightly, as Isaac eased her back down into her chair, she was quite overcome and taking a small kerchief from up her sleeve, she gently dried her eyes with it. Mr. Strong standing by watching, could see how the surprise and joy she had experienced upon seeing Isaac again, had overcome her.

When she had somewhat recovered, she turned to Isaac and said,*"Now who is this fine gentleman"*, Isaac acquainted her with Mr. Strong, who smiled and bowed his head to her. Slowly and with some difficulty Isaac acquainted the good lady the terrible situation he had found upon returning home , he told her of the great difficulty he found in his mourning and what the future held for him. When Isaac finished, the old lady again got to her feet and addressing both men, she said, *"Whilst in't fair Citie you both must stay here with me"*, the two garret rooms are available for your use". Despite protests from Mr. Strong, they were swept aside by Widow Cuthbert, who insisted their presence would be a pleasure to her. Turning to Isaac she said, *"Whilst you show Mr. Strong his room, I will prepare dinner and don't forget your bags"*.

After making their way up the garret Stair and upon being shown the rooms Mr. Strong nodded and said to Isaac, *"The room is perfectly adequate and I have a view over the Citie and I find Widow Cuthbert is a kind and charming old lady"*, Isaac nodded his head in agreement. Taking his leave from Mr. Strong, Isaac went to his own room and after emptying his bag he hung his few items of clothing tidily in the cupboard, making use of the jug of water and bowl in the room he refreshed himself by taking a good wash. He poured the sullied water into the leather bucket and after putting on his jerkin he wentout onto the landing at the top of the stairs.

He saw the door to Mr. Strong's room was closed, he knock lightly upon the door and Mr. Strong quickly appeared in the threshold, Isaac said,*"Can ah empty ya slops in mi bucket"*, Mr. Strong stepped aside and said, *"Thank you Isaac, I would appreciate that"*, after emptying the slops from Mr. Strong's bowl, Isaac said, *"We'd best get down stairs wen ya 'r ready, ah can smell Roast Pork"*. Widow Cuthbert, chattered throughout the meal asking questions of both Mr. Strong and Isaac and they were not able to give an answer to all of them. Apart from what Mrs. Hopkin had given them, which they had eaten at mid morning, they had not had a proper meal and it was apparent both men were enjoying what had been prepared for them.

When Mr. Strong had finished eating, he complimented Widow Cuthbert upon her cooking skills, she smiled and looking at the empty plate in front of each man, she said, *"Them emptee plates in front of ya both, is all I need ta si, then ah know that ya've enjoyed ya grub"*. Rising to his feet and turning toward Isaac, Mr. Strong said, *"Isaac, I would like you to accompany me to Ogleforth, in order I may visit the home of the Ladies who cared for our Master and deliver to them the letter from Squire Fewster"*. Isaac nodded and rose to his feet, after again expressing his appreciation to Widow Cuthbert, Mr. Strong followed Isaac to the door, which Isaac closed behind them. As they made their way past the King's Church in Gudramgate, there were few people walking in the street and only two pony carts were espied.

Isaac indicated to Mr. Strong that they were about to turn left into Ogleforth. halfway down Ogleforth, Isaac stopped and indicated to Mr. Strong the house they were seeking, stepping forward Mr. Strong pulled sharply upon the Bell chain and he heard the sound of the bell ringing, which came up from beneath him through the open door of the Kitchen below the stairs. In but a few moments the door opened, before him stood a woman of matronly appearance he assumed her to be the housekeeper, from the pocket of his waistcoat he gave her his card. She bade him to enter, before doing so she turned to Isaac and suggested he wait down below in the Kitchen, where he could be sent for if he was needed.

After descending the stairs, he knocked upon the open Kitchen door, the cook appeared in the doorway and much to Isaac's surprise, the lady recognised him from the occasions when Isaac and Will had visited to see the Squire when he was staying at the house. She asked him to be seated, he took a seat at the table until he was sent for, he watched as the good lady fussed around making preparations for Supper. She chatted to Isaac as she worked, she told him she was having to do all the work, she explained that the Kitchen Maid (a girl whom she herself had been teaching how to cook) had run off over a week ago with a soldier who had deserted from his post at Clifford's Tower. She went on to tell Isaac, she had told her Mistresses that she herself had only one pair of hands and a new Kitchen Maid was needed. Her Mistresses, she went on to say, don't see all the work that has to be done in the Kitchen, but they quickly complain if things get rushed.

The good lady was still bemoaning her problems as Great Peter tolled out 7 o' the clock, she commented to Isaac, that he would not have to wait much longer, her Mistresses would soon dismiss their caller in order to have their Supper. Shortly after the cook had expressed that thought, the housekeeper swept into the room, she said to the Cook, *"Supper will be required shortly upstairs"*, turning to Isaac, she said, *"Mr. Stackpole, I have a message from Mr. Strong asking that you await his presence outside the front door"*, she then turned about and left the Kitchen.

The Cook smiled warmly at Isaac and said, *"Ya'd best get a move on, she''ll be opening t' door afore ya get up there"*. Isaac smiled and thanked the good lady for her cheerfulness and set off to ascend the stairs, as he put his foot upon the top step, he saw the house door opening and Mr. Strong stepped out and joined him on the causeway. Looking quite pleased with himself, Mr. Strong said, *"Isaac, I have pleasing news, let us hasten back to the Fat Friar to discuss what I have learned"*. Their walk back to the Fat Friar was speedy and thoughtful. Within minutes they were stepping over the threshold of the Fat Friar and seating themselves in the area between the fireside and the Barrels and Casks set upon the gantry. When they had made themselves comfortable, they saw Widow Cuthbert entering through the doorway from the Kitchen, they both saw she was breathing heavily and looked wearisome.

She seated herself in her chair, at the fireside, made herself comfortable and then said, *"You both look as if ya need a tankard of Ale, help ya selves"*, Isaac rose to his feet and turning to Mr. Strong he said, *"Ah ya ya joyning mi Mr. Strong"*. The bailiff nodded and followed Isaac over to the Gantry, Isaac took up a tankard and allowed a small amount of the Ale to pour into it, turning to Mr. Strong, he said, *"Both Will and mi drank this last time"*, taking the tankard, Mr. Strong took a drink of the liquid, he looked at Isaac and nodded, saying,, *"That is a lovely flavour"*. Isaac turned the tap on again and filled the tankard up to the brim, the golden Ale spilling over the side he passed the vessel to Mr. Strong and then commenced to fill a tankard for himself.

They returned to their seats, Isaac pulled forward a small table which had been fashioned from a small Barrel (a firkin) which had been sawn in half. After savouring another drink from his tankard, Mr. Strong smiling broadly at his two companions said, *"I found my visit to the two good Ladies in Ogleforth very helpful and interesting"*. He paused and went on to say, *"They were pleased to have received the letter from Squire Fewster and were sad to read of the terrible circumstances awaiting you Isaac when you returned home, our Master had informed them of his wish for you to come and live in this Citie and hope they may be able to convey any advice or help"*. Mr. Strong reached for his tankard again took a long drink from it, adjusting his posture in his chair, he re-commenced his story, saying, *"The good ladies told me they were seeking* urgently to appoint a suitable young lady to become a Kitchen Maid in that very house and they told me they would be happy to offer the position to your Sister Nan". Glancing across at Isaac, Mr. Strong saw there was a beaming smile upon his face.

Taking another quaff of the beer, Mr. Strong emptied his tankard, he asked Isaac how he felt about the offer that had been made, Isaac, shaking his head a little, but still with a slight smile playing across his face, said, "Ah just didn't expect folk ta be so kind, ah think Nan, will be 'appy ta cum". Widow Cuthbert, after telling Isaac to fill up the tankards, then said, "When you get sat down again, I want to tell you something else". Isaac, who was standing at the gantry, turned his head and said, "Aye reet". After Isaac had returned to the table with the full tankards and made himself comfortable after resuming his seat, Widow Cuthbert, who was looking directly at Isaac said, "I too have been giving a lot of thought about the situation you are in Isaac, you know I have great difficulty with many things which need to be done in a Tavern like the Fat Friar".

She paused and shuffled about in her chair to make herself more comfortable and then said, "Isaac. why don't you come here and work for me, both you and your wee son will be most welcome". Isaac sat with a look of bewilderment across his face and seemed unable to speak, Widow Cuthbert could see the difficulty Isaac was having and she said, "Isaac, do you think my offer would help you, it would 'elp me if you said yes". Isaac, got to his feet and stepped over to where the old lady was sitting in her chair, she sat forward as Isaac bent forward and he placed his hand around her shoulders and gave her a hug. He straightened himself and said, "Mrs. Cuthbert, 'ave niver in mi life met any body as kind as you, i'll not be able to pay ya back, but yes ah'd like ta live here.

Mr. Strong rose to his feet and stepping forward to Isaac, heartily shook him by the hand saying, "Isaac I am very happy *for you, I am sure you have made the right decision"*. The events of the day were then discussed and they also talked of other arrangements that would have to be made, to enable Isaac to return back to York. Isaac was pleased Mr. strong was with him, that worthy gentleman was able to think of everything and was able to advise Isaac about what he should do. When finally they had covered and talked about everything, it was three thoughtful, but tired people who made their weary way to their beds.

Isaac rose at daybreak, after readying himself for the day, he made his way down the stairway and went round to the yard at the rear of the Fat Friar and whence there he descended the stone steps into the cellar where he busied himself making the barrels and casks ready to be moved upstairs into the tap room where, after he had removed the empty one's he could roll them onto the Gantry, upon completing his task, Isaac returned up the stone steps into yard above, when he reached the top and was stepping onto the yard, the aroma of bacon frying drifted into his nostrils, he entered the door and stepped into the kitchen and shouted a cheery, good morning to Widow Cuthbert who was cooking at the oven. As Isaac was taking empty casks from the gantry, Mr. Strong came through the door and shouted a "good morrow" to Isaac and Widow Cuthbert who was just coming in from the Kitchen.

After breaking their fast, Mr. Strong asked Widow Cuthbert to give him directions to Gudramgate in order for him to visit Parson Atkin to deliver Squire Fewster's letter. Isaac told him would go to Keit's yard and after feeding and watering the horse, he would would exercise it in Keit's paddock. When Isaac got to Keit's yard, he saw Luke Watt's just disappearing through the doors into the stable, he followed the path of the Cordwainer into the stable. As he passed through the doorway, Keit called out a "Good Morrow" greeting to him, as ever with a broad smile upon his face, as he turned around Luke also called out a greeting.

Isaac then explained to his friends of the offer Widow Cuthbert had made and of his decision to accept it, both men were pleased to hear the news and wished him well, they then went on to tell Isaac, that they had also discussed his plight and of the plan they had been making before the siege beset the Citie. Their plan they told him was to obtain a waggon and a horse or a pair of horses and jointly to use it as necessary, to transport the goods and materials of their trades about the Citie and surrounding countryside. Because Keith had the stabling and large paddock their costs would be small. They then told Isaac, that they had thought that he could be their groom/driver, Keit seeking re-assurance from Luke, went on to say, *"Even though you will be living at Fat friar and helping out Widow Cuthbert a bit, ya cud still do this job, if ya wants ta"*.

Isaac thanked his friends and told them he would be interested in joining them, but he would not be able to say yes, until things had been sorted out and he actually came to live in York and see how his new life fitted in. Both Keit and Luke understood his caution and told him not to worry, everything would work out for the best. Luke took his leave to return his workshop in Trinity Passage, after his departure Isaac fed and groomed the horse, Isaac heard Keit busy rummaging in the loft of the barn and then he saw his friends legs appear in the aperture at the top of the ladder. As Keit stood on the top of the ladder he reached his hands back inside in his hands he held two long handled wooden spades.

As he leaned downwards, he asked Isaac to take them from him, Isaac did so and Keit came down the ladder, when he stepped off the ladder he said to Isaac,*"When we get a waggon ah can use a bigga bath to mix mi plaister in, so ah need bigger shovels"*. Isaac smiled said, *"It cud be months afor ah get backta York"*, Keit said, *"Ah but i'm riddy fa wen ya do cum"*. Still smiling, Isaac went back to the horse and led the animal outside to the Paddock, returning back inside the stable, Keit was busy loading his cart, he said to Isaac, *"A'll 'ave that much work wi mekking gud mess on folk's 'ouses an' wukshop's that was 'it during siege, ah'll bi working fa years"*. Keit finished loading his cart, he told Isaac he was going to Clifton to make good the Daub and Wattle walls in some of the houses, Isaac told him that he was going back to the "Fat Friar" to tidy the cellar and do other jobs, which Widow Cuthbert had mentioned. They left the yard together and at the gate, Isaac left his friend and made his own way back to the "Fat Friar" as he approached the Tavern, Great Peter was tolling the midday hour (12 0f the clock) inside there were about a dozen who were quaffing their Ale as they struck deals with each other and discussed how trade in the Citie had increased since the end of the siege. Isaac had been very busy since his arrival and had helped Widow Cuthbert to serve the ale and dash back and forth to the cellar to change casks or barrels as they became empty, he wondered to himself how Widow Cuthbert managed to cope with the work demanded of her by running the "Fat Friar". He hoped he would be able to make her life easier when he came back to live in York and hoped it would not be too long. He was day dreaming as he walked back up the steps from the cellar and he heard Great Peter, toll two of the clock. He entered the tap room and saw Mr. Strong sitting at a table alone, a tankard of Ale was set in front of him, Isaac saw there were but two other men left in the room and they were Carpenters and were in deep conversation and were sitting at another table near the door.

Isaac took a seat opposite Mr. Strong, who was just replacing his tankard upon the table, turning to Isaac he smiled and said, *"I have had a very interesting morning in the company Parson Atkin, I now feel that everything is in place here in York and I think we can return to Leak to inform the Squire"*, pausing he took took another drink from his tankard, before going on to say, *"Isaac are you happy that we can return to Leake, have you any other worries that should be seen to first"*.

Isaac shook his head and then went on to tell Mr. Strong of the plans Luke and Keit had suggested and the job they had offered him, smiling broadly Mr. Strong said, *"I think your friends have made you a good offer, would you be happy joining them"*. Isaac nodded and said, *"Ah wud be 'appy doi'n that Mr. Strong"*. The Bailiff leaned across the table and shook Isaac's hand, before saying, *"I think you and your family, will have happiness, here in York, we will set off back to Leake tomorrow in the morning, can you have the horse and cart outside for an early start?"* Isaac nodded his head and smiled.

THE END

Epilogue

Tom along with his Father Keith, were standing in a field which had been part of the Battlefield upon which the Battle of Marston Moor had taken place on the 2nd July, 1644. The site was located between Tockwith and Long Marston and some three miles from York.

Tom had completed a Thesis on the events of the Battle and how the Civil War and the Siege of York for over three months had affected the Citizens, particularly the craftsmen and the poorer classes.

After Keith had read his son's Thesis he was pleased to see how well his son had researched the story and he was both pleased and delighted at what Tom had produced, they had made the trip to try to imagine what the horrors of that day may have been like for combatants on both sides and how the survivors may have had their lives altered forever.

Throughout their visit they had discussed History that Tom had dis covered, all the escapades that the main subject Isaac Stackpole had encountered, all the sadness and then eventually, happiness. Turning to his son Keith said, you have indeed in my opinion shown the best and worst of History.

Isaac was but a poor peasant, but he and his fellow peasants were pulled into a War over which they had no control.

Tom you have shown what life was like for people living in the country and also how conditions were for people living in a besieged Citie, you have shown the horror, sadness and kindness which befell many people.

The concern of the Squire and the simple country folk having the kindness to help Isaac in so many ways to overcome his grief, the wonderful friendship given to him by Luke Watts and Keit Starkey. It was interesting that you found that Isaac did return to York, with his sister Nan and his Son Willie and that Isaac had such a happy and rewarding time working with Luke and Keit with the horse and cart.

Nan too, seems have had a happy life working at the house of the two Gentle Ladies, but for you to find that she later married Keit Starky was a surprise to me. Both father and son looked once again across the surrounding fields, before Keith who was looking toward the Tockwith to Long Marston road where they had parked their vehicle on the small parking area. Looking at the Sun reflecting off their vehicle Keith said, *"I feel quite proud, Tom"*, Tom saw what his Father meant, shielding his eyes from the sun Tom looked at the side of vehicle where in bold lettering he saw painted on the side :-

KEITH STACKPOLE and SON,
HAULAGE CONTRACTORS